CHRIST IN EASTERN CHRISTIAN THOUGHT

CHRIST IN
EASTERN CHRISTIAN
THOUGHT

John Meyendorff

ST. VLADIMIR'S SEMINARY PRESS
CRESTWOOD, NEW YORK 10707
1987

Selected titles by the same author

GREGORY PALAMAS: Defense of the Holy Hesychasts
  Text and French translation (1959; 2nd ed. 1974)
A STUDY OF GREGORY PALAMAS (1964)
BYZANTINE THEOLOGY (1974)
ST. GREGORY PALAMAS AND ORTHODOX SPIRITUALITY
  (1974)
BYZANTINE HESYCHASM: HISTORICAL, THEOLOGICAL
  AND SOCIAL PROBLEMS (1974)
BYZANTIUM AND THE RISE OF RUSSIA (1980)
IMPERIAL UNITY AND CHRISTIAN DIVISIONS (1988)

Library of Congress in Publication Data:

Meyendorff, Jean, 1926—
    Christ in Eastern Christian thought.

    Translation of Le Christ dans la théologie byzantine.
    Includes bibliographical references and index.
    1.   Jesus Christ — History of doctrines.   2.   Theology,
Eastern Church.   I.   Title.
BT198.M4313   1975   232   75-31979
  ISBN 0-913836-27-3

55,629

CHRIST IN EASTERN CHRISTIAN THOUGHT

PRINTED IN THE UNITED STATES OF AMERICA
BY
EERDMANS PRINTING CO.
GRAND RAPIDS, MI

Contents

Foreword
To The Second Edition

Originally published in 1969 in French (Editions du Se, Paris) and in English (Corpus Books, Baltimore and Washington, D.C.), then translated into Italian (A. V. E., Rome), this book has now been updated and partially revised, with the addition of several references to recent studies and publications.

Still, the author makes no claim to exhaustiveness, and bibliographical references have been reduced to a minimum. A simple glance at H.-G. Beck's *Kirche und Theologische Literatur im Byzantinischen Reich* (Munich, 1959) will give an idea of the number of secondary Byzantine authors whose ideas I have not mentioned.

This book presupposes that the reader is acquainted with the basic facts of civil and ecclesiastical history of the late Roman and the Byzantine Empires. These are easily accessible in standard reference works such as J. Daniélou and H.-I. Marrou, *The Christian Centuries, I. The First Six Hundred Years* (1964), or A. Schmemann, *The Historical Road of Eastern Orthodoxy* (1963).

Originally written in French, the book was translated into English by Fr. Yves Dubois.

Preface

"Whom do men say that I, the Son of man, am?" This question, addressed by Jesus to his disciples on the way to Caesarea Philippi was answered by Peter: "Thou art the Christ, the Son of the living God" (Matt 16:13-16). Peter's answer, however, has been understood differently and did not prevent lasting schisms.

And indeed the debates about the identity of Jesus Christ, which lasted for centuries of early Christian history, were neither abstract nor purely academic. For both the words and the acts of Jesus have a different validity and different significance if they proceed from a mere man, or from the second person of the divine Trinity, if they represent a simple episode of human history, or should be seen and believed as unique words and acts of the Lord of history himself. It also makes a tremendous difference for the understanding of who God himself is, whether one sees him as an impassible ruler of a world where good and evil, joy and suffering, life and death are in constant opposition, or whether, on the contrary, one believes that he assumed the human condition, made it "his own" and was crucified as a criminal under Pontius Pilate, to rise on the third day, thus vanquishing evil and death. Does God save man simply by issuing decrees from heaven, as a ruler and a judge, or does he manifest himself through a loving identification with man and show himself as "being love"?

These are the alternatives involved in the debates on the personal identity of Jesus Christ.

Can the debate be solved by simple reference to historical data? Certainly not, because the historical facts about Jesus are not only "making" history, but also claim to transform history and to liberate man from categories and conditions which belong to the fallen world. Their true content and significance cannot be limited by "historical facts" as viewed by the "impartial observer." Even the closest disciples of Jesus understood what he did only when the Spirit taught them "all things."

Knowledge of Christ is undoubtedly based on the experience of eyewitnesses. But the Christian tradition trusts these witnesses only insofar as the Spirit has made them apostles: He is the one who taught them "all things" and made it possible for them to grasp the true meaning of the historical events they experienced. Their witness does not even claim the kind of infallibility of which the rationalist critique seeks to deprive them. It is not the testimonies of Mark, of Luke, or of Matthew, taken separately or together in opposition to Johannine theology, that give us the vision of Jesus which the Church proposes as true. Rather, the Church's vision is that of the New Testament as a whole, a collection of witnesses and theologians mutually confronted and grouped in conformity with the sole criterion of the Holy Spirit residing in the Church. The New Testament data may and must undergo the investigations of historical criticism, but such a criticism must take into account not only the views of the individual New Testament authors but also the vision of the New Testament as a whole, which is a collection of complementary witnesses.

Moreover, the New Testament message cannot be separated from the way in which it is proclaimed, at various times and within various cultures. In order to reach the minds of the Greeks, it not only had to be written in Greek, but its advocates had to employ categories of thought familiar to their audience. This book is an attempt to show that this *tradition* of the Church is indeed consistent with the New Testament in its christological formulations.

This is so because tradition is not a continuity of ideas only, but also of experience. It implies not only intellectual coherence, but also a communion in the ways of perceiving the truth. The truth that one thus recognizes is therefore not about objects—for God himself is not an object, perceived by the senses or the intellect—but about God and man together. For indeed, the Greek Fathers never separated theology from anthropology.

It is my firm conviction moreover that Byzantine christological thought—far from being, as it is sometimes conceived, a crypto-Monophysitic, Hellenized form of Christianity—is in fact meeting some of the most fundamental concerns of the contemporary search for a new theology. At a time when Christian theology realizes the insufficiency of the old Western concept of the supernatural for the understanding of man's destiny and salvation, and when the idea of grace as extrinsic to nature is increasingly challenged, it is important, before venturing into the dangerous paths of secularized Christianity, to rediscover the notion upon which the whole Eastern patristic understanding of salvation is based. Man is truly man when he participates in God's life. This participation, therefore, is not a supernatural gift, but the very core of man's nature.

An abundant literature exists on the spiritual tradition of Eastern Christianity, Eastern monasticism and asceticism. Very often, however, this spiritual tradition is considered independently of the biblical, neotestamental, i.e., christological and pneumatological, categories, and is then arbitrarily misinterpreted as esoteric or mystical. The concept of deification, for example, is often the victim of such misrepresentations. In a study of Christology in the Byzantine period the question "Who is Christ?" must precede our understanding of the Pauline concept of life "in Christ."

Since Christology is of necessity soteriological, I have not limited myself strictly to christological concepts as such. In some cases it has seemed necessary to answer the question: how is salvation understood by an author who has had considerable influence on the general trend of ideas, without, however, speaking of Christ? For a christological explanation is also needed when the understanding of salvation is not centered on Christology. In any case, such authors as Evagrius and Pseudo-Dionysius had a tremendous—even if negative—influence on the history of Christology, and I could not avoid giving them considerable attention.

JOHN MEYENDORFF

1.

Christology in the Fifth Century

The Council of Chalcedon (A.D. 451) opened a new era in the history of Eastern Christian thought. By its representative character, by the number of its participants, and by the scope of its debates, this assembly offered all the aspects that could be expected at that time from a true ecumenical council. Yet it caused within the Eastern Church a schism that endures to our own day.

Until Chalcedon, the schools of Alexandria and Antioch were the two foci of theological thought. Neither school, however, as a result of the fifth-century christological quarrels, preserved its characteristically independent thought. The intellectual authority of the school of Antioch was never re-established after the blows dealt it by the ebullient Cyril of Alexandria. In Alexandria, the majority either followed the leaders of the anti-Chalcedonian schism or confined themselves within the boundaries of the small Melkite imperial group. The Persian invasions and the Arab conquest, however, put an end to the existence of independent centers of creative Christian thought in Syria, Palestine, and Egypt. Constantinople, the brilliant capital of the empire, and an increasingly important center of Eastern Church life, had been originally largely dependent in intellectual matters on Alexandria and, above all, Antioch. But the circumstances following the councils of Ephesus and Chalcedon placed Constantinople in the position of an arbiter between East and West and led it to elaborate a theology of conciliation and synthesis. This type of theology was favored by the

13

emperors, who were seeking a reconciliation between the Chalcedonian and anti-Chalcedonian parts of their empire: such was the first task of the specifically "Byzantine" theology. The christological problems of the fifth and sixth centuries thus can be said basically to have shaped the Byzantine theological mentality and to have provided its main theme until about the ninth century.

In the lapse of time between Chalcedon and the era of Justinian, Byzantine theology accomplished a *creative* synthesis between the traditions of Alexandria and Antioch. It was no mere juxtaposition of opposing elements but the creation of a new line of thought, christened by modern Western writers, according to the expression of J. Lebon, "neo-Chalcedonism." These historians contend that the new tendency, interpreting Chalcedon in the exclusive light of the old Alexandrian theology and Cyril of Alexandria's utterances (however ambiguous), unduly favored Alexandria without succeeding in reconciling the Monophysites to the Church.[1]

If one looks at Justinian's reign in isolation, this conclusion may seem true. But from a wider perspective it can be seen that the theology of Justinian's time and the decisions of the fifth council (the last and permanent expression of neo-Chalcedonian theology), already contained the ferment of new developments that led to the christological system of St. Maximus the Confessor, in which the positive elements of the Antiochene tradition recovered their proper importance. Ephesus, Chalcedon, and the two Byzantine councils (553 and 681) *together* represent the great Byzantine christological synthesis; the later developments of Orthodox theology must be approached in the light of this synthesis.

Doctrinal conflicts between the various theologies from the fourth to the sixth century cannot be understood until their soteriological aspects are taken into consideration. During the Arian controversy, St. Athanasius and the Cappadocians firmly established that salvation was accomplished in the real meeting between God and man. The incarnate Word was truly God, not a creature, for God alone could reconcile fallen mankind to himself. And Christ's human nature was not deficient, deprived of intellect, as Apollinarius taught, but a complete human nature, "our nature," assumed in its totality by the Word, for "what is not assumed is not healed, and what is united to God is saved," as St. Gregory Nazianzen wrote.[2]

In order to understand the later development of christological debate, one must be aware that Nicene orthodoxy as expressed by the Cappadocians was defined by a simultaneous opposition to Arius *and* Apollinarius. Both taught that in Christ the Logos had taken the place of the human intellect; both understood Christ as one being or nature; but while this unity implied for Arius the "creatureliness" of the Logos, who was but a superior mind (νοῦς), for Apollinarius it meant the conception of Christ as a "heavenly man" whose whole vitality and dynamism resided in the Logos.[3] Arius and Apollinarius agreed in denying Christ a human soul. This negative agreement allowed both to assert in Christ a complete unity of Logos and flesh, a created unity for Arius, a heavenly unity for Apollinarius.

Although the anti-Arianism of the fourth-century Nicaeans took form in a positive definition of consubstantiality, excluding the identification of the Logos with a creature, their anti-Apollinarianism remained vaguer and produced no positive conciliar definition. All through the fifth century this anti-Apollinarianism dominated the theologies of the school of Antioch and determined their insistence on the fully *human* reality of Jesus. The extreme form of this position, Nestorianism, went so far as to regard Christ's human nature as an "assumed man" practically distinct from his divine nature. In contradistinction, the Alexandrians remained fundamentally anti-Arian. Their position, though deficient in that it remained for a long time insensitive to the Apollinarian deviation, had the advantage of always being in formal agreement with Nicaea. The two schools, formed by different mentalities and exegetical methods, produced ultimately contradictory Christologies.

The rigorist critical approach of Antiochenes like Diodore of Tarsus, Theodore of Mopsuestia, and Theodoret led them to study the Gospel text literally in order to describe the history of our salvation rather than to explain it. Since they maintained a literal interpretation of the Old Testament, these theologians tended, in their exegesis of the Gospels and Epistles, to take chiefly into consideration the historical Jesus, the aim and end of the history of Israel, in the full reality of his human nature. But the Word's divine nature, solemnly asserted at Nicaea, appeared to them as an entity obviously present in Christ yet independent in its essence and manifestations. The theological vocabulary of the times did not have at its disposal adequate terms to describe our modern concept of person as opposed to nature; and since the main concern of the school of Antioch was to preserve the full reality of both the entities present in Christ, it called them respectively "the Word assuming" the human nature, and the man Jesus, son of Mary, "assumed by the Word." This distinction had great advantages in exegesis, since it made possible the interpretation of various episodes of the Gospel text by attributing them sometimes to God, sometimes to man; it also avoided the problems of a Christology that spoke of such things as "the death of the Son of God." The great Theodore of Mopsuestia was aware, however, that the Antiochene Christology of the "assuming Word" and the "man assumed" was not sufficient to express the assertion of the Creed of Nicaea, "*one* Lord Jesus Christ," and could lead to a doctrine of two "subjects" in Christ. Consequently in all his writings he insisted on the Lord's unity, mistakenly thinking that he was expressing it adequately by this formula: one person (πρόσωπον) and two natures (φύσεις). Whatever meaning Theodore attached to the formulas he used, this terminology still lent itself to confusion insofar as the "person" common to both the divine and the human natures of Christ could in the vocabulary of the time be interpreted to mean a mere mask. The term "nature" always indicated a concrete reality and, at times, a personal reality. For Theodore, the divine reality "indwelt" in the man Jesus, but his system continued to exclude the notion of "the God-Word, born of the Virgin Mary."

This was precisely the object of the conflict between

Nestorius, a disciple of Theodore, and St. Cyril of Alexandria. In soteriology, the school of Antioch's main concern was to preserve Christ's whole human nature against Apollinarius because, as man, Jesus Christ had been totally assumed by the Word. One of the most obvious signs of the fullness of the Emmanuel's *human* nature was his *death* on the cross. Passibility is the essential characteristic of created human nature; impassibility characterizes the divine nature. For this reason the great Antiochene doctor Theodoret always rejected the "theopaschism" of Cyril and never accepted the expression "God died" on the cross. Theopaschism was for him the surest sign of Monophysitism and implied in Christ the absence of a genuine human nature, for only a man, never God, can die. Even after he had made peace with Cyril and accepted the notion of the divine motherhood of Mary, as well as the term *Theotokos* as a reflection of the mystery of the incarnation with a theological, not merely rhetorical, significance (the latter had always been accepted by Theodore and Nestorius), Theodoret never formally said that "God died." This would have meant for him not a union of the natures but a confusion of the one within the other, human nature transformed into the divine.[4]

However, this "anthropological maximalism" (in the words of G. Florovsky) of the Antiochene school was not sufficient for the construction of a coherent doctrine of redemption. In their view, Jesus Christ's human nature was autonomous: it maintained up to a point its free will and pursued an independent development and activity (yet in union with the Word); and to this human nature the Antiochenes attributed the merit of our salvation. The man Jesus, according to Theodore, "enjoys the cooperation of the Word in proportion with his determination (toward the good)."[5] From such an interpretation of salvation, one may easily draw conclusions favorable to a humanist asceticism that sees man's salvation in his own effort toward good and virtue as an imitation of the effort accomplished by Jesus. However, besides a practical and moralizing tendency that characterized the whole of their preaching, the Antiochene theologians did not draw all the possible conclusions from

their christological assumptions. In their desire to remain
faithful to the Church's tradition, they frequently returned to
the accepted themes concerning Christ as sole victor over
death and sin. This fidelity to tradition went together with
the desire to give a rational explanation of the incarnation
(in Theodore, and even more so in Nestorius). Such an
explanation required an adequate metaphysics manifestly
lacking in Nestorius.[6] His "rationalist" attitude brought him
into conflict with certain expressions of the accepted Christian vocabulary, such as the term *Theotokos,* and immediately
made him suspect in the eyes of the traditionalists. Confronted with their criticisms, Nestorius found himself lacking
valid theological and metaphysical arguments with which
to defend himself. Because he is considered today by some
as the most modern theologian of his day, and since his
intentions were beyond suspicion, he is sometimes presented
as the innocent victim of the intolerance of Cyril of Alexandria. Such a posthumous apology for Nestorius seems to this
author even less convincing than the often arbitrary charges
brought by Cyril, which continued to be accepted by later
theologians.[7]

In opposition to Antioch, Cyril of Alexandria tended to
stress mainly that salvation is given and accomplished by God
alone. The power of death and sin could not be defeated
by the human merits of the man Jesus. The Word assumed
the human nature and made it really *his own.* For a clear
understanding of Cyril, one cannot emphasize enough this
soteriological aspect of his thought.[8] He maintained that the
relationship between the divine and the human in Christ does
not consist of a simple cooperation, or even interpenetration,
but of a *union;* the incarnate Word is one, and there could be
no duplication of the personality of the one redeemer God
and man. Salvation consists precisely in the fact that the
Word was present in all the stages of the human life of
Jesus. To him the Virgin Mary gave birth. To refuse to call
her Mother of God amounts to a rejection of the mystery
of the incarnation, since in Christ *there is no other subject*
but the Word to whom she could have given birth. There
are not two sons, but only two births of the same Word,

who by nature remains immutably God, but adds a whole human nature to his being in order to restore mankind to its primitive state and free it from death and sin. It is also the Word who died on the cross. For this reason the death of the Word was really redemptive, since the death of a man, even the most righteous of all, would have remained merely the death of a human individual.

This fundamental christological intuition was expressed by St. Cyril within the framework of a still imprecise terminology. The term *hypostasis* especially, in Alexandria as in Antioch, and in spite of the very precise use the great Cappadocians had made of it in applying it to the trinitarian mystery, appeared as a synonym of nature (φύσις).

In order to assert that in Christ there is one single being, that before and after the incarnation the Word remained the only author of our salvation, Cyril spoke of one single hypostasis or of a "single incarnate nature of the God-Word" (μία φύσις Θεοῦ λόγου σεσαρκωμένη). The rather vague term πρόσωπον, used in Antioch to designate the union of the two natures in Christ, seemed to Cyril totally insufficient. Most of the time he opposed to it the idea of "hypostatic union," but with the synonymous use of the words ὑπόστασις and φύσις,[9] then accepted by both sides, he was led to speak also of a "single nature."

For more than one reason the Cyrillian terminology was insufficient to provide the framework of a universally acceptable Christology. First, it did not preserve the necessary role played by the human nature in the work of salvation. Since Origen's time it had a tendency toward "anthropological minimalism," which the Church had to keep in control and to which the Monophysites eventually fell prey. Cyril was not aware of the doubtful origins his formula μία φύσις Θεοῦ λόγου σεσαρκωμένη evoked in the minds of many. This formula had been borrowed by Cyril from a text that he believed to be from Athanasius but was in reality from Apollinarius.[10] The fraud to which the bishop of Alexandria had become an unsuspecting accomplice was discovered by the Byzantine authors of the sixth century, but they were unfortunately not able to prevent the Monophysites from using the unfortunate formula as an anti-Chalcedonian warhorse. For the Antiochene theologians, faithful in this respect to the first anti-Apollinarian polemicists, especially St. Gregory Nazianzen, the full human reality of Christ was not expressed with sufficient clarity in those expressions that spoke of "one incarnate nature of the Word"; the biblical notion of "flesh" ("the Word was made flesh," Jn 1:14) had lost in the Greek world its original sense of animated creature and was largely used as a synonym of body in opposition to the soul. The Apollinarian Christology implied, therefore, that Christ did not possess a full human nature but only a human body, the Word having taken the place of the rational and immaterial element in the human complex; and it was precisely this rational element that was for the Greeks the ἡγεμονικόν, the directing principle in the human individual. Deprived of the human mind (νοῦς), the human nature of Christ could not be a genuine human nature but only an inanimate body inhabited by the divine intellect.

Although he unwittingly used a vocabulary that sounded Apollinarian, Cyril himself, in his anti-Nestorian polemic, rejected Apollinarius. Expressions like μία φύσις Θεοῦ λόγου σεσαρκωμένη and μία ὑπόστασις seemed necessary to him especially in order to show *the unity of subject* that existed between the divine Word pre-existent from all eternity and the incarnate Word. It cannot be doubted that Cyril recognized in Christ a full human nature, the union of "two natures." In the first *Letter to Succensus* Cyril attacks those who wish to attribute to him the "opinions of Apollinarius" and continues:

> When we conceive the way in which the incarnation came about, we see that two natures became united without separation, without confusion, and without transformation; for the flesh remains flesh: it is not divine nature, though it be God's flesh; and similarly the Word is God, and not flesh, although on account of his "economy" he made the flesh his own.

After using this eminently Chalcedonian language, Cyril nonetheless goes back to his favorite expressions: "We say that there is one Son, and as the Fathers said, one nature incarnate of God the Word."[11] It is clear that φύσις and ὑπόστασις, according to Cyril, do not designate a "substance." In that case the substance of the God-Man would be a new substance, resulting from a mixture of divinity and humanity,[12] *complementary* realities from which the one hypostasis of the incarnate Word would be made. This idea of complementarity constituted Apollinarius's main error, as Diodore of Tarsus perceived,[13] and there was nothing of that in Cyril. On the contrary, in contrast to the later Monophysites, the great Alexandrian bishop refrained from demanding that the Antiochenes should adopt his terminology. In fact, the "single nature" appears neither in the *Anathematisms* against Nestorius nor in the text of the agreement that restored unity in 433 between the churches of Antioch and Alexandria.

Cyril's victory at Ephesus (431) did not merely have the negative effect of eliminating from Orthodox theology the "Nestorian" temptation. Its importance consisted not only of the assertion of a historical truth, that of Christ's unity, but also of the proclamation of a positive and theologically creative concept: that of a Christic humanity wholly human, wholly "appropriated" by the Word, and constituting the principle of the deification to which all those who are "in Christ" are destined. That is what the Council of Ephesus intended to preserve in making a dogma from the term *Theotokos* to designate the Mother of Jesus; for Mary could not be only the Mother of the "flesh" of Christ, because this flesh did not possess an independent existence but was truly the "flesh of God." In this flesh (κατὰ σάρκα) did the Son of God suffer, die, and rise again; with this flesh is the whole of redeemed mankind called to have communion with the Holy Spirit. The concept of "participation" in God and of the deification of man could not be attained in a strictly Antiochene context.

Cyril, however, lacked the terms that would have removed all suspicion of Apollinarianism and made his doctrine acceptable to the whole Church. His ebullient mind did not have the sober clarity with which, some fifty years previously, the great Cappadocians had disentangled the Arian controversy from the verbal confusions into which it had sunk and had reformulated the Nicene faith in a way acceptable to the majority of the Eastern episcopate. Faithful to Athanasius' theological system (the Apollinarian formulas he used were attributed to Athanasius), Cyril was either not able or did not want to apply to Christology the Cappadocian definitions of φύσις, οὐσία, and ὑπόστασις. This step was to be taken by the Council of Chalcedon, the essential merit of which was the formulation of Cyril's doctrine in a language theologically precise and understandable for the Antiochene theologians.

Such a development was made necessary by the very circumstances of the debates of Ephesus, and by the polemical nature of its decisions, which merely asserted Cyrillian orthodoxy without answering the real problems posed by Antiochene Christology. In his correspondence with Cyril, Nestorius had refused to admit that the Word, being God, could have "been born" of the Virgin and died on the cross. He agreed, however, to say that Christ—God made man—was born and suffered in the flesh.[14] Nestorianism was essentially ambiguous because it implicitly admitted a duality of subjects between the Word and Christ. In Nestorius' terminology it was obviously assumed that all that could be said of the Word, whether incarnate or not, could necessarily be attributed to the divine *nature* itself. Expressions such as "the Word died on the cross," or "was born of Mary," were prejudicial to the attributes of the divine nature, itself unchanged even after the incarnation. "By the contact of the temple in which it dwelt" (τῇ τοῦ ναοῦ συναφείᾳ), the Word's divine nature became itself subject to corruption.[15]

It is evident that only a clear distinction between the Word, as person or hypostasis, and the divinity as a nature impassible, unchangeable, and common to the whole Trinity could be of help in expressing, if not explaining, the mystery of redemption. But such a distinction was lacking in both St. Cyril and Nestorius. Its adoption by the Church at Chalcedon posed a certain number of new problems, which later Byzantine theology tried to solve; but in the middle of the fifth century it seemed that the Church had discovered, with the Chalcedonian formula, the only possible and orthodox way of wording the essential outlines of the mystery of the incarnation.

In an Eastern Church still impressed by the victory of Cyril over Nestorius, the heresy of Eutyches drew attention to the dangers of triumphant Alexandrianism. It brought to notice the absence in Cyril's vocabulary of a terminology able to cope with these dangers.

The Acts of Eutyches' trial by the Synod of Constantinople, presided over in 448 by Bishop Flavian, show that Cyril remained the only criterion of orthodoxy for the judges as for the accused. At first, Eutyches was not inclined to accept the formula of union that Cyril accepted in 433 at the time of the peace with the Easterners (Christ's perfect humanity and divinity, and "union of the two natures"), but he eventually consented. He refused, however, to confess two natures "after the union," in other words, the persistence and integrity of both natures in Christ. This doctrine was considered with good reason by the bishops who took part in the synod as Cyrillian in its contents, although Cyril had never formally endorsed it.[16]

Eutyches' condemnation appeared to many a relinquishing of Cyrillism. Dioscorus of Alexandria, with the Emperor's support, obtained without much difficulty the deposition of Flavian, the rehabilitation of Eutyches, and the condemnation of the consistent defenders of the "two natures after the union," namely, Theodoret of Cyrrhus and Ibas of Edessa, who were compromised a priori on account of their former friendship with Nestorius. This was the work of the "Robber" Council of Ephesus, under the martial leadership of Cyril's nephew and successor to the see of the Egyptian metropolis, and it acted in the name of Cyril's theology. Only the death of the Emperor Theodosius II made a reversal of the situation possible.

The Council of Chalcedon, with its 500 bishops, almost all Easterners (the largest Church assembly until then),

demonstrated that Monophysitism was fundamentally re-
pugnant to the Eastern Church, except Egypt alone. Once
the psychological pressures of Theodosius II and Dioscorus
had disappeared, the episcopate recognized the Catholic faith
in the person of Flavian, and not Dioscorus, even less
Eutyches. Yet no one challenged Cyril's absolute authority,
and no one championed a return to Antiochene terminology,
which was suspected of Nestorianism. The solution was found
in a recourse to Western Christology, and this meant a
terminological innovation—the distinction between nature and
hypostasis. Such a distinction had not been admitted until
then by the East, Antioch or Alexandria: it was Chalcedon's
essential and original contribution to Christology. This council
appears in the history of the Church as the most perfect
example of the "conciliarity" that enables the Church to
discover and formulate in a truly "catholic" language, understandable by all, a permanent truth that no isolated local
tradition can completely express.

Western theology, as expressed in Pope Leo's famous
Tome to Flavian, possessed, in comparison with the Alexandrian and Antiochene systems, the evident advantage of
insisting on the full reality of the two *substantiae* in Christ
without being in any way Nestorian. The tendency of Latin
thought, as it appears already in Tertullian, was to see Christ
above all as a mediator between God and mankind. Its
conception of redemption was more juridical, based on the
idea of sacrifice and reconciliation rather than on the Eastern
concept of deification. Therefore it could not avoid asserting
that Christ was *at the same time God and man* but was also
a single *person.*

The first result of Pope Leo's intervention in the East
gave the Antiochene theologians a chance of survival at a
moment when they risked being overwhelmed by the Monophysite wave. Yet the main insight of Cyrillian theology
about Christ's unity was not abandoned; nor was the idea of
communion excluded, which is central in the Eastern concept
of salvation. Leo's intention was not to speculate about the
very meaning of the union of the two natures in Christ but
to reintroduce the common sense of the Bible, in which

Jesus appeared clearly as both God and man. This common sense had been frankly abandoned by Eutyches; in the words of Leo, he was nothing but *multum imprudens et nimis imperitus* ("exceedingly thoughtless and sadly inexperienced"). The Gospel text shows us clearly that each of the natures of the incarnate Word preserves its own operations (*agit utraque forma quod proprium est*), but each does so only in communion with the other (*cum alterius communione*). This communion is no mere juxtaposition but is based on the identity of subject in the divine and human activities of Christ: the same is God and man (*qui enim verus est Deus, idem verus est homo*). Although Leo does not mention "deification," he admits its essential theological presupposition. Finally, there is in Leo's text a clear concept of *communicatio idiomatum*, the very thing that was the stumbling block for all the "nestorianizing" theologians of Antioch: the unity of person makes it possible to say that "the Son of God died" (*unitatem personae in utraque natura intelligendam Filius Dei crucifixus dicitur et sepultus*),[17] without the divine nature losing its natural impassibility. This was precisely the point on which Cyril had fought against Nestorius: God, without ceasing to be God, made human nature *his own* to the point of mortality.

Leo's Latin terminology could not, however, satisfy the East. The trinitarian quarrels of the fourth century had already shown what misunderstandings could result from the parallelisms *persona* (πρόσωπον) and *substantia-natura* (οὐσία-φύσις). The Council of Chalcedon therefore translated St. Leo's *persona* by ὑπόστασις and also put an end to Cyril's ambiguous μία φύσις ("one nature"). Here is the famous text of the Chalcedonian definition:

> Wherefore, following the holy Fathers, we all with one voice confess our Lord Jesus Christ one and the same Son, the same perfect in Godhead, the same perfect in manhood, truly God and truly man, the same consisting of a reasonable soul and a body, of one substance with the Father as touching the Godhead, the same of one substance with us

as touching the manhood, like us in all things
apart from sin; begotten of the Father before the
ages as touching the Godhead, the same in the last
days, for us and for our salvation, born from the
Virgin Mary, the Theotokos, as touching the manhood, one and the same Christ, Son, Lord Only-
begotten, to be acknowledged in two natures, without confusion, without change, without division,
without separation; the distinction of natures being
in no way abolished because of the union but rather
the characteristic property of each nature being preserved, and concurring into one person [πρόσω-
πον] and one hypostasis, not as if Christ were
parted or divided into two persons, but one and
the same Son and Only-begotten God, Word, Lord,
Jesus Christ; even as the prophets from the beginning spoke concerning him, and our Lord Jesus
Christ instructed us, and the Creed of the Fathers
was handed down to us.

Written on the basis of the formula of union (433)
and of the confession of Flavian (448), the Chalcedonian
definition was the result of a series of laborious compro-
mises between the opposing parties. It is all the more
remarkable to find in it elements of a *positive* solution of
the christological problem.

The vast majority of the Fathers were definitely Cyrillian, and the first version of the text presented at the council
merely took up the terms of 433: "from two natures"
(ἐκ δύο φύσεων), a Cyrillian formula that the Monophysites were prepared to accept because it allowed them to
say "one nature after the union." The term *nature* thus kept
its ancient sense of concrete being, synonymous with *hypostasis,* and the ambiguity of the whole Alexandrian terminology remained intact. It took an ultimatum from the
Roman legates and strong pressure from the imperial representatives to compel the Fathers to send the text back into
a commission. Fundamentally anti-Nestorian, the assembly

did not know how to formulate its anti-Monophysitism, which remained a vague instinct.

The eventual and unanimous acceptance of the final text, however, can not be explained merely by external pressures. It was no mere capitulation to Rome, as the Monophysites tried to depict it, nor did it give up Cyrillian theology.

To be convinced of this, one has only to read the Acts of the second session: while the majority of bishops, after the reading of the *Tome* of Leo, acclaimed it as an expression of the true faith, common to "Leo and Cyril," the latter remained for them the only reference worthy of confidence. The representatives of Illyricum and Palestine, however, still objected to Leo's orthodoxy. The Archdeacon of Constantinople, Aetius, finally obtained their agreement by reading to them other texts by Cyril; but the entire matter had to be sent back into a commission for five days, so that the *Tome* of Leo might be compared to the writings of Cyril, and especially to his *Anathematisms*.[18] The result of the investigation was announced at the fourth session, and only then did the vote take place, each bishop specifying that Leo's letter to Flavian was in his opinion only a new expression of the true faith proclaimed at Nicaea, Constantinople, and Ephesus, and in Cyril's letters.[19] Therefore, while condemning Eutyches, the Chalcedonian Fathers remained convinced that "Nestorianism was a force more dangerous to the Church than Monophysitism."[20] But, above all, they intended to remain faithful to Cyril.

The Latin formulas included in the definition ("each nature preserving its own way of being,"[21] "in two natures") and not contrary to the thought of St. Cyril,[22] are balanced by the remarkable insistence on the personal *unity* of Christ. The expression τὸν αὐτὸν ("the same") is intentionally repeated eight times in the text, underlining the unity of *subject* in all actions, whether divine or human, of Christ. The word Θεοτόκος, implying the *communicatio idiomatum*, is also used. The expression "in two natures"—foreign to Cyril, but generally accepted in Antioch and in the West, and frequently used by the members of the synod of 448 that condemned Eutyches—brought in the fundamental and emi-

nently constructive distinction between φύσις and ὑπόστασις that was lacking in earlier christological language.

Adopted in trinitarian theology by the Cappadocians,
this distinction had made a timid entry into the christological
realm through the intermediary of the *Tome* of Proclus of
Constantinople to the Armenians. Proclus already had deliberately preferred to say μία ὑπόστασις rather than μία
φύσις.[23] After Chalcedon, the distinction provided theologians with the proper terms to designate both the unity
and the duality in Christ. In conclusion, the council added a
touch of truly Catholic moderation and humility by maintaining in Christology the element of mystery amid the
intricacies and the phraseological subtleties into which they
had plunged. The union of the two natures was defined at
Chalcedon by four *negative* adverbs, which, while they condemned the two contrary heresies of Nestorius and Eutyches,
excluded any pretention to explain *fully* in human terms the
very mystery of the incarnation.

In spite of its extraordinary sense of balance and tradition, the Chalcedonian definition was rejected by a large
number of Eastern Christians. On the one hand, they were
opposed to it because it was forbidden in 331 to draw up
new confessions of faith and also because of the touchy
conservatism with which the Egyptians held on to the formulas that symbolized the triumph of their great Archbishop
Cyril over Nestorius. On the other hand, "for the theology
of the hypostatic union, [the Chalcedonian formula] was a
good beginning, but only a beginning." It did not affirm
clearly, "for example, who the subject of suffering and
crucifixion was...conversely, all the warnings against any
confusion of the two natures left the proponents of the
hypostatic union unsatisfied on their fundamental soteriological point: that the ultimate deification of man had its
inception in the union of the humanity of Christ with his
divinity in an intimate and inseparable wholeness of person."[24]

2.

Chalcedonians and Monophysites

The distinction established at Chalcedon between the terms φύσις and ὑπόστασις was too new and revolutionary in the theology of the incarnation not to bring about divergent interpretations and misunderstandings. Methodologically, the theologians of the time can be classified into four groups:

1. Strict Dyophysites who remained faithful to the Antiochene Christology and, while they rejected Nestorius, considered Chalcedon as a posthumous victory for Theodore of Mopsuestia and a partial disavowal of Cyril.

2. Monophysites who, following Dioscorus and Timothy Aelurus, considered Chalcedon as a return to Nestorianism and rejected the council. The Cyrillian formula, "one single incarnate nature of the God-Word," represented for them the only admissible christological formula; for them this single nature undoubtedly consisted "of two natures" (ἐκ δύο φύσεων), since the word "nature" additionally could have a generic sense; yet, concretely, the historical Christ was "one single nature." To agree with Chalcedon that he was "in two natures" (ἐν δύο φύσεσιν) after the union amounted to admitting the existence of two separate beings in Christ.

3. A group called today neo-Chalcedonian (after the suggestion of J. Lebon). To this group, Chalcedon did not disavow Cyril but merely condemned Eutyches. By saying "one hypostasis," Chalcedon adopted all the arguments of Cyril against Nestorius, and the Cyrillian phraseology itself, in-

cluding the formula "one incarnate nature of God the Word," which remained valid in an anti-Nestorian context. The formula "in two natures," used in Chalcedon, was essential only in order to assert the double consubstantiality of Christ and thus condemn Eutychianism.

4. None of these groups was able to solve the problems of terminology posed by the Chalcedonian definition. An effort toward a creative solution was undertaken only in the first half of the sixth century by a fourth school of thought, largely inspired by Origenist metaphysics. The main representative of this school was Leontius of Byzantium.

Although the existence of these various groups is presently recognized by historians specializing in that period, the evaluations about each group do not always agree. These judgments are determined, on the one hand, by the renewal of interest in and admiration for the work of Theodore of Mopsuestia, brought about by some recent studies.[1] On the other hand, these judgments are due to deeper theological reasons that, while not necessarily of a denominational character, are at the root of most doctrinal disagreements between East and West since the time of the fourth century. For some, Chalcedon merely confirmed Antiochene Christology in essentials by rejecting the polemical excesses of Cyril. Theodore of Mopsuestia, the great representative of the Antiochene school, was "Chalcedonian" before Chalcedon, and his condemnation by the council of 553 was based on unauthentic or corrupted quotations.[2] It is self-evident that neo-Chalcedonism does not enjoy the favor of these present-day historians. For them it represents only an artificial effort to conciliate Cyril with Chalcedon and was, in fact, a return to Monophysitism. The prefix "neo," therefore, is used by them in a definitely pejorative sense and represents for them a movement that practically betrayed Chalcedon by ratifying the underlying Monophysitism that, according to them, dominated later Byzantine Christianity. In contrast, the true Chalcedonism would have been preserved only by our first group, the strict Dyophysites and, obviously, by those Westerners who opposed the condemnation of the "Three Chapters" by the Fifth Ecumenical Council.[3]

The rehabilitation of Theodore of Mopsuestia implied in this thesis witnesses a modern predisposition in favor of Antioch—a predisposition that at the beginning of this century also favored Nestorius.[4] This tendency is considered unacceptable by other authors, who recognize a fundamental doctrinal opposition between Theodore and Cyril; they note that not only Ephesus but also Chalcedon firmly sided with Cyril, even though these councils may have qualified some of his formulas.[5] If, as it seems, an impartial examination of the Acts of Chalcedon proves them right, neo-Chalcedonism must be considered not as a disavowal of Chalcedon but as a return to true Chalcedonism.

The importance of the debate must be emphasized, since it concerns the very meaning of the Chalcedonian definition and, by implication, all later theological developments in both East and West.

The period between Chalcedon (451) and the beginning of Justinian's reign (527) was dominated by a fruitless debate between the Monophysites and the strict Dyophysites. The many imperial interventions in this debate contributed more than a little to its embitterment and the dead end into which it plunged. This initial debate immediately following Chalcedon will be the subject matter of this chapter.

On the Chalcedonian side, during the years immediately following the council, the great figure of Theodoret, Bishop of Cyrus and rehabilitated victim of Dioscorus, dominated the scene. Until his death in 466, Theodoret continued to publish theological works. He corresponded with numerous contemporaries, including Pope Leo and the Nestorians of Persia.[6] As a friend of Nestorius, Theodoret openly opposed not only Eutyches but also Cyril. His refutations of the *Twelve Anathematisms* and the Council of Ephesus were remembered by everyone. Antiochene in thought and education, Theodoret nevertheless had been able to recognize where Cyril had been right against Nestorius, and he signed the formula of union of 433. A genuine theologian, he was able to penetrate words and formulas and reach their meaning. He recognized that orthodoxy could also be expressed in Alexandrian formulas and that certain Antiochene formulas, such as the "assumed man," had to be rejected.[7] In 451, Theodoret's orthodoxy was recognized after he anathematized his former friend Nestorius. For fifteen years he remained the most important spokesman of the Chalcedonian party.

Yet Cyrillism, even in its Chalcedonian expression, remained foreign to the bishop of Cyrus. The old Antiochene formulas always came naturally to his pen, especially when he was writing to his former Oriental friends. His formulas, often correct, sounded Nestorian to the ears of the Monophysites. Besides, as has already been indicated, Theodoret remained steadfast in his refusal to use theopaschite formulas, i.e., to say that "the son of God died on the cross." In the great work that he composed after Chalcedon, probably about 453,[8] the *Haereticarum fabularum compendium,* the fifth book of which consists of an *Epitome* of Christian doctrine, he still objects with some polemical violence to any form of theopaschism. The resurrection, he argues, is manifestly the resurrection of Christ's body, not of his soul or of his divinity; Christ's soul, like any other human soul, is immortal. How could his divinity be mortal? Christ's death, therefore, consisted of the separation of the immortal soul from the mortal body, the divinity remaining attached to them both and guaranteeing in this way their reunion in the resurrection.[9] Manifestly, the hypostatic union remains outside Theodoret's perspective. Christ's actions are only considered in the perspective of the "two natures"; the words φύσις and ὑπόστασις remain synonymous.

Having rejected the theology of the "assumed man," which for Theodore of Mopsuestia constituted the true *subject* of the passion, Theodoret replaced it, in the name of the union with Cyril, with abstract terms like "humanity," "human nature," or "the things human" (τὰ ἀνθρώπεια). When asked who suffered, he answered: "the flesh." This suffering had been appropriated by the Word, since the flesh was "his own."[10] Undoubtedly, within Theodoret's system, to attribute suffering to the Word as *subject* would mean that the divine nature itself suffered. As he continued corresponding by letter with the Persian Nestorians, Theodoret gave an Antiochene interpretation to Chalcedon. His tendency was to identify the single hypostasis defined by the council (and on account of which the Nestorians rightly regarded Chalcedon as a Cyrillian council) with the concept of single πρόσωπον always accepted by the school of Theodore of Mopsuestia.[11] The identification of πρόσωπον and ὑπόστασις had in fact been accepted at Chalcedon, but only insofar as it reinforced and explained the meaning of πρόσωπον. The Antiochenes, however, tended to ignore this Chalcedonian Cyrillism and to interpret the synod as a victory over Alexandria. Ill at ease with the notion of hypostatic union, they continued to ignore it in their theological vocabulary, and their only justification for the term was to make it mean union κατὰ πρόσωπον. In other words, the dilemma remained complete. It is known that Nestorius, who was still alive in 451, gave his approval to the *Tome* of Leo.[12]

In 458, a consultation of the episcopate, undertaken by the Emperor Leo I as a result of Monophysite insurrections in Egypt and the episcopal consecration of Timothy Aelurus, brought about a general confirmation on the part of the bishops of Cyril and of Chalcedon, but it gave no constructive theological solution to the dilemma that opposed Cyrillian terminology to that of the council. In Constantinople, the Antiochene interpretation of Chalcedon dominated the Chalcedonian party, which always found in theologians of the school of Theodore of Mopsuestia, and especially in Theodoret, the essentials of their valid arguments against the Monophysites.

Patriarch Gennadius of Constantinople (458-471), who after Ephesus had published a violent refutation of the *Anathematisms* of Cyril, and who succeeded Anatolius as bishop of the capital, was another typical representative of that tendency. Like Theodoret, he was in correspondence with the Nestorians. In a *Praise* of St. Leo's letter to Flavian, obviously destined to defend Chalcedonian orthodoxy as he understood it, Gennadius translated the essential terms in such a way that it was impossible for the strict disciples of Cyril to accept them. While rejecting formal Nestorianism, the patriarch avoided the term Θεοτόκος and hypostatic union; in discussing the two natures of Christ and in emphasizing the particular identity of each one of them (ἑκατέρας φύσεως ἰδιότητα σωζομένην), he spoke of union only as "in a single πρόσωπον."[13] Undoubtedly, for Gennadius Antiochene Christology had lost none of its force, and he used it abundantly in his commentaries on Scripture.[14]

His successors to the patriarchal see had to give way several times to imperial pressure and betray Chalcedon. A notable example was Acacius, who accepted the *Henotikon* of Zeno, which proclaimed the Creed of Nicaea and the *Anathematisms* of Cyril as the only criteria of orthodoxy (482). But the political and non-theological character of the various imperial attempts at re-establishing religious unity in the East is evident. On the doctrinal plane, the Chalcedonian party of Constantinople unfortunately lacked eminent theologians and, in fact, remained faithful to Antiochene theology only.

This situation manifested itself during the so-called theopaschite controversies, which exploded in Constantinople during the first years of the sixth century under the Patriarch Macedonius (495-511). An unbending Chalcedonian, Macedonius was throughout his years as patriarch a courageous symbol of the pathetic isolation of the Church of Constantinople. Opposing both the Monophysite Emperor Anastasius and the Monophysite majority of Egypt and Syria, Constantinople was abandoned by Rome, whose centralizing formalism prevented it from overlooking the fact that Constantinople maintained in its diptychs the name of Patriarch Acacius, who had been implicated in the episode of the *Henotikon.* Taking his stand with the support of the Acoemetae ("Non-sleeping" monks) Macedonius rejected all compromise with Monophysitism; but this opposition remained purely negative and lent itself to criticisms. The doctrinal weakness of his position was illustrated by the theopaschite episode, largely provoked by the interpolation of the so-called *Trisagion* by the Monophysites.

The modification was introduced into the *Trisagion* by the Monophysite patriarch of Antioch, Peter the Fuller. The original text of the famous hymn, sung at Chalcedon, was: "Holy God, Holy Mighty, Holy Immortal, have mercy on us"; Peter added σταυρωθεὶς δι' ἡμᾶς ("crucified for us"). The interpolation was meant to proclaim, by using an expression from the Nicene-Constantinopolitan Creed, an essential aspect of Cyrillian theology. The Word as the only "subject" in Christ is also the subject of the death "in the flesh" which is "his own." Undoubtedly the *Trisagion* was interpreted as a hymn to the incarnate Word, and the interpolated form of it was formally orthodox. It would have been decidedly heretical had it been addressed to the Trinity, implying the passion of the three persons or of the divine essence.[15] The Chalcedonian opposition would have been justified, therefore, if it had limited its objections to the fact that the hymn was interpreted in a Trinitarian sense in many churches and that consequently the use of the interpolated form was dangerously ambiguous. However, if one reads certain Chalcedonian texts relative to this controversy, one finds, against theopaschism in all its forms, objections current in the anti-Cyrillian circles of Antioch before and after the Council of Ephesus. A notable example is to be found in the collection of (fake) letters to Peter the Fuller, published in 512.[16] The first letter, for example, attributed to Anteon, Bishop of Arsinoe, asserts that "Jesus Christ is one of the incarnate Trinity, but the cross can only be attributed to his human nature."[17] In this text, as in many others of the same collection, Dyophysitism, without being formally Nestorian, is expressed without reference to the hypostatic union.

The Chalcedonism of the Acoemetae, the main adversaries of Monophysitism in Constantinople during the first years of the sixth century, was also an Antiochene Chalcedonism. Even if one refuses to believe the Monophysite sources which declared that the monks officially celebrated the memory of Nestorius, it is certain, as the correspondence between Justinian and Pope John II in 533-534 demonstrates,[18] that they refused to accept the doctrine of *communicatio idiomatum*. They fought against theopaschite formulas, and, furthermore, it did not appear to them that the term Θεοτόκος had to be taken literally. In consequence they were called Nestorians by Pope John II himself.[19]

This same strictly Antiochene interpretation of Chalcedon was defended at Antioch by a certain Basil of Cilicia. Photius wrote of him that he was "contaminated with Nestorianism" without openly taking the part of Nestorius and without attacking St. Cyril to his face, and that he reproached John of Scythopolis for his exclusive devotion to Cyril's twelfth anathematism, which proclaimed "God's passion."[20] Basil's attitude seems to correspond exactly to that of Theodoret or Gennadius, with possibly a more clearly polemical emphasis against theopaschism.

These few examples are sufficient to demonstrate the existence in the East, in Syria and Constantinople especially, of a theological school that, while it accepted Chalcedon, professed essentially the Christology of Theodore of Mopsuestia, without, however, falling into formal Nestorianism. This school dominated the Chalcedonian party until approximately 518.[21] The Monophysite theologians saw Nestorianism in this party, and by associating Chalcedon with it they wrongly classified the council itself as Nestorian, in spite of the fact that Chalcedon had anathematized Nestorius and exalted the memory of Cyril. The main leaders of the Antiochene school, with Theodoret at their head, had been compelled to side with the council on this; but to Cyril's fervent disciples, these anathemas were hypocritical as long as the principles and the terminology that made possible the appearence of Nestorianism remained in full strength and were even being proposed as decisive arguments in favor of the council. For them, the surest sign of the Nestorianism of their adversaries was their refusal to say that "the incarnate Word suffered in the flesh."

Progressively, the problem of theopaschism was acquiring the same symbolic significance that the word Θεοτόκος had in the period from 428 to 431. For instance, while Severus was patriarch of Antioch (512-518), he deposed Epiphanius, Bishop of Tyre, who was repeating against theopaschism the precise argument Theodoret himself had proposed after Chalcedon in his *Epitome* (see page 32).

Christ's soul was immortal, and therefore, a fortiori, so was his divinity; consequently it was impossible to say that "God suffered."[22] That the Chalcedonians should have had recourse to such arguments in order to defend the council was in the eyes of the Monophysites justification enough for the accusation of Nestorianism. In spite of the distinction between φύσις and ὑπόστασις established at Chalcedon, the Chalcedonians continued to identify these two terms in practice. The incarnate Word's hypostasis could not have suffered in the flesh since it was a divine hypostasis, and divinity is by nature impassible. Yet, if one does not admit "the Word's passion in the flesh," the soteriological aspect of St. Cyril's theology disappears: God has not assumed the mortal condition of fallen mankind in its totality; for God alone could vanquish death by voluntarily assuming it.

Since Joseph Lebon's monumental work on Monophysitism was published, it has generally been recognized that the Monophysite doctrine of the incarnation, especially the scientific form given to it by Severus, is nothing but Cyrillian Christology. This point has been made abundantly clear during recent consultations between Chalcedonian and non-Chalcedonian theologians: "Monophysitism," i.e., adherence to Cyril's christological formulas, does not imply acceptance of Eutyches' views. Severus fighting against the "Grammarians" (Chalcedonian theologians in the sixth century) is but a continuation of Cyril's self-defense after the union of 433.[23] What has been said so far has shown clearly that an essentially Antiochene Christology dominated the Chalcedonian party. It is not surprising that it should have been difficult to bring about the union. The debate between Antioch and Alexandria begun at the time of the Council of Ephesus was merely continuing as if the councils of Ephesus and Chalcedon had not taken place. The solution found then had been made possible by the open-mindedness of both parties toward the legitimate preoccupations of their adversaries. They had both agreed to look beyond the formulas and had found unity there. Unfortunately, Cyril's successors in Alexandria and the theologians of Syrian Monophysitism did not have the theological pliability required to understand that Chalcedon had not betrayed the Cyrillian doctrine by adopting a new theology. As has been shown, some of the council's supporters only confirmed them in their suspicions.

During the second half of the fifth and the first half of the sixth century, the great Monophysite theologians, Timothy Aelurus, Philoxenus of Mabbugh, and more especially Severus of Antioch, clearly dominated the scene; and the Chalcedonian party had practically no noteworthy theologian to oppose them.

The starting point of their Christology was the contemplation of the identity between the pre-existent Word and the incarnate Word;[24] this identity was a soteriological necessity asserted by the Creed of Nicaea and by Cyril against Nestorius. For the Monophysites, it was expressed as an identity of nature or hypostasis, since these two terms were synonymous. It is known that they were also identical for St. Athanasius, to whom the Monophysites liked to refer, as did St. Cyril.[25] The simple logic of Monophysitism is well expressed in the words of Timothy Aelurus:

> No man whose heart is healthy in the faith teaches or believes two natures, either before or after the union, for when God the Father's fleshless Word was conceived in the womb of the Holy Virgin, then he also took a body from the flesh of the Holy Virgin, in a manner known to him alone, while he remained without change or modification as God, and was one with his flesh, for his flesh had no hypostasis or essence before the conception of God the Word so that one could give it the name of particular or separate nature, for the nature does not exist without the hypostasis, nor the hypostasis without the person [πρόσωπον]; therefore, if there are two natures, there are also necessarily two persons; but if there are two persons, there are also two Christs.[26]

The same logic is found also in Philoxenus of Mabbugh:

"By his nature," he writes, "he is God, and if he became what he was not, it is not from man that he became God, but from God that he became man, while remaining God as he was."[27] "He became and underwent no change, for he remained [what he was] even in his becoming."[28] To say that the Word "had become man by nature," would mean for Philoxenus that "God has become changing by nature...."

This insistence on the divine immutability is here opposed to the idea of change (τροπή) proper to creatures, especially fallen creatures. It is in order to save the latter that the immutable Word united it to himself. But the union, simply because it is a union, excludes all "number." St. Cyril was already writing: "In the union, what is united can no longer be separated: there is therefore one Son, and his nature is one, since the Word became flesh."[29] A nature means obviously a being or a person. "There is no nature without person," writes Philoxenus, "just as there is no person without nature. For if there are two natures, there must also be two persons and two sons."[30] To admit in Christ two concrete beings—and this is the only meaning of nature accepted by the Monophysites—amounts to suppressing the union, and therefore the very basis of salvation.

The incarnate Word is thus a single nature that, by condescension, and in the realm of "economy,"[31] took on "becoming," i.e., changing human nature, in order to become with it a single nature. The Monophysite theologians were, however, conscious of the danger of Eutychianism and Apollinarianism. If the Word was man only "by economy" and not "by nature," was not his manhood transitory and imaginary? This they unanimously deny: "He has become perfect man as to the soul, the body, and the intelligence, in order to renew the whole man. True God by nature, by essence and eternity, he made himself, as it has been said, with the exception of sin which is neither man nor nature, true man and, above nature and according to the flesh, consubstantial to us."[32] The Monophysites opposed any idea of mingling or tertium quid between the divinity and the manhood in Christ. Philoxenus writes:

The Word was not changed into flesh when he
took a body from it, and the flesh was not transformed into the Word's nature when it was united
to it. The natures were not mixed among themselves
as water and wine which by commixture lose their
natures, or as colors and medicines which, once
they have been mixed together, lose (each one of
them) the determination and the quality which
they possess by nature."[33]

One sees that Philoxenus considers Christ as fully human.
Even though the expression "one incarnate nature of God
the Word" has an Apollinarian origin, he refuses to interpret it in this sense. He also asserts against Eutyches that
Christ is consubstantial with us. The weakness of Philoxenus' position resides, however, in the fact that in his
Christology there exists no formula radically opposed to
Eutychianism. One has to believe his word when he condemns Eutyches, just as one has to believe Theodoret when,
under obvious pressure at Chalcedon, he condemns Nestorius.

It remained for the great sixth-century theologian Severus
of Antioch to formulate the Monophysite positions in a
more systematic way. Like Philoxenus, Severus opposes any
idea of the "mingling of the natures" in Christ. There is
therefore in Christ no manhood as a distinct nature. How
then can one say that Christ is man, that human nature
became fully his own in spirit, soul and body? Severus answered: through the fact that Christ's single nature possesses
all the natural qualities (ἰδιώματα) of manhood. He
writes:

We are not allowed to anathematize those who
speak of natural properties: the divinity and the
humanity that make the single Christ. The flesh
does not cease to exist as flesh, even if it becomes
God's flesh, and the Word does not abandon
his own nature, even if he unites himself hypostatically to the flesh which possesses a rational and
intelligent soul. But the difference is also preserved

as well as the identity under the form of the natural characteristics of the natures which make up the Emmanuel, since the flesh is not transformed into the Word's nature and the Word is not changed into flesh.[34]

This is why Severus always refused to say that Christ was a single essence (οὐσία). This would exclude all duality in the qualities (ἰδιώματα) and all possibility of conceiving Christ as consubstantial with us. He explicitly intended to maintain a real duality within the one being designated by the words "one nature," while avoiding confusion. He was thus led to speak of a composite (σύνθετος) nature or hypostasis. Before the incarnation, the Word was a "simple" nature, but by becoming man, he became "composite in regard to the flesh" (σύνθετος πρὸς τὴν σάρκα).[35] Severus was the only Monophysite theologian to speak of "composition" within the single nature of Christ, but he did so in a very consistent manner.[36] These two categories or qualities, divine and human, within the single nature (or concrete being) are undoubtedly what makes this "composite nature" inevitable. They suggest that Severus recognized in Christ two essences (οὐσίαι) conceived in an abstract sense, or in a sense in which they would be common to a genus (γένος) including numerous hypostases. Severus of course knew that the Cappadocians had made use of the term οὐσία in their doctrine of the Trinity, in order to designate what is common to several hypostases: thus he would not say that Christ, single and unique being, is one οὐσία. As for ὑπό-στασις and φύσις, he considered them either as synonymous, when they designate the mode of existence of a concrete person, or as distinct, since φύσις could also designate a collection of concrete beings with the same οὐσία. In the case of Christ, however, φύσις and ὑπόστασις must be synonymous since the being of Christ is concretely unique, while fully participating in the essence (οὐσία) of God and in the essence (οὐσία) of mankind.[37]

Although Christ is concretely one single nature, intellectually (κατ᾽ ἐπίνοιαν, or ἐν θεωρίᾳ) it is possible to conceive in him two natures, and even two hypostases and two persons (πρόσωπα).[38] The union of the divinity and of the manhood signify, without any doubt, that Christ is made "out of two natures" (ἐκ δύο φύσεων), but the union also specifically means that "two" is transformed into "one" and that the duality of natures can now only be contemplated "by the intellectual imagination."[39]

Undeniably Severus made a serious effort to answer the Dyophysites' objections. His doctrine of "two natures" ἐν θεωρίᾳ corresponds to that of Cyril, who uses precisely these terms to designate the duality in Christ,[40] and like Cyril, he always preserves the synonymous character of ὑπόστασις and φύσις whenever he speaks of the concrete being of Christ; this leads him to say that intellectually, one can also conceive in Christ two hypostases, even two πρόσωπα.

However, because the Christology of Severus evolved into a stricter system than that of Cyril, the words that had been used by the great Alexandrian bishop to designate soterio-logical and kerygmatic realities acquired with Severus a more precise philosophical sense. The word θεωρία sounded less docetic in the writings of Cyril than in those of Severus. It cannot be denied that Severus opposed Chalcedon out of faithfulness to Cyril. He refused to say "two natures after the union" because Cyril had never said it. But his need to defend his position and specify his terms led him to a Monophysitic rigor that Cyril did not have. By admitting in Christ two natures ἐν θεωρίᾳ Severus had of necessity to answer the question: how many natures were there ἐνεργείᾳ, i.e., "in fact" or "in actuality"? His obvious answer, "one nature," logically entailed a monoenergistic position. Besides, for Aristotle, one nature always entailed one energy.

This is why the formula in the *Tome* of Leo on the active properties of each nature—*agit utraque forma cum alterius communione quod proprium est*—taken over by the Chalcedonian definition, "each nature keeping its own way of being," was for the Monophysites most difficult to admit. In their eyes, two energies meant two active beings, and the hypostatic union was reduced to an illusion. "One is the agent (ἐνεργῶν), i.e., the incarnate Word," writes Severus "one is the activity (ἐνέργεια) ; but the works (τὰ ἐνεργη-θέντα) are varied, i.e., what is done by the activity."[41] This distinction between the agent, the activity, and the works can be found in pseudo-Basil (probably Didymus), quoted by Severus,[42] and is perfectly suited to his christological system. The agent's unity (Christ's single hypostasis-nature) entails the unity of energy, without making it impossible for the works, corresponding to the natural qualities of the human and divine natures, to be distributed into various categories, divine and human.[43] It was thus apparent that Severus was heralding with great precision the seventh-century monoenergistic movement. Both, moreover, were trying to reconcile logically the Chalcedonian and Monophysite positions.

Severus's position on the single energy is a good illustration of the very basis of the disagreement. The two opposing parties followed conflicting arguments. The Monophysites contemplated the Logos in his new "state," the incarnate state, and insisted on the absolute unity of subject, expressed by them with the word φύσις, in both states. No human energy could thus be found in the action accomplished by the Logos alone in the incarnation. The Chalcedonian argument, while admitting the soteriological inspiration of the Cyrillian theology and, evidently, the identity between the pre-existing Logos and the incarnate Word, was also pre-occupied with the human aspect of salvation. It could not be satisfied with a manhood conceived only ἐν θεωρίᾳ, as a "state" of the Logos, which was expressed in human acts without human existence. Severus, of course, admitted this existence, but only ἐν συνθέσει,[44] and he refused to designate it by the terms φύσις or ἐνέργεια, which according to him were necessarily linked to an existence that was separate, concrete, and hypostatic. But is a human nature without human energy a true human nature?

As for the Chalcedonian definition, it was the object of divergent interpretations. The Monophysite conservatism blamed it for abandoning Cyrillian terminology. Two natures still meant for the strict Cyrillians two concrete and distinct beings. Chalcedon had nonetheless used the term ὑπόστασις to designate Christ's unity, a term preferred to all others by Cyril. This was an important concession on the part of the Antiochenes, but the interpretation given by many Chalcedonians to the use of ὑπόστασις (considering it a mere synonym of πρόσωπον) did not help to convince the Monophysites that Chalcedon had in fact remained faithful to Cyril. Besides, as Severus did not fail to point out, the Chalcedonian definition did not use the expression hypostatic union (ἕνωσις ὑποστατική). It certainly insisted very strongly on Christ's unity and used in passing the word "union" (of the natures); but strictly speaking, the term ὑπόστασις designated there, in a way parallel to πρόσω-πον, the "point where the particularities of the two natures meet" (τῆς ἰδιότητος ἑκατέρας φύσεως καὶ εἰς ἕν πρόσωπον καὶ μίαν ὑπόστασιν συντρεχούσης). Therefore, the council did not say that *the hypostasis of the union was the pre-existent hypostasis of the Logos.* In order to acquire a fully orthodox sense, the definition had to be read in a Cyrillian context, and this was certainly the way in which the majority of the council had conceived it. But the Monophysites refused to do this. The fact that the strict Dyophysites, who understood the Chalcedonian ὑπό-στασις in the sense of the Antiochene "πρόσωπον of union," were the council's main adherents between 451 and 518 did not encourage Severus and his disciples toward conciliation. As has been shown, for the Monophysites the best proof of the Chalcedonian crypto-Nestorianism was the rejection by many supporters of the council of the formula "one of the Trinity suffered in the flesh." Did this rejection not mean that for them the hypostatic union was not really a union in the hypostasis of the pre-existing Logos?

In order to defend the formulas of the council's definition, the Chalcedonians invoked the trinitarian terminology of the Cappadocians. According to St. Basil, the hypostasis designated in fact the individual, while the essence, or nature, applied to what is "common." This argument, put forward between 514 and 518 by John the Grammarian in a long *Apologia* for the council, gave new weapons to Severus of Antioch. Orthodoxy, Chalcedonian as well as Severian, proclaimed that Christ was consubstantial to the Father in his divinity and consubstantial to us in his manhood. But the divine οὐσία, according to the doctrine of St. Athanasius that the Cappadocians adopted by identifying φύσις and οὐσία in God, represents a concrete reality in the Platonic sense. There is *only one* God in three hypostases. To identify essence and nature in Christology would presuppose, according to Severus, that the whole Trinity had become incarnate! The Cappadocians' Trinitarian terminology therefore cannot be applied as such to Christology. We have seen above how Severus made use of this terminology in connection with the data of his theology of the incarnation.

The christological controversies remained in complete deadlock throughout the second half of the fifth century. Except in Egypt, it does not seem that ethnic or political elements contributed much in drawing the distinction between the partisans of the synod and its adversaries.[45] Most of the controversy was taking place in Greek between theologians who thought and wrote in that language. Monophysitism, therefore, cannot be identified with an "Eastern" form of Christianity. Syriac Christianity seems to have been fairly equally divided among Nestorians, Chalcedonians, and Monophysites. Nor was Chalcedonism identified, as was the case case later, with the empire's religion. The two greatest emperors of the time, Zeno and Athanasius, had more or less openly disavowed the council, and the Monophysites were only too happy to use their support. The imperial interventions in the controversy, the most famous of which was the publication of the *Henotikon* by Zeno (482), produced no great results precisely because, instead of solving the theological problems raised by the definition of 451, they tried to ignore it, and finally provoked the opposition of both parties.

In the end, a specifically Byzantine theology had the merit of providing the Church with the elements of a genuine solution, which, unfortunately, came too late to conciliate the Monophysites. This solution consisted of a new awareness of the hypostatic union with all that it implied.

This re-interpretation of Chalcedon played in relationship to the council a role similar in all aspects to the role the Cappadocian Fathers played in relationship to Nicaea. A synodal formula, providentially exact but adopted by an assembly that could not be aware at the time of all the psychological and philosophical difficulties this decision would bring about, demanded a creative interpretation.

In the case of Chalcedon, this interpretation was provided by the Byzantine theology of the sixth and seventh centuries. It was determined not only, as is generally believed, by Justinian's unionist policy but also by the development of christological thought and a greater elaboration of Chalcedonian terminology.

3.

The Origenist Crisis of the Sixth Century

Origen's personality and ideas have always been the source of passionate controversies. Condemned in his lifetime by his bishop, supported by numerous disciples, he was attacked again in the fourth century by St. Epiphanius and condemned in 400 by a council presided over by Theophilus of Alexandria. The role played by St. Jerome and Rufinus of Aquileia in the Origenist quarrels of that time are also well known. The same quarrels were used as an excuse for the deposition of St. John Chrysostom.

Justinian's edict against the Origenists, published in 543, had for its immediate cause the troubles in the Lavra of Mar-Sabbas in Palestine. St. Sabbas himself visited the Emperor in 531 and asked for his intervention against the partisans of Abbot Nonnus, the leader of the Origenists.[1] The doctrines at stake in the dispute were not confined, however, to the local Palestinian situation, and Justinian had to initiate a general condemnation of Origenism and finally have it ratified by the Fifth Ecumenical Council. The condemnation concerned, on the one hand, Origenist cosmology and anthropology and, on the other, a certain Christology professed in Origenist circles and in earlier times by Evagrius Ponticus.

In his synodal letter of 400, Theophilus of Alexandria had already pointed out that for the Origenists, "the Word of the living God has not assumed the human body," and that Christ, "who was in the form of God, equal to God, was not the Word of God, but the soul which, coming down from the celestial region and divesting itself of the form of eternal majesty, assumed the human body."[2] The distinction between Christ and the Word presupposed by this curious Christology of the Origenists could not fail to recall, for sixth-century minds, the Nestorian distinction between the Word and the assumed man. In both cases, in completely different metaphysical frameworks, the being of Christ became duplicated. It is not strange, therefore, that St. Sabbas's biographer several times defined him as the supporter of orthodoxy "against the doctrines of Origen and of Theodore of Mopsuestia."[3] This unexpected association of the respective leaders of the Alexandrian and Antiochene schools was possible only within the context of the disputes of the sixth century, at a time when Justinian was above all preoccupied with presenting the Chalcedonian doctrine of the two natures as perfectly compatible with the Cyrillian Christology of the single being of the pre-existent and incarnate Logos.

The question has long been asked whether the Origenism of the sixth century was really the doctrine of the great Alexandrian doctor. It seems that recently published texts enable us to solve that problem.

Most historians who devote themselves to the study of Origen adopt a sympathetic and often admiring attitude toward him. Consciously or unconsciously preoccupied by the problem of Christian witness in a non-Christian world, they are led to admire Origen as a Christian thinker who managed to make himself understood by the pagan Greeks and who created a Christian theology that studiously expressed itself in philosophical categories acceptable to non-Christians. Origen's merits in this respect are undeniable and most genuine. On the historical level, this personal rehabilitation of Origen has raised the problem of distinguishing between his own ideas and those of his disciples. Was Origen himself, or only a few "Origenists," the cause of the troubles of the fourth and the sixth centuries? The problem consists of knowing whether these Origenists were faithful to their master or had, in fact, corrupted his teaching.

Some historians tend to present the disputed questions

of the fourth century, which were finally condemned in the sixth, as having nothing to do with Origen himself. They are made out to be the inventions of polemicists, heresy hunters interested in compromising Origen's memory. An objective study of the facts, and especially the reading of the περὶ ἀρχῶν (*De principiis, On the First Principles*), which the modern apologists of Origen usually overlook, leads to different conclusions. For instance, M. Harl, in his brilliant analysis of the περὶ ἀρχῶν, does discover there the points of the Origenist doctrine that the Church's tradition formally rejected.[4] These are precisely the propositions condemned under Justinian. According to M. Harl, their existence in the sixth century arises from the fact that "disciples less intelligent than the master insisted upon Origen's more questionable theories instead of remaining faithful to his main ideas, to the principles of his thought."[5] This judgment, though it admits that authentic Origenism is susceptible to an unorthodox interpretation, still seems insufficient to explain the fate of Origenism in the Christian tradition. The condemnations of which Origen was the object in the sixth century did not concern only accidental traits of his thought that were "exaggerated" by disciples; it was precisely the main ideas of the περὶ ἀρχῶν, especially Origen's cosmology and anthropology, that were the targets. Such are the conclusions of historians of Origenism, and especially the learned editor of the περὶ ἀρχῶν, P. Koetschau.

If Origen as exegete and mystic is not implicated in the sixth-century condemnations, the same is not true of Origen as theologian; and the Origenists who entered into conflict with the Church in the time of Justinian based their teaching on perfectly authentic ideas of Origen. His trinitarian doctrine did not attract them, since the formulas of the Alexandrian doctor had been clearly superseded and replaced by the terminology of Nicaea and of the Cappadocian Fathers. No Origenist of Justinian's time thought of returning to them.[6] Foremost were his cosmological, anthropological, and eschatological ideas, which constituted precisely the cornerstone of Origenism as a system.

In the sixth century, Origenism was especially widespread

in monastic circles, where it served as the basis of a certain spirituality. One should read, for example, passages in the letters of St. Barsanuphius, a celebrated ascetic of the region of Gaza in Palestine, in order to realize with what passion the ideas of Origen and those of his disciple Evagrius were discussed at the beginning of the sixth century.[7] In Egypt the intellectualist current of Evagrian works was also fighting with the adherents of a more "incarnate" and christocentric spirituality.[8]

The Origenist traditions were stronger in the Great Lavra of St. Sabbas in Palestine than elsewhere. In Egypt they had been formally condemned since 400. From its origin, monastic asceticism had suffered the temptation of Platonic spiritualism. Essentially a popular movement, monasticism originally expressed the eschatological nature of Christianity. Thousands of Christians had spontaneously consecrated themselves to perpetual prayer in isolation and poverty to prepare for the kingdom to come (for which they were acquiring a foretaste through prayer), which was more important to them than any worldly reality. For this spontaneous movement Origenism provided a philosophy that undoubtedly made monasticism more understandable to the Hellenic world, but which also modified the very nature of monasticism. In a biblical perspective, the different aspects of monastic asceticism—celibacy, fasts, mortifications—sought to purify the flesh corrupted by sin and prepare it for the resurrection. Monasticism was understood as a prophetic ministry that anticipated the realities of the kingdom to come. In the Origenist perspective, the material body in which the soul was imprisoned as a consequence of sin had no place in the kingdom. The monk sought therefore not only to purify it but to detach himself completely from it. Perpetual prayer itself became an "intellectual" prayer having for its aim dematerializing of the intellect and bringing it back to its primitive state. The linear perspective of biblical spirituality seeking the kingdom to come was thus replaced by a vertical perspective, the search for dematerialization.

Several modern historians (such as de Lubac, Daniélou, Bertrand), preoccupied by their desire to re-establish Origen among the ranks of the great Christian doctors, have brought into relief the importance of the theology of history in Origen's exegesis and the central role he attributed to Christ. The περὶ ἀρχῶν, however, as well as many exegetical passages, remains to show that the conception Origen had of man, his doctrine of the incarnation, and his eschatology must be understood in the framework of a spiritualist and essentially Platonic monism. This system of metaphysics provided some monks in Palestine and Egypt with the basis of a dubious spirituality and led some Origenists to the most aberrant doctrines. Whatever the adaptations brought by later disciples to Origen's doctrine, there is no doubt that this doctrine, in its most characteristic features, issued from the περὶ ἀρχῶν. It was therefore inevitable that the condemnation of Origenism engulfed the Alexandrian master himself.

Recent studies have shed new light on Evagrius Ponticus, who was the great interpreter in the fourth century of Origenist ideas to Egyptian and Palestinian monks. The recent publication of the *Gnostic Chapters* of Evagrius (in their Syriac version, the original Greek having been lost) makes it possible to see very clearly the direct origin of the doctrines condemned by the fifth council; that is—in addition to what is properly called Origenism—Evagrius' Christology.[9] His name does not appear in the text itself of the anathematisms pronounced in 553, but numerous contemporary and later sources, which used the now-lost Acts of the assembly, mention the condemnation of Evagrius by the fifth council.[10]

Besides the fifteen anathematisms approved in 553, two important letters of Justinian describe the doctrinal problem posed by Origenism in the sixth century. The first of these letters, addressed in 543 to the five patriarchs, but better known as the *Letter to Menas* (Menas was then patriarch of Constantinople), constitutes a real theological treatise drawn up by the Emperor on the subject of the Palestinian controversies and ends with ten anathematisms. The letter received approbation from a local Constantinopolitan council the same year.[11] The second imperial letter was addressed to the council of 553 and contained the essentials of the decisions that the assembly ratified in its fifteen anathematisms.[12]

In 543, Justinian began his indictment by attacking the trinitarian subordinationism of Origen.[13] It is interesting to note that the Emperor was not followed on this point by the council, which did not pronounce any anathema against Origen's trinitarian doctrine. This doctrine, in fact, does not seem to have interested the Palestinian Origenist monks, who had provided the motive for conciliar action. The ambiguity of Origen's trinitarian system resulted, in any case, largely from philosophical presuppositions and from his doctrine of creation, which was considered as co-eternal with God and excluded the distinction, established by post-Nicene theology, between the eternal generation of the Son and the creation of the world in time.[14] Cosmology and anthropology, the most vulnerable points of Origen's system, were the council's main targets, together with Evagrius Ponticus' strange Christology, which was derived from Origen's philosophy.

Anathematisms 1-5, 10-11, and 14-15[15] refer to the Origenist doctrine of creation, fall, and apocatastasis, which supposes, on the anthropological level, the pre-existence of souls. It is well known that in the περὶ ἀρχῶν Origen considers creation as eternal; God did not "begin" to exercise his goodness; from all eternity, he created a succession of worlds[16] whose eternal unity is on the intellectual level, since God creates only reasonable and equal beings.[17] The diversification and eventually the materialization of minds happens in virtue of their free will and as a consequence of the fall. This process of diversification and materialization applies to the angels, the demons, human beings, and even the heavenly bodies, equally considered as fallen rational beings.[18] Anathematisms 2, 3, 4, and 5 of 553 condemn very precisely these Origenist ideas on the origins of the world and on the nature of the hierarchy that diversifies beings.

> Whoever says: the creation of all reasonable beings
> included only bodiless and completely immaterial
> spirits...; having no longer wanted the vision of

God, they gave themselves over to bad things..., they took more or less perfect bodies and received names...; therefore the ones have been called Cherubim, the others Seraphim..., be he anathema (*Anathema* 2).

Whoever says that the reasonable beings in whom the divine love had grown cold hid into gross bodies like ours, and were called men, while those who reached their last degree of evil partook in cold and obscure bodies and were called demons and evil spirits, be he anathema (*Anathema* 4).

According to Origen's essential intuition, a righteous God could originally create only reasonable beings, by nature equal among themselves; this necessarily led him to the doctrine of the pre-existence of souls and apocatastasis. In the sixth century this doctrine of pre-existence, particularly widespread among the monks,[19] seems to have provoked a chain of anti-Origenist reactions. The first anathematism of the fifth council is devoted to it:

Whoever venerates the fabulous pre-existence of the souls and the apocatastasis which is linked with it, be he anathema.

The doctrine of apocatastasis is again condemned in the terms that Origen liked to use in the περὶ ἀρχῶν:[20]

Whoever says that the life of the spirits will be analogous to the life which existed at the beginning, when the spirits were not yet fallen and lost, so that the end and the beginning are similar, and that the end will be the true measure of the beginning, be he anathema (*Anathema* 15).

In Origen's system, the cyclic conception of time implied an eternal return of new worlds towards a single world of "intellects." The anathematism that relates to this view underlines one of Origen's contradictions. While attaching importance to free will in the creatures' hierarchical self-determination (after they had been created identical and equal), he limits their ultimate freedom by his anxiety to push aside all ontological dualism, whether Manichean or Gnostic. We know that, according to Origen, Satan himself would have his place as a spiritual creature of God in the restored intellectual universe, evidently after ceasing to be God's enemy.[21] This point is condemned by name in the twelfth anathematism.[22] Only the material bodies are fated to disappear, according to Origen.[23] Hence the eleventh anathematism:

> Whoever says that the future judgment announces the annihilation of the bodies and that the end of the fable will be an immaterial nature, after which there shall be no longer any matter, but only pure spirits, be he anathema.

Undoubtedly, the *Letter to Menas* of the Emperor Justinian and the anathematisms of the fifth council do not always present a faithful picture of Origen. Their criticisms are based always and solely on the περὶ ἀρχῶν; as is well known, Origen was generally far more reticent in his other works, especially his *Commentaries,* about the more dubious points of his doctrine, for example, the problem of the resurrection of the body. Some of the condemned doctrines, especially relating to the spherical form of the risen body of Christ (*Anathema* 10), have no parallel in the known texts of Origen.[24] It must, however, be pointed out that the name of Didymus is attached to those of Origen and Evagrius in the contemporary sources that speak of the condemnations of 553. It is therefore a priori possible that the tenth anathematism is concerned with one of his lost writings.

Until recent years the problem remained complete as far as the christological anathematisms of the fifth council were concerned (6, 7, 8, 9, 12, and 13); they contain a conception of Christ and of salvation whose dualistic undertones could not be discovered in the basic doctrine of the περὶ ἀρχῶν.

The recent publication of Evagrius Ponticus' *Gnostic Chapters,* in which the doctrine condemned in 553 is found, makes it possible to measure all the significance of the decisions of the fifth council. The assembly's target was not a phantom Origenism but the genuine doctrines of one of the spiritual masters of Eastern monasticism, Evagrius.

The anathematisms 6, 7, 8, 9, 12, and 13 condemn a doctrine that distinguishes between God the Word and Christ. The latter is conceived as an intellect (νοῦς) that alone among created intellects remained "steadfast" (ἀκίνητος) in the contemplation and knowledge of God (γνῶσις οὐσιῶδες), that is, was not overcome by the fall. He is, therefore, a creature who remained in the state that existed previous to the world's diversification and materialization. There was, therefore, no incarnation of the Word. There was an abasement of the νοῦς-Christ for the salvation of all creatures, in the various degrees of their fallen existence, in order to restore them to their primitive unity. For Christ "has become all in all, Angel among the angels, Power among the Powers..., man among men" (*Anathema* 7). Christ can only be called *Logos* because he is united to the Logos before all worlds (as were also the other intellects before the fall), and, similarly, the Logos can receive the name of Christ; but this is only a catachresis:

> Whoever says that it is not the God-Logos..., one of the holy Trinity, who is properly Christ, but that he is so by catachresis, because, they say, of the *mind* which stooped (διὰ τὸν κενώσαντα ἑαυτὸν νοῦν), being attached to the God-Logos himself (συνημμένον αὐτῷ τῷ Θεῷ Λόγῳ), and which is properly called Christ, but whoever says that the Logos is called Christ because of the mind and that the mind is called God because of the Logos, be he anathema (*Anathema* 8).

This text only takes over one of Evagrius' chapters: "Christ is not the Word at the beginning, so that he who has been anointed is not God at the beginning, but that one, because of this one, is Christ, and this one, because of that one, is God. . . ."[25]

Final salvation will consist of the restoration of all minds to their pre-existent unity and equality. The angels, demons, and men will then be, in relationship to the God-Word, in the same unity as that of Christ, who, even in his abasement, was never deprived of it.

Consequently, anathematism 13 condemns the doctrine according to which "there will be (on the last day) absolutely no difference between Christ and the other reasonable beings (λογικά) neither by the essence (τῇ οὐσίᾳ), nor by knowledge, nor by the power and energy over the universe"; the minds will therefore be "united by essence to the Logos," exactly as Christ is today, and will even receive his creative powers. And, in fact, Evagrius wrote: "When the mind will receive the essential science, then it will also be called God, because it will also be able to found varied worlds."[26]

It is now clear why the Origenist monks of the New Lavra of Palestine were commonly called *Isochrists* ("equal to Christ") or *Protoctists* ("created at the origin"). These apellations reflect the doctrine of salvation that determined their spiritual life. According to Cyril of Scythopolis, they pretended that the final human destiny was to obtain "equality with Christ" in the apocatastasis.[27]

The importance of the condemnation of Origenism at the Fifth Ecumenical Council was overwhelming for the later development of thought and spirituality in the Byzantine world. The anathematisms directed against Origen and Evagrius attacked spiritual authorities who had left their mark on whole generations and who continued to have numerous followers, especially among the monks. It therefore is not surprising that for many later Byzantine writers the decisions concerning Origen took first place in the work of the council of 553;[28] their essential character underlined once more, perhaps permanently as far as Byzantium was concerned, the inner incompatibility between Hellenism and the Gospel. As the Quinisext Council of 692 (canon 1) put it, Evagrius, Origen, and Didymus were condemned for having

"restored the Hellenic myths" (τὰς ἑλληνικὰς ἀναπλα-
σαμένους μυθοποιίας).

After reading the fifteen anathematisms, one cannot help
wondering how the notion, spread by Harnack, that Byzantine
Christianity was Hellenized Christianity can have been so
popular. The anathematisms present a very clear diagnosis
of the most obvious differences between Hellenism and
biblical Christianity and indicate as clear a choice as is
possible for the latter. As O. Cullmann has shown, the
symbolic expression of time in the Bible is the *ascending
line,* while for Hellenism, it is the *circle.*

> The Greeks cannot conceive that deliverance could
> result from a divine action within temporal history.
> For them, deliverance resides in the passing from
> our existence here below, which is linked to the
> cycle of time, into the beyond, freed from time
> and always accessible. The Greek representation
> of bliss is therefore spatial, defined by opposition
> of the beyond to the here-below; it is not temporal,
> defined by opposition between present and fu-
> ture. . . .[29]

This is not the place to discuss in detail this judgment of
a general nature expressed by Cullmann. It is, however,
interesting to note that the criticism of Origenism, as expressed in Justinian's letter to Menas and in the condemnation of 553, deals precisely with these essential Greek
doctrines that determined Origenism: the eternity of the
intellectual world, and the cyclical return of created beings
to their origin, which make useless and incomprehensible the
redemptive act of Christ in time.

"Educated in the mythology of the Greeks," wrote
Justinian, "[Origen] posed as exegete of the divine Scrip-
tures, starting with their methods. . . . What else did he
expound but the doctrines of Plato?"[30] The eternity of a
spiritual world that is only diversified and materialized by
successive falls in order to come back always to its primitive

natural state implies a sort of determinism that excludes the necessity of redemption:

> If punishment and reward have an end, why the incarnation of our Lord Jesus Christ? Why the crucifixion, the death, the burial, and the resurrection of the Lord? What will be the reward of those who will have fought the good fight and witnessed for Christ, if the demons and the impious receive through apocatastasis the same dignity as the saints?[31]

To Origen's doctrine of the pre-existence of souls, their natural immortality, and their incarnation due to the fall, Justinian opposed a biblical conception of man: "God at the same time made a body and created the soul, forming in this way perfect man: for a body without soul is not a man, nor a soul without body."[32]

The soul is not immortal because it naturally and eternally participates in an intellectual essence, but by the grace of God, in order to be able to direct earthly creatures.[33] Man's presence in the material world is therefore no punishment for sin: on the contrary, Genesis tells us that man, the culmination of all creatures, was introduced last, as a king, to whom the whole creation was already prepared to pay homage.[34] To the cyclic and spiritualist determinism of Origenism, Justinian opposed a conception of man whose proper dignity consists precisely in being at the same time spiritual and material and whose free will could not be limited by the metaphysical necessity of an "apocatastasis."

Evagrius's condemnation had an equally important historical significance, for it attacked one of the spiritual writers most widely read in Eastern monasteries. After 553, his works were officially excluded from Orthodox monastic libraries. Only a small number of them are still available in the original Greek. Translations, especially in Syriac and Armenian, were preserved, however, by the Nestorians and the Monophysites, who were not bound by the decisions of the fifth council. But the official banishment was not sufficient to exclude Evagrius completely from the spiritual tradition of the Greek East; several of his works, especially a treatise *On Prayer,* remained extremely popular under a borrowed name: that of St. Nilus.[35] Fierce anti-Origenists, like St. Barsanuphius, while formally condemning the Evagrian doctrines, those "Hellenic myths," admitted that the soul could find useful teaching in the purely spiritual and non-dogmatic parts of his works.[36] This was to prove more or less the attitude of the whole tradition toward Origen and Evagrius.

The Evagrian conception of perfection as gnosis, and of prayer as "an activity proper to the mind," was linked to his anthropology: man, a fallen intellect, is called to come back to his primitive state, that is, a state of purely intellectual activity. This is why Evagrius was able to write the whole of his remarkable little treatise on prayer practically without mentioning Christ, since for him Jesus is but an intellect whose equal man is called to become. The monk's "pure prayer" is not addressed to Christ. One familiar with Evagrius's metaphysics will not be surprised that the incarnation has practically no place in his system of spirituality, which can be summarized in this precept: "Hold thyself as immaterial before the Immaterial, and thou shalt understand" (*On Prayer,* 66). The monk's prayer, for Evagrius, has as well a framework of Origenist eschatology; it is the "prelude to the immaterial and uniform gnosis" (*ibid.,* 85) that constitutes the ultimate aim of created intellects and will be granted them at the time of their "apocatastasis" into primitive unity.

Once the essential elements of the Evagrian metaphysics and theology were rejected by the council of 553, what was still "useful to the soul" in his writings? Essentially, the actual concept of perpetual prayer; for Evagrius was the originator of the spiritual school that made the "monologic" prayer—the constant mental invocation of the name of God— the center of monastic life in Byzantium. St. John Climacus, St. Maximus, and the great Byzantine mystics merely took over his teaching on detachment from the passions, continuous concentration, the fight against all distraction, the superiority of mental prayer over psalmody, the fear of any concept provoked by imagination, and the return of the mind upon itself as a condition of its union with God. But they did this within a different context: the "intellectual prayer" became in the Byzantine tradition the "Jesus prayer." The spiritual writings attributed to St. Macarius the Egyptian, Evagrius's master, played a corrective role in regard to Evagrian spirituality. Suspected today of being a Messalian document, this collection of *Spiritual Homilies,* dating from the beginning of the fifth century, became just as popular as Evagrius' writings. The heart—and not the intellect—takes there the central place in the human composite, conceived no longer as an intellect chained to matter as a consequence of the fall but as a psychosomatic whole that participates in its entirety in prayer. The "intellectual prayer" (νοερὰ προσευχὴ) becomes the "custody of the heart" (φυλακὴ καρδίας), and the result of this is a contemplation of the divine light given already here below to those who are worthy of it.[37] In the background, one distinguishes a very different anthropology from that of Origen and Evagrius, a biblical conception of man, who from the beginning has been created as a psychosomatic unity that has been taken over as such and deified in its entirety by the Word. The result is that the spiritual life, far from being reduced to a dematerialization of the intellect, is centered on union with Christ, the sacraments, prayer, and works.

The predominance of the Macarian tendency and the reinterpretation of Evagrius were caused, or at least facilitated, by the condemnation of Origenism under Justinian. From then on, the aim of monastic ascesis was conceived not only as an intellectual contemplation of God but as a transfiguration, or deification, of the whole man by participation in the deified body of Christ. Even where the Evagrian vocabulary was preserved almost intact, the christocentric sense given it deeply modified its meaning. The choice taken by the Byzantine Church in 553 essentially consisted in preferring the Bible to Hellenism, and, as a result of this choice, several other crises also found their solution in the eleventh, and then in the fourteenth, century. Byzantine hesychasm was not merely the continuation of the Origenist and Evagrian schools.[38] It borrowed only their mystical phraseology and their psychology of prayer. The latter, however, became integrated into the anthropology of pseudo-Macarius and into the monumental christological synthesis of Maximus the Confessor. Although officially condemned, Origenism left its mark on the development of christological doctrine. This was effected through the intermediary of Leontius of Byzantium. Until recently, the influence this author exercised on the christological concepts of Maximus and John of Damascus was acknowledged; but his identity was almost unknown. Critical studies have made it possible to distinguish him from Leontius of Jerusalem, the contemporary author of the treatises *Against the Monophysites* and *Against the Nestorians;* similarly, the work known under the title *De sectis* is not attributed to either of the Leontii any longer. Therefore, Leontius of Byzantium can be considered as the author of only three known pamphlets: *Contra Nestorianos et Eutychianos,* in three books; thirty *Chapters* against Severus; and the *Epilysis,* which takes up the anti-Severian arguments of the first book,[39] which had been criticized by a contemporary. This clarification of the literary legacy of Leontius makes it possible to identify him more precisely and to define the true significance of his doctrine. He was the principal lieutenant (ὑπουργὸς) and the comrade-in-arms of the famous Abbot Nonnus, chief of the Palestinian Origenists who revolted against St. Sabbas, and he is mentioned as such by the documents of the time.[40]

These three pamphlets were written during the years preceding the condemnation of Origenism by Justinian (543), at a time when discussions about the orthodoxy of Evagrius already were taking place in Constantinople. Leontius undertook then to offer his contemporaries *his* solution, an Origenist solution, to the christological problem that divided Monophysites and Chalcedonians, probably thinking he thereby could show the usefulness of Evagrian metaphysics. His careful attempt to hide the heterodoxy of his solution[41] helped prevent his condemnation.

Quoting Nonnus from the beginning of the first pam-

phlet,[42] Leontius unveiled his program to show that the
Council of Chalcedon represented the *via media,* the only
true one, between the opposite heresies (ἐναντιοδοκῆται)
of the Nestorians and the Eutychians. He then undertook a
presentation of his own Christology, based on an Origenist-
Evagrian ontology. Later he devoted the second and third
books of the *Contra Eutychianos et Nestorianos* to the refutation of what he considered the two extreme christological
errors: the ideas of Theodore of Mopsuestia and aphthartodocetism.

Two capital points provide a good illustration of the
Christology of Leontius:

1.   The comparison between the union of the two natures
in Christ and the union of body and soul in man. Leontius
certainly did not have a monopoly on this comparison. The
Monophysites, for instance, used it profusely, but precisely
in order to show that the union between the divinity and the
manhood in Christ is a natural (φυσικὴ) union; neither
the soul nor the body exist independently, but both are part
of the one human nature; in the same way Christ after the
union is "one nature," the elements of which cannot be
separated.[43] As for Leontius, not only does he reject the
notion of a physical union, but he explains that the soul is
"an independent incorporal essence" (οὐσία ἀσώματος
αὐτοκίνητος) and that soul and body are ontologically
perfect in themselves (οὐκ ἀτελῆ καθ᾽ ἑαυτά).[44] The
analogy is therefore suited to a Dyophysite, not a Monophysite, conception of the incarnation. The objection immediately leveled against this conception was that it supposes, on the one hand, a union of two hypostases and, on
the other hand, the pre-existence of Christ's humanity; and
indeed, as we shall see later, Leontius himself defines the
hypostasis as an existence "by itself" (καθ᾽ ἑαυτόν).
Answering these objections in the *Epilysis,* the author admits
that the pre-existence of the humanity of Christ is ontologically possible (οὐκ ἀδύνατον); a hypostasis can very
well be formed from pre-existing entities—for example, the
reunion of body and soul at the resurrection. In the exceptional case of Christ, however, *it was not fitting* that he ever

should have existed as "mere man" (ψιλὸς ἄνθρωπος)....[45]

In this way Leontius narrowly escapes the accusation of
heresy, probably by using consciously ambiguous language;
he does not formally confess the fact of pre-existence. Yet
he remains faithful to Evagrius; for he denies only pre-
existence as far as Christ's "manhood" (ἀνθρωπότης) is
concerned, that is, the fallen state or the intellect after it
has become a soul (ψυχή). In Evagrius's conception, only
this fallen state is, properly speaking, "man." This is the
human nature Christ received from Mary at the incarnation,
since he had come in order to save it,[46] and it certainly was
not pre-existent to him. But Leontius does not deny the
pre-existence of Christ as an intellect, eternally united to the
Logos καθ᾽ ὑπόστασιν and κατ᾽ οὐσίαν.

2. The definition of the union of the divinity and the
manhood in Christ as an "essential union" (ἕνωσις οὐσιώ-
δες) or "according to the essence" (ἕνωσις κατ᾽ οὐσίαν).
This definition is used by Leontius in all his pamphlets,[47]
while the following expressions are found but once in all his
works: ἕνωσις καθ᾽ ὑπόστασιν (col. 1348 d), ὑποστα-
τικὴ (col. 1308 c), and ἐνυπόστατος (col. 1300 a).
Furthermore, in the last two cases, the expression implying
a hypostatic union was only added to the notion of union
"according to the essence," which remains the essential
christological definition.[48]

This definition obviously was not made to please the
two opposing Byzantine parties. For Severus and the Monophysites, on the one hand, the term οὐσία had in Christology
an abstract sense, and they admitted, as we have seen, two
"essences" in Christ united into a "natural" (φυσικὴ) unity,
that is, an existentially concrete unity. The terminology of
Leontius was obviously on this point just as suspect for the
Chalcedonians. On the other hand, in Evagrian thought the
"essential knowledge" (γνῶσις οὐσιῶδες) is precisely the
primitive state of pure intellects and the expression of their
unity with the Logos; this is the unity in which the Christ-
intellect has remained, while the rest of the intelligible world
started to "move" toward the different fallen states, "angels,"

"man," "demons," which constitute the diversified world after the fall. It is true that Leontius speaks nowhere of essential *gnosis*, but of union. This may have been a means of adapting to the problems of his time; and such was his aim, namely, to apply Evagrian ontology to the christological problem of the sixth century. One should notice that the anathematisms 2 and 7 of 553 also speak of the "union in the identity of essence" of the minds with the Logos, Christ being one of these minds. Such was the vocabulary of the Palestinian Origenists. In any case, Leontius never designates the Logos as the "subject" of the union; that "subject" is always "Christ" or, more frequently, the "Lord" who, "having appeared from the Virgin, was also called God and Son of God in the Logos and according to the Logos."[49]

The same distinction between the Logos and Christ appears in the manner in which Leontius deals with the death of Christ. The subject of the "passion" is, according to him, the "flesh," which suffered "by the will of the Word" (βουλομένου τοῦ Λόγου).[50] And the "flesh," according to Leontius, is certainly not synonymous with the "manhood," since immediately afterwards he opposes it to the "reasonable soul" that, in the case of Christ, remained above sin and death. Yet the flesh does not sin by itself but only after a free choice made by the soul; the result is that in Christ the passion took place in the nature of the flesh and after a free choice of the soul.[51]

The parallel that can be established between this conception of the passion and that predominating in Antiochene circles is immediately apparent, as we already have seen.[52] Theodoret invoked against theopaschism not only the natural impassibility of the Logos but also the impassibility of the soul. No wonder the neo-Chalcedonian triumph of 553 attacked at the same time both those with Nestorian leanings and the Origenists, in other words, all those who refused to admit that "the Word suffered in the flesh." Moreover, Leontius tells us himself that he was "Nestorian" in his youth, meaning, in the language of the time, merely that he venerated the memory of Theodore of Mopsuestia.[53] The common rejection of theopaschism shows the meeting point of both schools of thought, Antiochene and Origenist, otherwise so different, and explains their common opposition to Monophysitism and consequently their attachment to Chalcedon. Both, therefore, had to be rejected with the reaffirmation of theopaschism in 553.

But if, in Leontius' view, Christ was essentially the non-fallen intellect, united to the Logos (κατ᾽ οὐσίαν), who had willingly taken on human nature in order to restore it, how did he manage to integrate the Chalcedonian definition into such a Christology? He had to build an original system of metaphysical thought.

The term οὐσία, for instance, means for him primarily mere *existence,* "not the what, not the how."[54] This term can, therefore, be applied to God, to the angels, men, animals, plants, to say in general, that they exist. One can also talk of the "essence of a particular being," with regard to what is *distinct* or *different* from other beings; but in that case οὐσία becomes synonymous with φύσις, nature; the proper function of the term φύσις is in fact to suggest a *difference* (τὸ παρηλλαγμένον) but not division or number (τὸ διῃρημένον).[55] It thus can be seen immediately how the term ἕνωσις κατ᾽ οὐσίαν could mean to Leontius a unity of existence, while the duality of natures maintains the difference that remains between the divinity and the humanity, between the Logos and the Christ-Mind.

The term ὑπόστασις, lastly, designates division (τὸ κεχωρισμένον), the individual (τὸ ἄτομον), the particular (τὸ ἴδιον),[56] and also the "someone" (τὸν τινα).[57] The hypostasis can in this way designate individual beings identical by nature and therefore able to be counted, and also beings constituted by different natures but existing "the ones in the others": for example, each man is a hypostasis, although he is formed of two different natures, soul and body.[58] After death, the soul being separated from the body, two hypostases appear, but they are again united at the resurrection.[59] The characteristic of the hypostasis is therefore to be "by itself" (καθ᾽ ἑαυτὸ ὑφεστός).[60] One could in this way say that there is *one nature* in Christ, if there existed a "species of Christs" (εἶδος Χριστῶν);[61] but there is only one Christ, and the only term suitable to designate him is "one hypostasis," which is an individual whole made out of parts, each one of which is a complete nature.[62] The term *hypostasis* reflects essentially and only a connection and a relationship. V. Grumel writes:

> The man in Jesus [i.e., his individual nature] is other and distinct in connection with other men (ἄλλος ἀπὸ ἄλλον) and on that basis is a hypostasis in opposition to them, but he is not such in relationship to the Word; similarly the Word in relationship to the Father and the Holy Spirit, is ἄλλος ἀπὸ ἄλλον, and on that basis is a hypostasis in relationship to them, but he is not such in respect to Jesus' humanity. The reason is that, while nature by itself does not cause division, but indicates only difference, the hypostasis indicates no difference, but only distinction and division: it distinguishes and separates one from the other the ὁμοούσια by their properties, but unites with one another the ἑτερούσια by their community of being.[63]

It goes without saying that for Leontius the only hypostasis is not that of the pre-existent Logos but that of Christ, formed at the time of the incarnation, finding itself in "essential union" with the Logos and "made of" natures, which are its parts. If one considers Christ as God and man, one must say with Chalcedon that there are two natures, the divine and the human; but one logically can also say three natures, Logos, soul, body, or even more, since the soul's functions can also be considered as natures.[64] Theological vocabulary admits, according to Leontius, that the parts should be called by the name of the whole; for instance, that the man Jesus should be called Lord, or, conversely, that the whole should be named after the parts: in this way it can be said that the Word is the "Son of Man" or that the "Lord of Glory has been crucified."[65] This is the only content of what he calls *communicatio idiomatum* (ἀντί-δοσις ἰδιωμάτων): a dialectic.

The proper meaning of the famous term *enhypostaton*—Leontius' major contribution to Christology—inserted into the Chalcedonian system, must be understood in the light of what has just been said. Discussing the dilemma that faced Nestorians and Eutychians, who both admitted the postulate "no nature without hypostasis" (οὐκ ἔστι φύσις ἀνυπό-στατος) and were reduced to admit in Christ either one nature and one hypostasis or two natures and two hypostases, Leontius introduces a new notion: that of existence "within something," which he designates as ἐνυπόστατον when he deals with an existence within a hypostasis, and as ἐνούσιον or the οὐσιῶδες when he deals with an existence "within an essence." He writes:

> The hypostasis is not an equivalent of the ἐνυπό-στατον, just as the essence is distinct from the ἐνούσιον: for the hypostasis designates *someone* while the ἐνυπόστατον designates the essence; the hypostasis defines a person with the help of particular characteristics, while the ἐνυπόστατον indicates that one is not dealing with an accident (συμβεβηκὸς) existing within another being and not contemplated in itself.[66]

It is obvious that Leontius' dialectic does not correspond at all to the Cappadocian trinitarian vocabulary, to which, however, he refers occasionally out of a sense of obligation.[67] The hypostases were for St. Basil and the two Gregories the direct and concrete objects of trinitarian contemplation, objects whose unity of being they had admitted under the influence of Athanasius, but not without difficulty.[68] If, according to St. Basil, the definition of essence and hypostasis is often limited to the concepts of "common" and "particular," the expressions used by St. Gregory Nazianzen reflect better their personal mode of existence and in any case exclude their interpretation as simple "relationships"; the

hypostases "possess" the divinity (τὰ ὧν ἡ θεότης) and
the divinity is "in them" (τὰ ἐν οἷς ἡ θεότης).[69]

When the Leontine *enhypostaton* had been integrated
into a perspective quite foreign to that of Leontius; when
it had been admitted that the hypostasis of Christ is not
different from that of the Logos, pre-existent and having
assumed the human nature (which in this sense is an *enhypostaton*); when, with all clarity and in conformity with
Cyril, it had been defined that the Chalcedonian duality of
natures does not suppress the fact of the unity of subject in
Christ and that subject was the pre-existing Logos; then
Leontius' true contribution took its appropriate place in the
history of Christology. His name thus survived the condemnation of Origenism in 553.

4.

"God Suffered in the Flesh"

The preceding chapters have shown that, when Justinian became Emperor (527), the theological position of the Chalcedonian party dangerously lacked coherence. Since the death of Theodoret, there had not been one theologian of importance. The Monophysites, on the contrary, could justly pride themselves in reckoning within their ranks a Philoxenus of Mabbugh and a Severus of Antioch. To the latter's pretention of being the authentic representative of the great tradition of the Fathers, the Orthodox could generally oppose nothing but the old arguments drawn from Theodore of Mopsuestia, highly suspect since the case of Nestorius.

Some theologians, while remaining faithful to the council, were beginning to notice the weakness of Chalcedonian apologetics, manifested especially in the radical opposition in some circles to the interpolated *Trisagion*. As we have seen, the text of this hymn in the form proposed by the Monophysite patriarch of Antioch, Peter the Fuller ("Holy God, Holy Mighty, Holy Immortal, *crucified for us,* have mercy on us") was not formally heretical, since it was addressed to Christ, not to the Trinity. It could be considered as subversive only insofar as it had become the rallying cry of the Monophysites. But the Chalcedonians did not limit themselves to this argument. Some also denied the very principle according to which the pre-existing Logos could have suffered, been crucified, and died; they named the subject of the suffering as being "the Christ" or "the flesh," or the "manhood" of the Logos.[1] The problem was un-

69

deniably the same one that had been debated during the years
preceding Ephesus and concerned the term *Theotokos*: could
the Word really "be born" of the Virgin, or was it only
the man Jesus who was "son of Mary"? Consequently, Cyril
of Alexandria, asserting against Nestorius the full theological
validity of the term *Theotokos,* was also led to declare in
his twelfth anathematism that "the Word had suffered in
the flesh"; conversely, the Acoemetae monks, who were
the main adherents of Chalcedon in Constantinople,[2] not
only objected to the theopaschite formulas but interpreted the
term *Theotokos* as a pious periphrasis, that is, in a sense that
Nestorius himself had accepted.

The problem went beyond simple apologetic considerations
or the question of *communicatio idiomatum.* At stake were
Christ's *identity* itself and the nature of the union "according
to the hypostasis" defined at Chalcedon. There was also a
question of knowing whether the terms "nature" and
"hypostasis" designated really distinct realities, or whether
ultimately the hypostasis was merely a manifestation of the
nature's existence. Since everyone agreed that the divine
nature was impassible, a real distinction had to be admitted
between nature and hypostasis if one were to say that the
hypostasis, the subject of the passion, was that of the Logos,
who remained impassible in his divine nature.

It is, therefore, fundamentally inaccurate to represent the
theology of Justinian's age, as well as the council of 553,
which was its outcome, as a series of superficial efforts
undertaken by Justinian to conciliate the Monophysites.
Chalcedonian theology itself could no longer delay the solution of its inner contradictions, and the Church owed it to
itself to take sides in a debate that was stirring the general
populace, as the controversy over the interpolated *Trisagion*
had demonstrated. The theopaschite formulas used by Cyril
had to be either accepted or rejected; and if they were
accepted, a christological vocabulary had to be constructed
that would remain Chalcedonian while integrating Cyril's
basic soteriological intuition, of which theopaschism was
the key element.

The historians who have little sympathy for what they

term Justinian's neo-Chalcedonism place great emphasis on the fact that the formula "One of the Trinity suffered in the flesh" had been used in Zeno's *Henotikon* and that it is found in Apollinarian texts.[3] That documents with Monophysite tendencies should have used it was inevitable; but this use is by no means limited to these documents. Not only does St. Paul himself speak of the "princes of this world" who "crucified the Lord of Glory" (1 Cor 2:8), but theopaschite expressions can be found in pre-Nicene theology as well,[4] and St. Gregory Nazianzen already makes it the essential element of his doctrine of salvation: "We needed a God *made flesh and put to death* (ἐδεήθημεν Θεοῦ σαρκου-μένου καὶ νεκρουμένου)[5] in order that we could live again"; and there is no problem for him about using such terms as "blood of God" (αἷμα Θεοῦ) and "crucified God" (Θεὸς σταυρούμενος).[6] Does not the Nicene-Constantino-politan Creed itself explicitly proclaim the faith of the Church in "the *Son of God*...incarnate of the Holy Ghost and the Virgin Mary..., *crucified* for us under Pontius Pilate"? St. Cyril's major preoccupation in his struggle against Nestorius consisted precisely in preserving the faith of Nicaea, which seemed to him to be endangered as soon as one ceased to say that Mary was "Mother of God" or that the Word "suffered in the flesh."

Thus, at the beginning of the sixth century there was nothing new in the renewed insistence on the theopaschite formula among the Chalcedonians, especially John Maxentius and the Scythian monks.[7] The embarrassment of the Chalcedonian party came rather from the reserve toward the formula expressed in Antiochene circles, although the latter were orthodox and not Nestorian. These reservations were of a philosophical rather than a theological nature. When Theodoret himself had made peace with St. Cyril and anathematized Nestorius, the Antiochene theology perfectly admitted the unity of being in Jesus Christ, expressed at Chalcedon by the term "hypostasis." But the difficulty resided in the notion of passibility applied to God, who is impassible by nature; for the Antiochenes the passion was still attri-buted to the flesh. But did not God have to make death truly "his own" in order to vanquish it? This is precisely the soteriological argument we have just seen in St. Gregory Nazianzen and which was the very essence of St. Cyril's thought. The Antiochene theologians admitted, no doubt, that God had appropriated the flesh by becoming fully man; but their training, going back to Theodore of Mopsuestia, still forbade them to say that "God died in the flesh" and, by implication, that Christ's single hypostasis was not a "hypostasis of union" newly appeared at the moment of the incarnation but the very hypostasis of the Logos; that it designated not only the concrete being of Christ but the *personal and pre-existent identity* of the eternal and incarnate Word. The pre-existent Word is the *subject* of the death of Christ, for in Christ there is no other personal subject apart from the Word: only *someone* can die, not something, or a nature, or the flesh. Here lay the subject matter of the debate.[8] Antiochene thought was still unable to admit a distinction between nature and hypostasis.

The beginning of the sixth century saw the development of a concern to equate the Chalcedonian definition with Cyril's theology, and no longer with Antiochene theology alone. With the help of Justinian, this tendency soon dominated the scene in Constantinople and culminated in the decisions of the fifth council in 553. The advocates of this outlook were the chief source of trouble for the great Monophysite theologian Severus of Antioch.

In the period 514-518 there appeared in Cilicia an *Apology* for the council by John the Grammarian. The text is known to us only through the quotations included by Severus in his refutation of the *Apology*. It seems that the Grammarian, like Leontius of Byzantium, dedicated himself especially to the construction of a dialectical terminology.[9] His defense of the council rested above all on the necessity, acknowledged by the Monophysites, to assert Christ's double consubstantiality: to the Father and to us. If this double consubstantiality is fully real in Christ, then there are two natures or substances after the union, since the *same* nature could not be consubstantial to God and creatures. For the Grammarian, the term "nature" (φύσις) designates first of all the common substance, as in trinitarian theology; the Chalcedonian definition must therefore be understood in connection with the Cappadocians' trinitarian terminology. Yet in order to eschew Monophysitism, John maintains that it is not only possible, but necessary, to give also to the word φύσις the sense of concrete existence that it had with Cyril. For the Grammarian, orthodoxy resides in the *synonymity* of the Chalcedonian definition about the two natures with the Cyrillian formula "one nature incarnate of the God-Word."

He undoubtedly admitted theopaschite formulas on which Cyril so strongly insisted. As for the term hypostasis, according to him it means the separate existence (κατά μέρος). Its main use is to insist on the fact that Christ's humanity never existed *apart from* his divinity and that the two constitute a concrete and single hypostasis, or nature. It can now be seen that the thought of John the Grammarian prepared the framework into which fitted Leontius of Byzantium's christological terminology after it had been shorn of its Origenic context.

No genuine progress was accomplished in the dialogue with the Monophysites until the Chalcedonian party formally agreed to identify the hypostasis of union with the *pre-existent* hypostasis of the Logos. This identification made possible the recognition of a genuine doctrinal continuity between Cyril and Chalcedon. The chief merit for this identification seems to belong to Leontius of Jerusalem, an author who was writing between 532 and 536 and was long identified with Leontius of Byzantium. In fact, his Christology is radically different from that of his namesake, and it seems that one might even discern in him a direct attack on the Origenist positions of the latter.[10]

For instance, he radically rejected the possibility of the pre-existence of Christ's manhood, a possibility that Leontius of Byzantium admitted on the strength of the parallel he had established between an Origenist conception of man and the mystery of the incarnation. Leontius of Byzantium conceived body and soul as entities ontologically perfect in themselves (οὐκ ἀτελῆ καθ' ἑαυτόν) and yet defined the hypostasis as an existence "by itself" (καθ' ἑαυτόν). Logically, he should have admitted two hypostases in Christ, or even three, since he refused to identify the Logos and Christ. As for Leontius of Jerusalem, he violently attacked the ontological presuppositions of such a Christology.

He wrote: "The Word in the latter times, having himself clothed with flesh his hypostasis and his nature, which existed before his human nature, and which, before the worlds, were without flesh, *hypostatized human nature into His own hypostasis*" (τῇ ἰδίᾳ ὑποστάσει ἐνυπέστησεν)."

Christ's humanity therefore possesses no proper hypostasis. It exists only as part (μέρος) of a whole that is Christ, the incarnate Word; although individualized, it is not particularized, as are human hypostases. Leontius writes: "Christ does not possess a human hypostasis which, like ours, is particularized and distinct in relationship to all beings of the same species or of different species, but the Word's hypostasis, which is common to and inseparable from both his [human] nature and the [divine] nature which is greater than [his humanity]."" Leontius of Jerusalem insists that Christ's hypostasis, since it is that of the Logos, is not "particular" (ἰδικὴ) but "common" (κοινή)," and that this is the reason why Scripture designates Christ's manhood as being simply flesh; for Christ unites "all of mankind" (πᾶσαν τὴν ἀνθρωπότητα), and not only one individual of the human race, to the divinity." The term "flesh" is a generic term designating human nature as a whole."

It is clear that Leontius of Jerusalem intends here to incorporate into his christological system the Pauline notion of the new Adam and the related notion of the Church as the Body of Christ. This biblical idea, which is not limited to the New Testament, since Isaiah's "servant" can also be interpreted at the same time in an individualized messianic sense and in the sense of a "corporate personality" of suffering Israel, is also taken up in different forms in patristic thought. For instance, St. Gregory of Nyssa conceived the "image of God" as belonging not to every man as an individual but to the whole of mankind," and St. Irenaeus built his doctrine of salvation on the notion of "recapitulation," a notion taken up again by Cyril in his theology of the incarnation.[17] For St. Cyril, the incarnate Word "possesses us himself, since he took over our nature and made of our body the body of the Word."[18]

It is within the framework of this Cyrillian thought that one understands what Leontius of Jerusalem meant when he spoke of the common hypostasis of Christ: a hypostasis that, instead of being another isolated and individualized hypostasis among all the hypostases that constitute the human nature, is the hypostatic archetype of the whole of mankind, in whom "recapitulated" mankind, and not merely an individual, recovers union with God. This is possible only if Christ's manhood is not the human nature of a mere man (ἀνθρώπου ψιλοῦ or γυμνοῦ)[19] but that of a hypostasis independent of the limitations of created nature.

The problem that immediately arises here is that of Christ's concrete manhood. The synonymity of the terms nature and hypostasis in the works of Cyril, and the absence in the great Alexandrian doctor of a stable metaphysical system, may have led to the belief that for him, as for Gregory of Nyssa, all mankind was an indivisible ideal reality in the Platonic sense, of which each individual was but the immanent manifestation.[20] One knows that Cyril was generally not aware of the Apollinarian danger and freely used expressions that went back to Apollinarius. In the case of Leontius, however, neither of these reproaches is justified.

On the one hand, Leontius rejects Apollinarius formally and by name and asserts that human nature cannot be "animated" by the Logos but must be animated by a truly human soul. If Christ possessed a human nature, he must have had a soul.[21] On the other hand, he does not in any way doubt the historical reality of the manhood of Christ, which is for him "a sort of individual nature" (φύσις ἰδική τις).[22] The very hesitation implied in this definition well reveals Leontius' embarrassment when he has to express in general terms the unique reality of a manhood whose hypostasis is not a human hypostasis. He therefore speaks of a "particular nature" but refuses to say "a particular hypostasis." His attempt at defining the mystery in a system of concepts does not succeed. After defining the hypostasis

(following St. Basil in this) as "a nature limited by particular characteristics" (φύσις μετὰ ἰδιωμάτων),[23] he goes
on to describe the hypostasis of the incarnate Word as a
hypostasis that assumed, besides all the characteristics (ἰδιώματα) that defined it originally, new characteristics. The
result is that after the incarnation it is defined by "a more
composite character" (συνθετώτερον)[24] than the one before
the incarnation. The characteristics of the human nature have
in fact been added to those of the divine nature.

The incoherence of the reasoning is obvious. On the one
hand, the hypostasis is defined as "a nature with particular
characteristics," and, on the other hand, the "individual
nature" of Christ's manhood is not a hypostasis. Leontius is
clearly unable to conceive a metaphysical definition of the
hypostasis. However, he still contributes to a certain clarification of the notion of hypostasis, because he is groping in the
right direction. His thought is therefore an advance on the
Christology of St. Cyril.

Since Chalcedon, which had established the distinction
between nature and hypostasis in Christology, it had become
quite natural for the council's apologists to apply to the
theology of the incarnation the concepts that the Cappadocian Fathers had used to express the mystery of the Trinity.
This passage from the order of *theologia* to that of economy
was not, however, without its difficulties, and the Monophysites obstinately refused to make use of it. According to
St. Basil there were three hypostases and one nature in God,
while for Chalcedon there was in Christ one hypostasis
and two natures. In both cases, the hypostasis designated the
"who" and the nature the "what." Yet other definitions,
more philosophical, made the analogy more difficult. If one
considers, as Leontius of Jerusalem did, that the hypostasis
is but a "nature with particular characteristics," one has
inevitably to admit two natures in Christ. If one defines the
hypostasis as an existence "by itself," as Leontius of Byzantium did, one tends to transform the Trinity into three gods.
Finally, if one accepts the Thomist position that the divine
hypostases are but "relations" within the divine essence, the
theopaschite position of Cyril must necessarily be interpreted

as implying the passion of the divine nature itself; and, to explain the passion without using theopaschism, one then tends to admit in Christ, as did Theodore of Mopsuestia and Nestorius, a human "ego," subject of the passion and generally of the whole human experience of the incarnate Word.[25]

Neither the Trinity nor the incarnate Word can be defined within the sole framework of the Aristotelian or Platonic opposition of abstract and concrete. The theological development that took place gradually from the time of the Cappadocians until Justinian clearly defined the concepts of nature and hypostasis as both being at the same time concrete and really distinct. We have seen above[26] that, according to the Cappadocians, the concept of hypostasis cannot be reduced to that of "particular" nor to that of "relation." The hypostasis is not the product of nature: it is that in which nature exists, the very principle of its existence. Such a conception of hypostasis can be applied to Christology, since it implies the existence of a fully human existence, without any limitation, "enhypostatized" in the Word, who is a divine hypostasis. This conception assumes that God, as personal being, is not totally bound to his own nature; the hypostatic existence is flexible, "open"; it admits the possibility of divine acts outside of the nature (energies) and implies that God can personally and freely assume a fully human existence while remaining God, whose nature remains completely transcendent.

In the explanation Leontius of Jerusalem gave the formula "one of the Holy Trinity suffered in the flesh," he established the absolute distinction between hypostasis and nature, a distinction that neither Cyril nor the Antiochene theologians had fully accepted: the Word remains impassible in his divine nature but suffers in his human nature.[27] Since, from the moment of the incarnation, the human nature had become as fully *his own* as the divine nature, one may (and one must) say that the "Word suffered" hypostatically, in his own flesh, because his hypostasis is not a mere product of the divine nature but is an entity ontologically distinct from the nature, the ego that "possesses" the divine nature and "assumes" the human nature in order to die and to rise again. "The Word," writes Leontius, "is said to have suffered according to the hypostasis, for within his hypostasis he assumed a passible essence (οὐσίαν παθητὴν) besides his own impassible essence, and what can be asserted of the [passible] essence can be asserted of the hypostasis."[28]

In this way the formula "one of the Holy Trinity suffered in the flesh" clarifies the Chalcedonian formula, which simply asserted the union of the natures "into one hypostasis." The hypostasis is the pre-existing one of the Logos, who before the incarnation in the womb of Mary, and on the cross, preserved without alteration his personal identity. In this hypostasis resides the union of the natures or essences which otherwise cannot ever be confused. The ambiguity of the formulas of St. Cyril ("one single incarnate nature of the Word") and of Leontius of Byzantium (essential union)[29] is in this way definitely clarified. For, on the one hand, Chalcedon's legacy is perfectly preserved: the natures, even after the union, are two, because the uncreated divine essence can never as such be partaken of in any form by the created nature. (This was a fundamental element of later Byzantine theology.) But, on the other hand, the humanity assumed by the Logos, hypostatized in him, deified by his energies, becomes itself the source of divine life, because it is deified not simply by grace but because it is the Word's own flesh.[30] Here is the difference between Christ and the Christians, between hypostatic possession of divine life and deification by grace and participation.

Leontius of Jerusalem's understanding of the dynamism of salvation is in continuation with that of Cyril. It is splendidly expressed in this passage:

> Because of the organic union (συμφυΐα) with God, effected in an immediate way by an intimate union (συνανακρατικῆς) on the level of the hypostasis, the wealth of deification entered the man who was the Lord (τῷ κυριακῷ ἀνθρώπῳ), in his particular [human] nature (εἰς τὴν ἰδικὴν φύσιν αὐτοῦ); as for the rest of mankind, the other brethren who originated from Abraham's seed,

the Body of the Church,... they only partake by way of mediation in the natural union with the man who was the Lord, and who, the first from among us, received the benefit, as the leaven of the dough, as the only Son (Jn 1:18), but also first born (Rom 8:29), as member of the Body, but also Head (Eph 1:22)..., the only Mediator between God and men, the man Jesus Christ our Lord (1 Tim 2:5).[31]

The Word's manhood, hypostatized in him, filled with his energy and "leaven" within the "dough" of the whole of mankind, is the very foundation of the doctrine, so dear to the Greek Fathers, of the deification of man as the true content of salvation. For salvation is not obtained by means of a "created grace" justifying nature; the notion of created grace is completely foreign to Greek patristics, according to which nature itself is made to be in real communion with God, to participate in his uncreated life.[32] Later Byzantine theology, especially that of St. Maximus, showed that this participation in the divine did not imply the passivity of human nature but, on the contrary, the restoration of its authentic activity. This was the meaning of the doctrine of the two energies or wills of Christ. However, even if Leontius of Jerusalem was mainly concerned with showing that the Chalcedonian dogma did not destroy the unity of Christ, and if as a result the emphasis of his theology is not on the manhood as such, his text quoted in the preceding paragraph is sufficient to show that the absence of a human hypostasis in Jesus in no way implies that his manhood ceases to be an existential reality.

The position of Leontius of Jerusalem, equally opposed to the Evagrian Origenism of Leontius of Byzantium and to the Nestorian interpretation of Chalcedon, was shared by several theologians of the first half of the sixth century.[33] The "Scythian monk" John Maxentius, whose culture was completely Latin and who intervened both in Constantinople and in Rome in order to have the theopaschite formula approved, must be mentioned here as a witness to the unity that could then still unite East and West in christological questions, in spite of diverging tendencies already fore-shadowing the later separate developments.

The Emperor Justinian intended to impose this unity on the whole Empire and made it the cornerstone of his religious policy. His main preoccupation was to conciliate the Monophysites by making them accept Chalcedon. This was the task he assigned to the Fifth Ecumenical Council, whose decisions, although they essentially ratified the Christology of Leontius of Jerusalem, are bound up with the episode of the "Three Chapters."

One of the most frequent reproaches addressed to the great synod of 451 was that it received into the communion of the Church two former friends of Nestorius, Theodoret of Cyrus and Ibas of Edessa. For the Monophysites, this provided the most tangible proof that the synod had rejected the faith of Cyril, since Theodoret and Ibas had both fought against him. Could the very definition of Chalcedon be interpreted after that in any but a Nestorian sense? This was the question the Monophysites asked the Chalcedonian theo-logians during the conference organized in 533 by Justinian in the palace of Hormisdas. A court bishop, Theodore Askidas, then suggested that the Emperor complete Chal-cedon by a new conciliar act. This was the context in which the episode known as that of the "Three Chapters" came about. The main purpose of its promoters was to achieve union with the Monophysite masses of the East. Nestorianism as such had for a long time ceased to represent a real danger, but the Monophysites *thought* they were meeting it again in the Chalcedonian definition; it has been seen above that the Chalcedonian apologetics of the second half of the fifth century gave some substance to this accusation, since they used the arguments that the theologians of Antioch had formerly leveled against St. Cyril.

In the language of the time, the "Three Chapters" were designated as:

1. Theodore of Mopsuestia and the whole of his work.

2. The writings in which Theodoret of Cyrus had at-tacked the anathematisms of Cyril of Alexandria and the

Council of Ephesus (431), and in which he specifically rejected any form of theopaschism.

3. The letter in which Ibas gave an account to Mari the Persian of the reconciliation of 433 between the Easterners and Cyril; this reconciliation was represented as a capitulation of the bishop of Alexandria.

In 544, Justinian published an edict proclaiming an anathema against each of these "Chapters" (κεφάλαια). Theodoret and Ibas were not personally affected since they had been rehabilitated at Chalcedon and had there explicitly anathematized Nestorius. It was, therefore, considered that they had themselves renounced whatever might have been Nestorian in their previous writings. Justinian's caution was providential; without it, the school of Antioch would have been condemned as a whole and tradition would have been deprived forever of the Antiochene balance to the posthumous triumph of Cyril.

Justinian's decree initiated a mechanism both political and doctrinal that brought about the council of 553. The dramatic circumstances of this assembly and the pressures the Emperor was obliged to exercise on Pope Vigilius and the Western episcopate cannot be related here; but the final outcome and its consequences for the history of theology must be investigated.

The *Confession of Faith* (ὁμολογία πίστεως) composed by Justinian in 551 and addressed to "the whole fulness of the Catholic Church" describes the program and the essential motivation of the decisions of 553.[34] The Emperor strongly asserts the orthodoxy of the theopaschite formulas, which had become for him a real criterion of orthodoxy. But he does not do it to the detriment of Chalcedon; vigorously objecting to the confusion (σύγχυσις) of the divinity and the manhood in Christ, he strongly insists, in opposition to the Severian Monophysites, on the necessity of admitting *two* natures. He refutes their dislike of "counting their numbers" (ἀριθμός).[35] The unity of Christ is designated by the notion of hypostasis and not by that of nature; thus Justinian (following Leontius of Jerusalem) fully recognizes the distinction between nature and hypostasis,

and remains fundamentally Chalcedonian. Without adopting
the whole terminology of Leontius, he accepts its central
idea: the nature can only exist *within* the hypostasis, for
otherwise it remains an indeterminate abstraction (ἀόρι-
στον).[36] It is by the hypostasis of the Logos that the
humanity of Christ received all its existence in the womb
of Mary. It is therefore possible for a hypostasis to become
a composite hypostasis (ὑπόστασις σύνθετος) since, being
the *source* of existence, the hypostasis can never lose its
identity (τὸ ἴδιον), while within a composite nature (φύσις
σύνθετος) the components would lose their particular existence.[37] Christ, having a composite nature as Severus would
have liked, would be neither God nor man but a new nature;
while in fact he is *both* God *and* man in his composite
hypostasis. In order to define this unity, Leontius of Byzantium had made use of the image of the human individual,
within whom the soul and the body, two distinct natures,
are united in one hypostasis. Justinian perceives all the
inconveniences of this image, which the Monophysites, who
did not share the Origenist opinions of Leontius, had immediately used in their own favor, since the soul and the
body constitute *one* human nature; he therefore states that
the image may be used to describe the hypostatic unity of
Christ but not that of its composite character, for the two
natures of Christ are neither complementary, as the soul and
body are, nor simultaneously created, since his uncreated
divinity pre-existed the incarnation.[38]

Clearly opposed to Monophysitism by the firm way in
which he maintains the peculiar meaning of hypostasis, and
waging a polemic against Severus on the questions of the
"number" of the natures, Justinian, however, makes important
terminological concessions to the latter. In particular, he
admits that the natures of Christ can only be distinguished
"by way of speech and thought, and not as two distinct
things" (λόγῳ μόνῳ καὶ θεωρίᾳ, οὐ μὴν αὐτῶν τῶν
πραγμάτων ἔχει τὴν διαίρεσιν).[39] In precisely this sense,
Severus also accepted "two natures" (δύο φύσεις ἐν θεωρίᾳ).[40] Above all, the imperial confession of faith proclaims
the intrinsic orthodoxy of the Cyrillian formula (μία φύσις

Θεοῦ Λόγου σεσαρκωμένη). After a brief exposition of
Dyophysite Christology, the Emperor goes on to say: "While
professing these doctrines, we accept the expression of St.
Cyril who said that there is but one incarnate nature of the
God the Word..., for whenever the Father said μία φύσις
τοῦ Λόγου σεσαρκωμένη, he used the word nature instead
of the word hypostasis."[41]

Following this come quotations from the *Letters to Succensus* of Cyril that tend to prove that the Cyrillian Monophysitism was only verbal while his deeper thought agreed
with that of the Council of Chalcedon.

Justinian's position went as far as his necessary fidelity
to Chalcedon allowed in meeting the Monophysites. Many
a Chalcedonian—for example, Hypatius of Ephesus at the
colloquium of 532—accepted without reservation from Cyril
only the writings formally brought up and approved at
Ephesus and at Chalcedon.[42] Justinian's religious policy consisted, on the contrary, of having the Monophysites accept
Chalcedon by re-establishing the *entire* authority of Cyril
among the Chalcedonians. Under these conditions the only
means of making both sides accept union in the faith was to
make them recognize that the opposition between Cyril and
Chalcedon was merely verbal. In 553 this policy was ratified
officially by the condemnation of those who, being already
dead, could not present a defense, but whose writings represented a serious obstacle to the final triumph of Alexandrian
theology.

The *Confession of Faith* of Justinian already contained
the fourteen anathematisms that the council of 553 merely
elaborated, without modifying their sense. Their meaning
becomes clear in their actual phrasing. In having them approved by the council, Justinian wanted to acquit Chalcedon of the accusation of Nestorianism (see especially the
anathemas 5, 6, and 14). This renewed condemnation of
Nestorianism as it appeared, or was supposed to appear,
in the "Three Chapters," is expressed in the repeated assertion of the unity of subject in the incarnate Word (anathemas
2, 3, 4, and 5), in the solemn proclamation of theopaschism
(anathema 10), and above all in the prohibition (implied in

anathema 13, which deals with the writings of Theodoret)
against opposing in any way the writings of Cyril, especially
the *Twelve Chapters* against Nestorius, which Ephesus and
Chalcedon had omitted to sanction officially. There was only
one restriction to Cyril's triumph. The council proclaimed
that the expression μία φύσις ("one nature") could not and
must not, under pain of anathema, be understood otherwise
than as a synonym of μία ὑπόστασις (anathema 8). Cyril
is, therefore, orthodox, but must be understood in the light
of Chalcedon; and, conversely, Chalcedon must not be considered as a disavowal of Cyril. This, of course, was the
stumbling block for the Monophysites, though the council
was extending a hand toward them by ratifying Justinian's
expression according to which the difference between the
natures in Christ can only be contemplated "in thought"
(ἐν θεωρίᾳ, anathema 7). Did not Severus of Antioch in
fact speak in the same way?

The condemnation of the "Three Chapters" is included
in the three last anathematisms. Only Theodore of Mopsuestia was condemned in his person and in his work. The
persons of Theodoret and Ibas were covered by the formal
authority of the fourth council. The former continued to
be read and quoted among the great doctors of the Greek
Church; as for Ibas, the text that concerned him cast
unjustly into doubt the authenticity of the letter to Mari,
and therefore left his personal authority untouched.

It is clear, however, that the importance of the doctrinal
decisions of 553 went beyond these matters concerning
persons. Even if the theology of Theodore were really open
to an orthodox interpretation, which is doubtful, the proclamation by Justinian and his council of Cyril of Alexandria
as the almost absolute *regula fidei* in christological matters
constituted in itself a very important fact for the East,
where it determined the later theological developments,
and for the West, where it was accepted only after long
hesitation.[43]

Far from having resolved all the problems that the
mystery of the incarnation poses, the fifth council, by fully
rehabilitating the Cyrillian concept of the unity of *subject*

in Christ, focused attention on the great importance of the hypostatic unity of the incarnate Word. The council maintained against Apollinarius that the human nature, enhypostatized into the Word, was "a flesh animated by a reasonable soul" (σάρκα ἐμψυχωμένην ψυχῇ λογικῇ καὶ νοερά, anathema 4) and that, in consequence, the humanity of Christ remained fully human, that Christ, in conformity with Chalcedon, was fully consubstantial to us by his humanity, but that his hypostasis was the divine and pre-existing Word. This position of the council, as of the neo-Alexandrian theology of which it was an expression, made it impossible to identify the hypostasis with the concepts of (self-) consciousness or of intellect. As man Christ possessed all that, but he was not a human hypostasis. Birth, temptations, passion, and death—all that was fully human in him. But the ego that was in him, the source and the agent of these necessary aspects of the freely assumed human nature, was the Word, who was also the foundation of the *communicatio idiomatum* and of the ultimate deification of human nature. All this was possible only if the conception of hypostasis preserves its "open" character, as source and foundation, and not as content, of every being, and is not identified with a simple aspect of the natural existence, human or divine. The fact that the human nature was "enhypostatized into the Word" did not prevent his energies or actions from being fully human.

This very notion of hypostasis made it possible for Byzantine theology to preserve in its interpretation of the incarnate Word the positive content of Antiochene thought and the fundamental insight of the *Tome* of Leo, according to which each nature "acts according to its properties."

Byzantine Christology as defined in Justinian's time is criticized, however, for "leaving too much in the dark the reality of the psychological life of the Savior's soul" and for "modifying the properties of human nature as such."[44] And since it is obvious that all the subsequent destiny of Eastern Christianity is implicated in this judgment, the question is of some importance.

In order to solve it one must remember that the decisions

of the fifth council do not constitute a final conclusion but
only a stage in the development of Christology. Their dogmatic content must be considered in the light of later stages,
and especially of St. Maximus's doctrine of the two wills
and his conception of deification. The critics of the Christology of the fifth council seem to base their judgment on the
Thomist concept of "pure nature," which cannot be reconciled either with the patristic conception of sin or with that
of deification; deified human nature, human nature having
come into communion with the divine nature, is not "modified as to its natural characteristics," but restored to the
divine glory to which it was destined from the creation.
Human nature, at the contact of God, does not disappear;
on the contrary it becomes fully human, for God cannot
destroy what he has made. The fact that the human nature
of Jesus was hypostatized into the Logos does not suppress
that human nature but, on the contrary, guarantees its own
human perfection and therefore its consubstantiality with
the whole of the human race. The role of St. Maximus was
to be the development of these cosmic dimensions of salvation.

Even before the seventh century, however, Byzantine
theologians, such as the author of the *De Sectis* (a treatise
attributed in the past to Leontius of Byzantium,[45] written
between 581 and 607), are fully conscious of the implications of Christ's consubstantiality with mankind. The unknown author just mentioned, for instance, recognizes
genuine ignorance in Christ. He writes: "Most Fathers
admitted that Christ was ignorant of certain things; since
he is in all things consubstantial to us, and since we ourselves are ignorant of certain things, it is clear that Christ
also suffered ignorance. Scripture says about Christ: 'He
was progressing in age and wisdom' (Lk 2:52); this means
that he was learning what he did not previously know."[46]

This position of the author of the *De Sectis,* taken over
by the anti-Iconoclastic writers of the eighth and ninth
centuries, proves that the Christology defined in 553 in no
way excludes the existence in Christ of a fully human
consciousness; furthermore, it shows that the notion of

hypostasis, which in Christ is that of the Logos, is not identifiable with that of consciousness, which remains a phenomenon of nature.

Most Byzantine writers, however, have refused to recognize in Christ any ignorance, and explained such passages as Lk 2:52 as some pedagogical tactic on the part of Christ. This was most probably due not so much to their Christology as to their conception of ignorance, which for a Greek mind was automatically associated with that of sin. This is especially true of Evagrian thought. For instance, Leontius of Byzantium, who was not a neo-Chalcedonian, and who, as has been seen, did not admit the hypostatic union in the Logos, refused to recognize that Christ could "be ignorant," since Christ was without sin.[47]

The concept of hypostatic union and the absence in Christ of a human subject, the only ego being the Logos, were not the essential reasons that led the Byzantine authors to deny ignorance in Christ. There was also a certain philosophy of gnosis, which made knowledge the sign par excellence of unfallen nature. Christ could not be ignorant because he was the new Adam. One did not have to be neo-Chalcedonian to assert that.

The author of the *De Sectis* did not share this philosophy, and his position was perfectly tenable in the Byzantine Church, even after 553. Actually, even Cyril, who was not himself an Evagrian,[48] admitted that the "proper" of the human nature united to the Word and invested through obedience with the condition of a servant was to worship the Father and to remain ignorant.[49] Undoubtedly for St. Cyril this ignorance was a willingly "assumed" ignorance in the framework of "economy," but it was a genuine ignorance; and the author of the *De Sectis* was thus able to refer to the authority of the great Alexandrian doctor.[50]

It is typical that his beautifully clear text on ignorance in the *De Sectis* is part of a chapter in which the author also objected to the so-called Aphthartodocetae, who asserted that the body of Christ, born of the Virgin Mary, was the body of the new Adam and therefore without sin, and consequently incorruptible (ἄφθαρτος). The problem here is in fact similar to that of Christ's ignorance. It is a problem of anthropology more than of Christology. R. Draguet has shown clearly that "the doctrine of incorruptibility [of the body of Christ] accommodated equally well with the formula of two natures and with Monophysite Christology; it can be noticed from the mere fact that it drew followers as much from the ranks of those who favored the Council of Chalcedon as among the Severian or Jacobite Monophysites."[51] Was not the Emperor Justinian himself, who all his life professed Chalcedonianism, tempted by Julian's "Aphthartodocetic" doctrine?

The problem was to know whether man, *by nature,* was corruptible, and if in consequence the Word, by assuming human nature, necessarily also assumed corruptibility (and ignorance). We have seen that Cyril included ignorance among the proper characteristics (ἰδιώματα) of the human nature assumed by the Word. Severus of Antioch, in unison with Chalcedonian orthodoxy, also asserted against Julian that corruptibility belonged to human nature proper, that Adam before the fall was incorruptible only insofar as he participated in divine incorruptibility, and that only by his resurrection did Christ give incorruptibility back to human nature.

Julian of Halicarnassus' discussion on Aphthartodocetism and his condemnation not only by the Byzantine Orthodox Church but also by the moderate Monophysites illustrates, as has been pointed out several times,[52] that the Christian East ignored, as a whole, the doctrine of original sin "of nature." Because Julian shared this conception of original sin, implying the corruption of human nature itself as a consequence of Adam's transgression, he wanted to shield Christ from it. But Severus answered him by calling him a Manichee and by denying vigorously the doctrine of original sin as a transmission of guilt. It is rather a natural *mortality* transmitted from generation to generation, as a consequence of the separation between God and man after the sin of Adam.[53] It is not itself a state of sin, but a "condition" of the human nature that the Word, by his incarnation, came to assume and, by his resurrection, re-established into the grace of immortality.

This argument shows that fifth-century Christology, and in particular the theopaschite formulas, did not interfere with the full reality of Christ's human nature, which is also our human nature, limited, ignorant, corruptible. By saying "God suffered in the flesh," one confesses precisely the corruptible state of human nature that the Word came to save by assuming it in the very condition in which Adam's sin had left it.

Thus the age of Justinian represents a real progress in Christology. Also, by clarifying the Chalcedonian position for the sake of Christian unity, the fifth council realized the only possible basis for a reconciliation between Monophysites and Chalcedonians: the common faithfulness to Cyril of Alexandria.[54]

5.

Pseudo-Dionysius

Byzantine thought never escaped from the great problem of the relationship between Greek philosophy and Christian revelation. The condemnation of Origenism under Justinian, however, constituted an important stage in the history of Byzantine Hellenism, which was always in conflict with itself. It was a serious blow for what is presently called the "Alexandrian vision of the world," a combination of Aristotelianism and Platonism that made up the essentials of the neo-Platonic system, and which, since Clement and Origen, gained respectability in Christian circles, after it was widely adopted by the Gnostics. This view presented a hierarchical world in which all the elements proceeded from God, the higher ones serving as intermediaries for the lower ones, and in which all tended toward God. In an effort to resolve the problem of the relationship between the absolute and the relative, the neo-Platonists' philosophical "method" principally multiplied the intermediaries with revelatory and theurgic functions. Such a method satisfied the typically Hellenic need to conceive the world as a harmonious whole (κόσμος) submitted to an order both permanent and metaphysically necessary (εἱμαρμένη); but insofar as all idea of creation *ex nihilo* was excluded, this method made it impossible to avoid a monistic and essentially pantheistic view of the universe.

Following Philo, Origen had tried to adapt this system to biblical revelation. To that effect, he had explained the existence of hierarchies by the original fall. The diversifica-

91

tion of intelligences into the angelic, the human, and the satanic arises from their self-determination toward evil and not from divine necessity. On an essential point, Origen therefore abandoned the neo-Platonic system and brought a corrective to it: the doctrine of free will. Deprived of any clear doctrine of creation, however, he did not escape from the essential neo-Platonic monism: hence his conceptions of the pre-existence of the souls and of apocatastasis which were condemned in 553.

But at the very moment of this condemnation, the same "Alexandrian vision" appeared in a new form, availing itself of the authority of Dionysius the Areopagite, a disciple of St. Paul in Athens. As the author's identity is unknown, it is difficult to trace the historical place that could link Pseudo-Dionysius with Origenism. The question deserves careful study. It is generally accepted today that the unknown author of the *Corpus Areopagiticum* belonged to the Severian circles of Syria, in other words, to the moderate Monophysites.[1] We know from other sources that in those circles the neo-Platonic system of thought common to Origen, Evagrius, and Pseudo-Dionysius was current, with its preoccupation to integrate within a Christian system the hierarchical world of neo-Platonism. This essentially apologetic preoccupation appears to be the best possible explanation of an altogether exceptional phenomenon in Christian thought: the *Corpus Areopagiticum.*[2] Directly inspired by Proclus, the last of the great neo-Platonists, the author of the *Areopagiticum,* instead of resorting like Origen to the biblical idea of the fall in order to explain the hierarchies, gave them a permanent value amid a world willed by God and assigned to them a positive role in his conception (which he intended to be Christian) of the relationships between God and creatures. He thought he had safeguarded the essentials of Christian revelation in bringing to the neo-Platonic system which he had adopted the corrective of the doctrine of God's absolute transcendence.

There is no intention to present here a complete analysis of the Dionysian system.[3] It merely will be placed in the context of the Byzantine doctrine of salvation, on which it exercised a certain influence; the insistence will be particularly on the Dionysian conception of God, "theology" properly so-called, and the doctrine of the hierarchies.

In Greek patristics before Dionysius the problem of the knowledge of God was dominated by the polemic against an Arian extremist of the fourth century, Eunomius, and the sect of the Anomoeans. The three great Cappadocians, as well as St. John Chrysostom, had taken part in this great debate. According to Eunomius, the divine essence, identified by him with the Father only, the Ungenerate, was accessible to the human mind; man could know God as God knew himself. Against this doctrine, the Fathers had recourse to apophatic, or negative, theology: the divine essence cannot be known; it is impossible to say what God *is:* only what God *is not* can be known. Any positive definition of God implies his identification with something. But the Fathers' preoccupation was precisely with elevating God *above all* and in this way excluding any limitation to his being. A known God is necessarily limited, since our created intelligence is limited by its very creation.

By identifying the being of God with the Father's essence, Eunomius faced Christian thought with the following alternative: either to recognize that the divine essence *is* knowable or to fall into agnosticism. The Origenist school, of which Eunomius himself represented an intellectualistic and simplified expression, tended to adopt the first solution. Origen spoke, of course, in the manner of Philo, of the "divine darkness," but he intended by that to exclude from the knowledge of God any material or sensible image. Negative theology corresponded in his thought to a "platonizing" anthropology, which put as the condition of true knowledge the dematerialization of the mind. The mind, once freed from its bodily fetters and from its fallen state, recovered for Origen its original divinity and attained to the vision of God in his essential being. God was, therefore, unknowable not in his essence but because of the imperfection of fallen minds. The Cappadocian Fathers, on the contrary, upheld an *absolute* transcendence of the divine essence. The negations of apophatic theology, far from being simply relative to *fallen*

man's incapacity to know God, reflect the unknowability of
God *himself,* who is absolutely transcendent because he is
Sovereign and Creator. Did they accordingly fall into
agnosticism? Not at all. Gregory of Nyssa, noting the
apparent contradiction that exists between the vision of God
promised to those who have a pure heart (Mt 5:8) and
the words of Paul that assert "no one ever saw God" (1 Tim
6:16), wrote: "He who by nature is invisible becomes visible
through his energies, appearing in what is around him."[4]
And St. Basil asserted that "the energies [of God] descend
toward us, while his essence remains unapproachable." His
opponent retorted: "If you ignore the essence of God, you
ignore God himself." But Basil answered: "How am I
saved? By faith. But faith can know that God *is,* but not
what he is."[5]

In the controversy with Eunomius, the Fathers clearly
defended the biblical conception of a living and acting
God against a philosophical and intellectualistic conception
of Deity-Essence. On this point their thought is very clear,
although the terminology they use to express their doctrine
is far from stabilized.

On the level of theology (θεολογία) in the strict sense,
Pseudo-Dionysius continues and develops this patristic
thought. While he adopts the language and the conceptual
system of the neo-Platonists, he separates himself from them
very clearly when he speaks of transcendence as belonging
properly to the divine essence. For Dionysius, God is a
"super-essence" (ὑπερούσιος) and therefore can be identified with no being as object of knowledge: he is beyond
any knowledge. In the first chapter of his treatise *On the
Divine Names,* Dionysius writes:

> In the same way as things pertaining to the mind
> cannot be grasped by the senses, simple and shape-
> less objects escape all form and outlines; and as
> nothing having put on the shape of a body can
> touch what is bodiless or draw the undescribable,
> according to the same true reasoning, all essence
> is transcended by the super-essential Indefinite.[6]

In the Platonic and Origenist tradition, the mind, in order to know God, must rid itself of its fallen state and of the beings around itself; in other words, it must become its own self again. For Dionysius, this "casting off" remains insufficient; the mind itself must come out of *itself*,[7] for the knowledge of God "is beyond the mind" (ὑπὲρ νοῦν).[8] A very particular way of knowing, "through unknowing" (δι' ἀγνωσίας), is then given to it. The angelic hierarchies themselves, which by definition and nature are pure spirits, permanently enjoy this mysterious contemplation, but they also are unable to possess the final stage of it. Their knowledge is presented by Dionysius as a perpetual progress,[9] for God remains, even for them, unknown in his essence while revealing himself to them through his theurgic operations. These operations are "unifying," but they do not lead simply to that which, for Plato, was One by essence, opposed to the multiplicity of beings; for God "is knowable neither by ourselves, nor by any being, neither as Unity, nor as Trinity," yet he is at the same time One and Three, transcendent cause of what is for us unity and multiplicity.[10]

Pseudo-Dionysius detaches himself therefore completely from two neo-Platonic postulates: the natural divinity of the νοῦς and the knowability of the divine essence. His God remains the transcendent and Creator God of the Bible, and not the One of Plotinus. This does not exclude, however, the meeting between God and created beings; on the contrary, this meeting constitutes the aim and ultimate meaning of beings. It supposes a descending movement on the part of God, out of himself, to make himself approachable and knowable, and an ascending movement on the part of beings who first of all recover their "analogy" with God,[11] that is, their capacity to participate in the virtues of God; then, coming out of themselves, to participate in the very being of God (but not in his essence), and "go back" (ἐπιστροφὴ) to God.

The descending movement of God toward beings is expressed by Dionysius in terms reminiscent of the Platonist "processions." God is not only "One" and "Silence": he multiplies himself, he expresses himself and he appears. He is not only transcendent essence, but also the cause of beings, and the revealing operation. This duality of the divine being is expressed in Dionysius by a very particular language, always designed to be understood by his neo-Platonic contemporaries. Dionysius says:

> As I said elsewhere, the holy initiates of our theological tradition call divine unities (ἑνώσεις τὰς θείας) those secret and incommunicable realities, deeper than any foundation, and which constitute this unicity of which it is insufficient to say that it is ineffable and unknowable. And they call distinctions (διακρίσεις) the proceedings and manifestations suitable to the beneficent thearchy (τὰς ἀγαθοπρεπεῖς τῆς Θεαρχίας προόδους τε καὶ ἐκφάνσεις).[12]

Precisely, according to Dionysius, because the divine essence is not identified with the Platonic "One," it is possible to speak of distinctions in God, which are the bases of his omnipresence and omnicausality. This is exactly the essential theme of the treatise *On the Divine Names:*

> The Deity is the More than Good (ὑπεράγαθον), the More than God (ὑπέρθεος), the Superessential (ὑπερούσιον), the More than living (ὑπέρζωον), the More than wise (ὑπέρσοφον), because it does not enter within *our* concepts of the good, the divine, the essential, the living, and the wise, and we must attribute to it all these names which express a negation by *transcendence;* yet it is also genuinely *cause* of whatever exists; one can therefore attribute to it the names Good, Beautiful, Being, Source of Life, Wise, as well as all those relating to the beneficent gifts of this Deity, called for that reason Cause of all Good.[13]

It therefore can be said that God "penetrates" the universe, that the ideas of beauty, of good, of wisdom discovered by our experience of the world put us truly in contact with God. However, God cannot be identified with them: he remains transcendent, he is their cause.

Two dangers faced Dionysian thought, like any Platonism, when it developed its conception of unions and distinctions in God. The first was pantheism, and the second, Platonic emanationism. The idea of a transcendent and "super-essential" God avoided from the beginning the pantheistic danger. Yet Dionysius firmly preserved a conception of causality that asserted the participation of beings in their cause. This participation was made possible by the doctrine of divine "processions" and "powers," thanks to which the Deity put itself on the level of its creatures and made itself partakable. For Plotinus, these processions implied a diminution of the Deity; the emanations, from the very fact that they emanated from the One, lost the fullness of divine being. Dionysius deliberately avoided this pitfall, which would have implied a fragmentation of God. He writes:

> It is common, synthetic, and unique for the whole Deity to be participated in fully and entirely by all the participants, and never by any of them in a partial way,[14] as the central point of a circle is participated in by all the radii which make up the circle, and as the many imprints of a single seal participate in the original, which is immanent entirely and in an identical way in each imprint, without being in any way fragmented. As for the unpartakableness of the Deity, universal cause, it also transcends [these participations], for there is with it no sort of contact, no sort of community, nor any synthesis between it and its participants.[15]

In his description of the descending movement of God, implying a "going out" of his own essence by God, as well as in his description of the ascending movement of man toward God, based also on an "ecstasy" outside any properly human function of body, mind, and sight, Dionysius certainly approached very closely the mystery of a *personal* meeting with God. Who is this God, present with all of himself in the processions or acts *ad extra,* while he remains in transcendence, if not the personal God of the Bible? Similarly, the man who, in order to know God, casts off all things, including his own mind—in what would he remain truly man if not in this first and fundamental principle of existence that Christian theology calls hypostasis? It becomes evident that this is Dionysius' fundamental insight in certain passages where the neo-Platonic jargon generally prevailing in the *Areopagitica* allows more traditional expressions to come through, and in which christological and eschatological themes appear:

> Then, when we shall become incorruptible and immortal, and when we shall have attained to the state conformable to Christ and the perfectly blessed, we shall be always with the Lord, as Scripture says (1 Thess 5:17), enjoying fully in very pure contemplations his visible theophany which shall enlighten us with its dazzling rays, like the disciples at the time of the very divine transfiguration, partaking by our impassible and immaterial intelligence in his intelligible illumination, and by the unknowable and blessed display of these more than bright rays, to the supra-intelligible union, in an always more divine imitation of the supra-celestial spirits. For as the Word of Truth has it, we shall be like the angels and sons of God, being sons of the resurrection.[16]

The purely Christian inspiration of this passage, which summarizes the points on which Dionysius clearly divorces himself from neo-Platonism and expresses the Christian conception of the knowledge of God in a language he intends to be intelligible for neo-Platonists, explains why the whole of Dionysian thought has been able to exercise such an influence on later Christian theology. It must be noted, however, that Dionysius cleverly avoids any explicit reference to the personalist concept of hypostasis, which the

Cappadocian Fathers had applied to the Trinity and which had been used in the famous christological definition of Chalcedon. In a well-known passage from *On the Divine Names,* Dionysius speaks of God as at the same time Trinity and Monad, but only in order to assert immediately that our knowledge cannot really reach God either as Monad or as Trinity, since God is the cause, anonymous and transcendent, of all number and all unity.[17] Therefore, nothing remains here of a meeting with the personal and triune God. This reserve in Dionysian speculation before the well-established concept of hypostasis may come from his belonging to Monophysite circles, fiercely anti-Chalcedonian, which refused to distinguish between nature and hypostasis, and also from his apologetic interest, which always made him adopt in his expositions a neo-Platonic point of view. Only by starting from that point of view does he sometimes reach conclusions in which the biblical notion of the living God becomes transparent.

Dionysius himself complains of being accused of "using against the Greeks the Greeks' own goods."[18] This is in fact what he is always trying to do, and he has the great merit of being successful in at least two essential areas. First, in the area of mystical theology he demonstrates successfully that the knowledge of God cannot be identified with any natural process of the senses or of the mind but transcends them and represents a mode of knowledge *sui generis,* supraintellectual or mystical. Second, in the realm of the conception of the relationships of God with the universe, he goes beyond pantheism and Origenist emanationism in showing that the divine manifestations, or "names," that represent a real and necessary presence of God in the world do not interfere with his essential transcendence.

However, as Jules Lebreton has pointed out, "all these speculations do not get us beyond natural theology."[19] Dionysius always remained a philosopher, and not a mystic in the modern sense of the word.[20] His aim was to build a theory of knowledge that would answer both the demands of neo-Platonic philosophy and those of Christianity. If he was successful in the area of *theologia,* his success was much more questionable in the realms of cosmology and ecclesiology, in which the absence of common christological references made illusory his effort to bridge completely the gap between the Gospel and neo-Platonism.

The Greek conception of the world was essentially that of a hierarchical and unmovable order; this was the condition of all harmony and of all beauty and the expression of the divine origin of the universe. Accepting the principle of this Hellenistic cosmology, Origen and Evagrius had tried to explain the hierarchical structure of the universe by the free self-determination of beings, and the fall that was the consequence of their freedom. Dionysius, against Origen, maintained the divine origin of the hierarchy and gave it an essential place in his conception of the relationships between God and the world, while "making it up" with the help of biblical, liturgical, and sacramental concepts taken from the Christian tradition. It is almost certain that in this also his aim was to protect the Christian tradition and to make it acceptable to the neo-Platonic intellectuals. This preoccupation sometimes even took the shape of a direct polemic. For instance, after briefly describing the baptismal liturgy, he seems directly to address a pagan interlocutor:

> This initiation in some way symbolizes the holy birth of God in us and contains nothing indecent or profane; it even contains no sensible images, but rather reflects the enigmas of a contemplation worthy of God in natural mirrors adapted to human faculties. In what could this ceremony seem defective, which. . . inculcates the initiate, by its holy instructions, with the precepts of a holy life. . . ?[21]

This apologetic attitude in a writer of the sixth century is explained by the very nature of neo-Platonism at that time. After Iamblichus and Proclus, and under the influence of Eastern religions, the neo-Platonic movement gave more and more importance to the mysteries and to theurgy. It encouraged its followers to seek contact with the divine, more than philosophical satisfaction for the mind. It tended to take over, in a total system, both philosophy and religion. It was seeking, as Emile Bréhier puts it, a method

> which would allow the rediscovery, by deduction and in their proper place in the intelligible world, of the thousand religious forms which in paganism distinguish gods, demons, heroes, etc. This vast classification is empty of the spiritual life which animated the *Enneads* [of Plotinus] and which now falls to the level of, on the one hand, the diligent work of the theologian, and on the other hand, the practice of the *theourgos*.[22]

Dionysius' enterprise is identical, with this difference, that the religious forms he incorporates into the intelligible structures of late neo-Platonism are Christian. Here lies the explanation of the Dionysian system of the two "hierarchies," celestial and ecclesiastical.

The arguments about the true identity of Pseudo-Dionysius, although they lead to no satisfactory conclusion, at least make it possible to define clearly the author's dependence on the neo-Platonic writers of the fifth century, in particular Iamblichus and Proclus. All reality proceeds from the One, transcendent and unpartakable, and is determined in a rigorous system of gradations, in proportion to the remoteness of each being in relation to its origin. Each superior order (τάξις) serves, on the one hand, as an intermediary for the inferiors, and, on the other hand, is itself divided into three elements: the unpartakable (ἀμέθεκτος), the partakable (μεθεκτός), and the participating (μετέχων),[23] and constitutes a triad. For Proclus, the divine procession (πρόοδος) is communicated through this system of intermediaries and the conversion (ἐπιστροφὴ) of each being toward the One takes place. As we have seen, Dionysius remains fundamentally Christian in maintaining that God is still above the One, of which he is the cause, and that the concepts of being, life, wisdom, and intelligence are divine names and therefore do not belong to lower hierarchical orders; that the procession is not a diminution of the divine

being but a presence of God in his fullness in each being.
Yet the parallelism with Proclus remains complete in the
very principle of a system of intermediaries, classified in
groups of three and destined to transmit deifying science to
the lower orders. Their function is to "bring God out of
silence,"[24] to initiate the lower orders into the science of the
higher ones, and in this way to serve as a channel to the
descending procession of God and also to the ascension of
the being toward the transcending Good.

Dionysius is the source of the classification, which became
classical, of the angelic ranks into nine "orders" subdivided
into three triads. The first triad, which "is seated immediately
around God in a greater proximity than all the others" and
"is immediately contiguous with the primordial illumina-
tions of the thearchy,"[25] comprises the Seraphim, the
Cherubim, and the Thrones; the second celestial triad is
that of the Dominions, Virtues, and Powers; the last one
includes the Principalities, Archangels, and Angels. Although
it is possible to find in the Bible almost all these appellations
taken individually, it is evident that the structure itself of
the Dionysian angelic world has no foundation in Scripture.
Cyril of Jerusalem, John Chrysostom, and the author of the
book called *Apostolic Constitutions* mention the whole series
of nine Dionysian appellations, but in a different order.[26]
A certain tendency toward the classification of angelic
beings no doubt existed, but Dionysius gave it a systematic
form and a metaphysical foundation.

The celestial hierarchy corresponds, according to Dionysius, to an ecclesiastical hierarchy, which is the continuation
and reflection of it. Nowhere in his thought is Dionysius
more clearly dominated by the Platonic opposition between
the sensible and the intelligible than in his conception of the
Church. His starting point seems to be the allegorical and
symbolic interpretations of the Old Testament by the
Alexandrian exegetes. Without lingering too long over it
and without studying it for its own sake, Dionysius often
mentions the "hierarchy according to the law" (ἡ κατὰ
νόμον ἱεραρχία), the aim of which was to represent in
sensible types and symbols the intelligible realities of the

celestial hierarchy.[27] Since Philo, this was the method generally used to make the Hellenistic world accept the Old Testament. As for Dionysius, he finds in it the preliminary intellectual step that introduces his ecclesiological conceptions. The legal hierarchy directed the mind toward "a more perfect initiation," which is "our hierarchy" (ἡ καθ' ἡμᾶς ἱεραρχία). The latter is

> at the same time celestial and legal, participating by its middle situation in both extreme hierarchies, sharing with the one the intellectual contemplations and with the other the use of varied symbols of the order of the senses by whose mediation it is elevated in a holy fashion towards the divine.[28]

This strange definition of the ecclesiastical hierarchy shows that Dionysius remains fundamentally prisoner of the sense-mind dichotomy, and that he lacks the philosophical means to express the realities linked with the incarnation. He maintains, however, the unity of the cosmic structure by making the ecclesiastical hierarchy enter into the system that is dominated by the celestial orders. "Our hierarchy," he writes, "is assimilated as much as is possible [to the celestial hierarchy] so that it can possess the angelic splendor, receive its imprint and be elevated by it toward the super-essential principle ordering every hierarchy."[29]

The parallelism and dependence of the ecclesiastical hierarchy in relationship to the celestial hierarchy having been established in this way, one surprisingly finds only two triads or six "orders" in the ecclesiastical hierarchy: the triad of the initiators, corresponding to the clergy, and the triad of those initiated, or lay people.[30]

The initiating triad includes the bishops, called "hierarchs" by Dionysius to emphasize that they are literally "chiefs of the hierarchy"; the priests (ἱερεῖς); and the deacons, usually called ministers (λειτουργοί). The triad of the initiated includes the monks, the holy people, and the purified orders (catechumens or penitents). In this way Dionysius incorporates some traditional elements into his system, for instance, that which recognizes in the bishop the center of all sacramental activity in the local Church. But the difficulties of the system are obvious. Is it possible to maintain rigorously, in the order prescribed by Dionysius, the relationship of initiator to initiated between the various degrees of the ecclesiastical hierarchy? Is it possible to build a precise theology of ecclesiastical orders by saying with Dionysius that the bishop "consecrates and perfects," the priest "enlightens," and the deacon "purifies"? It is evident that in Dionysius, who was well acquainted with the respective Church functions as practiced in his time, the sacramental role of the bishop, the mainly educational function of the priest, and the deacon's catechetical and liturgical function linked with baptism are isolated from their original context and serve merely as an artificial form for a preconceived hierarchical system.

In addition to its arbitrary character, the main disadvantage of Dionysius' system is that it twisted the general perspective followed by the ecclesiology of the Church of the first few centuries. Fenced in within the structure of the hierarchies, the relationships between God and man are conceived in a purely individualist manner and are completely determined by the system of intermediaries. The episcopate, for example, is defined not as an element of the inner structure of the church-community, a function of the Body of Christ, but as a personal state. Dionysius writes:

> Whoever says *hierarch,* designates a deified and divine man, instructed in all holy knowledge, in whom the whole hierarchy depending on him finds the pure means of perfecting and expressing itself.[31]

> The deiform hierarch (θεοειδὴς ἱεράρχης), who participates in a full and total way in the hierarchical power, is not content with receiving by divine illumination the authentic knowledge of all the ritual words and of all the hierarchical sacraments, but it is he moreover who transmits them to others, according to their rank in the hierarchy,

and it is he who, because he is gifted with the most divine requirements of knowledge and with the highest power of spiritual elevation, accomplishes the holiest consecrations of the hierarchy.[32]

The Dionysian hierarch (and it must be noticed that this word designates not only the bishop but also great figures like Melchizedek, Moses, Zachariah, the Seraphim of Isaiah 6)[33] is essentially a gnostic and one who is initiated into a mystery, who transmits knowledge and illumination to individuals. The conception of a church-community of which he would be the head is absent from the Dionysian perspective. The conception of sacrament is reduced in this way to the transmission from one individual to another of a personal illumination. It is true that Dionysius uses to designate the Eucharist the traditional term synaxis, which implies an assembly of the faithful and a community action, but this use is not reflected in his conception of the sacrament; the rite has only a symbolic and moral significance: "The very divine distribution, operated in common and peacefully, of the same bread and of the same chalice prescribes them, since they have been nourished by the same foods, to unify their manners in living altogether in God." And Dionysius immediately limits its scope:

> But let us leave to the imperfect these signs, which, as I said, are magnificently painted in the vestibules of the sanctuaries; they will be sufficient to feed their contemplation. For us, in considering the holy synaxis, let us return from the effects to their causes, and thanks to the lights which Jesus shall give us, we shall be able to contemplate harmoniously the intelligible realities in which is clearly reflected the blessed goodness of the models.[34]

The Areopagite's writings represent a historical witness to the liturgical practices of the Eastern Church in the fifth and sixth centuries. For instance, the inclusion of the reception of the monastic habit and of the funeral rites among the sacraments of the Church reminds liturgiologists and modern theologians that the doctrine that limits to seven the number of sacraments is relatively recent, that it was only very recently adopted by certain Byzantine authors, and that until today it has not received any precise ecumenical sanction in the East. However, Dionysius' interest in the history of liturgy and of sacramental doctrines is not limited to the realm of facts. The doctrine of the hierarchies, with its dualism of sense-mind, implies in Dionysius himself a sacramental doctrine that can fit in with the rest of his system; and for those who have seen in him a disciple of St. Paul, and have accepted his writings as an integral part of tradition, it implied a problem of interpretation and selection.

The sacrament of communion, for example, the very rites of which are interpreted as an ethical lesson, necessary only for the "imperfect," appears in its very essence as an "image" of an intelligible communion; having described the distribution of the Eucharist to the faithful by the bishop, Dionysius, comments: "By offering Jesus Christ to our eyes he shows us in a tangible way and, as in an image, our intelligible life."[35]

The bread and the wine are for the Areopagite nothing but "the sacred symbols by which Christ signifies and communicates himself."[36] Quotations could here be multiplied, but it is sufficient to adopt the conclusion of R. Roques: "The loftiest sense of the Eucharistic rites and of sacramental communion itself is in symbolizing the union of our minds with God and with Christ.... Dionysius never formally presents Eucharistic Communion as a participation in the body and blood of Christ."[37] No tangible, ritual, or material reality can, therefore, according to Dionysius, have any other relationship with the intelligible world than a symbolic one.

How were these different elements in Dionysius' thought integrated by Dionysius himself and by later generations into the Christian tradition? This question is an important one, since the influence of the *Corpus Areopagiticum* has been considerable in the West as well as in the East.

We have seen that on the level of *theologia* Pseudo-

Dionysius was perfectly in the tradition of the great Cappadocians; he overcame the fundamental antinomy between the transcendence of God and the fact of his presence in the world. The treatise *On the Divine Names* thus became an inalienable element of Eastern patristic tradition, although the different interpretation it received in the West has caused many misunderstandings about the real sense of Dionysian thought. This misunderstanding was at the center of the fourteenth-century controversy between Barlaam of Calabria and Gregory Palamas. In any case, the influence exercised by the treatises on the theologians and religious of the following centuries is sufficiently well known, and we shall return to it in studying the later developments of Byzantine theology.[38]

It is important to mention here an aspect of Dionysius' influence that has attracted less attention, namely, that which relates to ecclesiology and liturgical piety, two essential elements of Christian spirituality. There is no doubt that Dionysius intended to express in his doctrine of the hierarchy the simple idea that all beings were created *in view of* their union with God, a central idea of patristic anthropology since St. Irenaeus, which was later to be magnificently developed by St. Maximus. In Dionysius' writings, the word hierarchy expresses first of all the universal tendency of beings to draw closer to God:

> The hierarchy is, according to me, a sacred order, a science, an activity which assimilates itself as far as possible to deiformity and, according to the illumination given it by God, elevating itself in proportion to its forces towards the imitation of God.[39]

But side by side with this dynamic definition of the hierarchy, Dionysius proposes his concrete conception: the scale of intermediaries, destined above all to incorporate into the system the neo-Platonic triads. A conception peculiar to Dionysius of the salvation of the Church and of the sacraments results from it, and in fact presents them in complete separation from the central mystery of Christianity, the incarnation.

Undoubtedly Dionysius, who probably belonged to the Severian Monophysite party (hence the mono-energetic formula he used once), mentions the name of Jesus Christ and professes his belief in the incarnation,[40] but the structure of his system is perfectly independent of his profession of faith. "Jesus" is for him the "very thearchic and super-essential spirit (θεαρχικώτατος νοῦς), the principle, the essence, and the very thearchic power of all hierarchy, of all holiness and of all divine operation."[41] The incarnation consists of the fact that

> Jesus himself, super-essential cause of the supra-celestial essences, having come down to our level without losing his immortality, does not move apart from the beautiful disposition instituted and chosen by him according to the human convenience, but obediently submits to the designs of God his Father transmitted to him by the angels.[42]

In other words, he who was already chief of the celestial hierarchy condescends to take the head of the earthly hierarchy in order to become the "Illuminator," "Sanctifier," "Initiator," and first Hierarch of it,[43] but it is always through the intermediary of that immovable hierarchy that the light of Jesus comes down to us.

Is this immovable character of the hierarchies reconcilable with the direct and supra-intelligible union that is the object of the "mystical theology"? It does not appear so. On the contrary, it seems that for Dionysius there are two distinct modes of union with God: on the one hand, theology, mystical, individual, and direct; and, on the other hand, theurgy, which is the "activity of the hierarchy" and of its numerous intermediaries.[44] The two modes of knowledge only coincide at their summit, insofar as their common aim is union with God. Dionysian *theologia* clearly belongs to the realm of personal holiness, what modern theology calls the "event"; *theurgia* could not, however, be simply relegated to the realm of pure "institution," since it rests, according to Dionysius, on the same neo-Platonic ontology as *theologia:* its aim is to transmit a gnosis, and the sacraments themselves are reduced to the role of initiating symbols.

On the ecclesiological level, the consequences of these conceptions are inevitably of great importance. If, for example, one grants objective value to the ecclesiastical hierarchy, the Dionysian system leads to a sort of magical clericalism, and it would be well worthwhile to examine whether a conscious or unconscious Dionysian influence played a role in the development of ecclesiology in the West in the scholastic and post-scholastic period. On the contrary, if one keeps the hierarchies in their anagogic and initiating role, the function of the sacrament is reduced to that of a symbol, and there cannot be any distinction between the objective presence of grace and the personal perfection of the "Initiator." This confusion, which was the especial tendency of the line of spirituality linked with Evagrius, appeared particularly tempting to certain Byzantine monastic circles; thus Nicetas Stethatos, a commentator on Dionysius, formally arrived at the conclusion in the eleventh century that the real "bishop" is the one who has "knowledge" and who is capable of initiating people into it, not the one who has been "ordained by men."[45] This extreme tendency, which finds an undeniable foundation in all the spiritual road from Origen to Evagrius and to Dionysius, was only overcome by theologians like Maximus and Palamas by a return to a christocentric conception of the grace of the sacraments and of human synergy. This return excluded the Dionysian system of hierarchies by limiting it strictly to the realm of natural theology. The most recent studies tend to confirm the judgment given by J. Vanneste on the influence of Dionysius:

> Although it cannot be denied that the imprint of Dionysius has been left on Western theology and doctrine, we are bound to acknowledge that in the East, whence his work came to us, the influence

of Pseudo-Dionysius remained mediocre. Involved at a very early stage in the theological controversies which divided the East in the sixth century, the Dionysian doctrine found few disciples to proclaim it. Unquestionably, the Cappadocians had already formed in the East a spiritual doctrine which would profoundly mark Byzantine theology and spirituality.[46]

Maximus the Confessor and John of Damascus obviously used Dionysius, mainly, however, by integrating him into a system of thought fundamentally independent of him.

The liturgical realm is probably the only one in which Dionysius and his vocabulary kept their originality and their importance in the Byzantine world.[47] Since the fourth century, the Christian liturgy, ceasing to express the religion of a persecuted minority, had to satisfy the needs of the masses, and it underwent an important transformation, if not in its essence at least in its forms and especially in the piety it expressed. This phenomenon, well known to historians of the liturgy,[48] brought about the adoption by the Church of concepts and terms borrowed from the vocabulary of the mysteries. Preaching insisted on the sanctity of the sacramental action, which the mass of nominal Christians, now thronging the churches, easily might forget. The idea of an esoteric initiation, borrowed from the neo-Platonists and the *Corpus Hermeticum,* began to be widely used to communicate to the faithful the sense of the sacred and to remind them how difficult it is to approach it. This tendency, certain aspects of which can find some basis in the Pauline conception of the *mysterion,* found its fullest expression in Pseudo-Dionysius. Only by ascending the steps of the hierarchy by way of initiation does one reach the mystery that remains always essentially hidden. In the absence of an initiation, one possesses only an indirect knowledge through hierarchical intermediaries and symbols. For Dionysius, this was essentially the role of the liturgy and of the sacraments, whose corporate, christological, and eschatological sense was left obscure. The necessary correctives to Dionysius were fairly rapidly incorporated in the realm of pure theology, but his symbolic and hierarchical conception of the liturgy marked forever Byzantine piety: hence the conception of a symbolic drama that the assembly attend as spectators, the mystery of which can only be penetrated by initiated individuals.

6.

The Spiritual Writers: Salvation, Asceticism, and Deification

The preceding chapters dealt mainly with problems and crises that Eastern Christian theology had to resolve successively from the fifth century: the christological crisis itself, the Origenist crisis, and the problem of the integration of neo-Platonic thought. The passionate character of the controversies arising from these problems witnesses to the existential importance contemporaries gave to them. The basic truths of the Christian religion were at stake: those truths dealing with the salvation of man, his relationship with God, and his final destiny.

God "became man in order that man might become God in him," said St. Athanasius,[1] and the whole of his anti-Arian polemic rests on this fundamental soteriological assertion, which would lose all its sense if the Word were nothing but a creature. Similarly, the Fathers' argument against Apollinarianism and Eutychianism can be summarized by the following insight of Gregory Nazianzen: "What is not assumed can not be healed, and what was united to God is saved."[2] If the Son of God has not "assumed" and made his own a true and whole human nature, salvation would remain a vain word.

In the present chapter the theological debates that have been considered so far in isolation will be left to one side, and the conception of salvation itself will be considered, as it appeared to the Byzantine spiritual writers, some of whom also took part in the theological debates of the time. For the christological debate was, in the East, always inseparable from the essential elements of Christian spirituality. Its capital role in the system of St. Maximus the Confessor and in the later developments of Byzantine theology require that we give it a prominent place in our general study of Christology.

Three elements make it possible for us to understand the conception of salvation dominant in the East: the patristic doctrine of the image of God in man and of his original destiny, its interpretation of original sin, and finally its teaching on redemption. We shall dwell briefly on each of these three points before turning to the Byzantine spiritual authors of the post-Chalcedonian period.

There is no *consensus patrum* for a complete exegesis of Gen 1:26-27. Does the notion of "image" include the whole of the human composite—soul and body—as St. Irenaeus thought, still preserving an anthropology close to that of the Bible; or does it reside only in the mind (νοῦς), as a later tradition said, having been influenced by Platonic anthropology? Is there a fundamental distinction to be drawn between the conceptions of image (εἰκὼν) and of "resemblance" (ὁμοίωσις), as asserted by Irenaeus and Origen; or should we consider them as synonymous, with Athanasius and Cyril of Alexandria? There is, however, an absolute consistency in Greek patristic tradition in asserting that the image is not an external imprint, received by man in the beginning and preserved by human nature as its own property independently of its relationships with God. "Image" implies a *participation in the divine nature.* Some passages will be quoted here from an author whose thought dominated the period we are considering: St. Cyril of Alexandria. For Cyril, the image of God resides essentially in the fact that man is "reasonable" (λογικὸς) and is, in this, distinct from all other creatures.[3] But this reasonable character *supposes* a participation in the divine Logos. Adam, before the fall,

> preserved in himself, pure and without stain, the illumination God had granted him, and did not

prostitute the dignity of his nature; thus the Son enlightens, as Creator, since he is himself the true light, while the creature is enlightened by participation in the light, and thus receives the name of light and becomes light, in going up towards the supernatural by the grace (εἰς τὰ ὑπὲρ φύσιν ἀναβαίνουσα διὰ τὴν χάριν) of him who has glorified it, and crowns it with various dignities.[4]

It appears from this passage that the proper dignity of human nature, as conceived by God and realized in Adam, consists of going beyond itself and receiving illuminating grace. The unknown author, called "Macarius the Great," who enjoyed great influence in the East, writes: "If human nature had remained alone in its nakedness and had not profited by a mingling and a communion with the supra-celestial nature, it would have resulted in nothing good."[5] These texts remind one that in the East the notion of grace is identified with that of participation; grace is never a created gift but is a communion with divine life. As R. Leys writes about St. Gregory of Nyssa, "grace makes man in the image of God," and he admits as indisputable that Gregory "ignores a historical state of pure nature: the world was created by grace."[6] Evidently the same judgment can be made about Cyril.[7] In Greek patristics, nature and grace are not opposed, but presuppose one another. Nature stops being really "natural" if it abandons its own destiny, which is to communicate with God and to rise ever higher in the knowledge of the Unknowable.

This conception of the image and the primitive destiny of man determines the dominant patristic interpretation of freedom. It belongs to the reasonable creature to be free. Freedom is part of God's image in man and *presumes* participation in the divine life. St. Basil writes very clearly that the soul of Adam was "free from all compulsion, that it had received from the creator a free life (αὐθαίρετον ζωήν), *because it had been created after the image of God.*"[8]

No more than the idea of nature is the idea of freedom opposed to the idea of grace, but it supposes it. Only insofar as he communicates with God is man really man, reasonable and free. "Man," writes St. Cyril, "from the origin of creation, received control over his desires and could freely follow the inclinations of his choice, for the Deity, whose image he is, is free."[9]

But original freedom also supposes the possibility of the fall, which the Fathers interpreted as a revolt against God and *therefore* as a sort of suicide, for a crime directed against God necessarily deals a blow at man himself. By this sin, Adam was deprived of his communion with God; his nature, once corrupted, lost the properties it owed to that communion, in particular freedom and immortality. Adam became the slave of the inferior elements of his own nature (the passions), instead of dominating them by his intellect, which linked him with God. The original existence of man presupposed a free participation in God through the intermediary of the superior elements of the human composite, essentially the intellect; the fall entailed slavery to Satan through the intermediary of the passions, made inevitable by the corruptibility of man separated from God.

Cyril of Alexandria writes:

> Adam was created for incorruptibility and life; in paradise, he had a holy life: his intellect was wholly and always devoted to the contemplation of God, his body was in security and calm, without the manifestation of any evil pleasure, for the tumult of stupid propensities did not exist in him. But when he fell because of sin and slid into corruption, then the pleasures and impurities invaded the nature of the flesh, and that law of savagery which is in our members appeared [Rom 7:5, 23]. Nature fell ill from sin through the disobedience of one [Rom 5:19], Adam. And the multitude was made sinful not through having partaken in Adam's sin —they did not exist yet—but through partaking in his nature fallen under the law of sin [Rom 7:23; 8:2]. As in Adam, man's nature contracted the illness of corruption (ἐρρώστησεν τὴν φθορὰν)

through disobedience, because through disobedience passions entered man's nature, in the same way in Christ it recovered health; for it became obedient to the God and Father, and committed no sin [1 Pt 2:22; Is 53:9].[10]

This text shows that in the thought of Cyril, sin is conceived as an illness (φθορὰ) contracted by Adam and transmitted by heredity to posterity. It is a deadly illness that affects the whole human nature and leads to sin.[11] Sin itself, however, remains a culpable act accomplished by the individual; it can be transmitted in its consequences, but not in its guilt. The human race possesses a nature corrupted insofar as it descends from Adam, but each human hypostasis, that of Adam as of every one of his descendants, remains totally responsible for its actions; it does not partake in Adam's fault, it "imitates" it;[12] even in its fallen state it preserves its freedom, which, as has been seen, is the essential aspect of God's image in man. Sin simply darkened that image and limited that freedom.

The redemption of human nature accomplished by Christ the new Adam consisted essentially in the fact that a sinless hypostasis, even that of the Logos, freely took over human nature in the very state of corruption in which it was (and this implied death) and by the resurrection re-established its original relationship with God. In Christ, man participated again in the eternal life destined for him by God. He is freed from the slavery that Satan had imposed through the intermediary of death. In the same way in which corruption appeared to the Greek Fathers as a disease contracted by man rather than a punishment inflicted by divine justice, so are the death and resurrection of the incarnate Word (the sacrifice for which Christ was both the priest and the victim) understood by them as, first, the accomplishment in Christ of our common destiny, and then as a new creation that could not be achieved unless the human nature of Christ had really become ours, in death itself. St. Athanasius writes:

The body of Christ was of the same substance as

that of all men ... and he died according to the
common lot of his equals.... The death of all was
being accomplished in the body of the Lord, and
on the other hand, death and corruption were
destroyed by the Word which dwelt in that body.[13]

This general outline of the thought of the Greek Fathers
on the original participation of man in the divine life, on
freedom as an *expression* of that participation, on sin as a
consequence of servitude to the demon and to the flesh, and
finally on redemption, which recapitulates human nature
in the risen Christ, determines the major aspects of the
spirituality and asceticism of the Christians of the Byzantine
era. Many hasty, and therefore incorrect, judgments have
been passed on this spirituality by authors who considered
it from a Western point of view, determined by the Pelagian
controversy and Augustinianism, or else by the Anselmian
theory of redemption. The main outlines of this spirituality
will be given here, free from these Western viewpoints,
but in connection with the problems proper to Eastern
Christianity.

In the fifth and sixth centuries, at the time of the great
controversies between Chalcedonians and Monophysites, Byzantine monasticism was in the process of overcoming a deep
inner crisis, certain elements of which have been encountered
in dealing with Origenism. From its origins, the monastic
movement had a central place in the religious life of the
Christian East. By leaving the world and the new Christian
community that had accepted and utilized the framework of
the empire, the monks took as their mission the incarnation
of the Church in its heavenly aspect, in opposition to the
institutional structures rooted in "this world." Since Christian
life as a whole was conceived as a participation in the divine
life, the process of deification, of which Adam had been
deprived by the fall, but which became accessible again in
Christ, the monks' essential preoccupation was to give to that
participation its full reality. Such a preoccupation implied,
however, a metaphysics, an anthropology, a theory of the
world; and neo-Platonism offered a ready-made system of

thought that, by its contemplative character, its scorn for
the tangible, its theocentrism, seemed marvelously adapted
to the particular insights of the monastic movement. Herein
lay the success of the Origenist movement, expressed especially
in the writings and the personality of Evagrius Ponticus.
Evagrius presented a coherent system of philosophy that
justified monastic asceticism and the fight against the "passions" of the flesh; the spirit (νοῦς) needed liberating because, although created incorporeal, it had misused its freedom and had fallen from the height of its original dignity
to a bodily state.

Evagrius' system and terminology were taken up by
later generations of monks. They are based first of all on
the distinction between *praxis* (or πρακτικὴ μέθοδος)
and *theoria* (or *gnosis*). The *praxis* consists essentially of
the fight against the passions (τὰ πάθη), and the practice
of the evangelical commands. Any bad action is considered
as the manifestation of an inner state of the soul: passion.
Passion is not only a state of the soul but a means used by
the devil to enslave man. One must go to the spring of
evil to obtain the liberation of the intellect. The analysis
of the world of passions, of their mutual relationships and
of the means of ridding oneself of them, illustrates Evagrius'
remarkable knowledge of the human soul. An example of
this is his description of spiritual indifference, or "acedia":

> The demon of acedia, also called the midday demon
> [mentioned in Ps 91:6], is the most oppressive of
> all the demons. He attacks the monk towards the
> fourth hour and besieges the soul until the eighth
> hour. He begins by giving the impression that the
> sun is hardly moving or not moving at all, and that
> the day has at least forty hours. After this, he
> continually draws the monk to his window; he
> forces him to go out of his cell, to look at the sun
> and calculate how much time still separates him
> from the ninth hour (the hour of vespers and of
> the meal), and finally to look about here and there
> to see if some brother is not coming to see him. . . .

The demon makes him disgusted with the place he is in, with his way of life, with his manual labor. Then he makes him think that the brothers are lacking in charity, that he has nobody to console him. And if anyone at such a time has given pain to the monk, the demon makes use of this to increase his hatred. Again he drives him to desire some other place, where he would easily find what he needs, where he could do some work that would be easier and more profitable. He adds that one can be pleasing to God anywhere. Together with this, he reminds the monk of his family and his previous way of life. He describes the long time that the monk still has to live and sets before his eyes the efforts of asceticism; finally, so to say, he sets the machine going that will drive the monk to leave his cell and flee from the arena.[14]

This passage, so down to earth, so close to the life of the monks in the desert which Evagrius shared, shows not only that the author is a neo-Platonic intellectual, but that he expresses a lived experience. He similarly analyzes other passions—gluttony, lewdness, avarice, sadness, anger, vainglory, pride—describing the various stages each one goes through in taking possession of the soul, and opposes against them the corresponding virtues. All can be vanquished by faith, which leads to continence and finally to *apatheia,* the supreme aim of the *praxis.* Thanks to *apatheia* (impassibility), man becomes free and can develop in himself the divine agape and consecrate himself entirely to *theoria,* of which "intellectual" and perpetual prayer is the most adequate expression.

Prayer, the essential activity of the monks, who took literally the Pauline precept "Pray without ceasing," (1 Th 5:17), was conceived by Evagrius as the principal means of that liberation of the mind:

Distractionless prayer is the mind's highest achievement...the mind ascending toward God.... The state of prayer is an impassible state, which by a supreme love carries off to intellectual mountain tops the spiritual mind in love with wisdom.... Prayer is the activity which suits the dignity of the mind, in other words, the best and most adequate use of it.[15]

This liberation implies for Evagrius a dematerialization. Prayer is also for him the "prelude to the immaterial gnosis" (προοίμιον τῆς ἀΰλου γνώσεως):[16] "Immaterial, go towards the Immaterial, and you shall understand,"[17] is his advice to the monk. As Vladimir Lossky writes: "We are there in the presence of a thoroughly Origenist conception: as for Origen, the ψυχὴ (soul) would be for Evagrius a distortion of the νοῦς (intellect), which moves away from God by becoming material. It becomes 'intellect' again by contemplation, of which the perfect stage is pure prayer."[18]

Once it has returned to its primary function, the intellect can contemplate creatures (φυσικὴ θεωρία) not through the distorting glass of the passions that held him captive, but in the light of the divine Logos with whom from henceforth he is in communion. And finally he can contemplate and know God himself, that is, have access to true theologia, the gnosis of the Holy Trinity, identified by Evagrius with the kingdom of God. This supreme stage of the soul's ascent towards God does not require "going beyond" the intellect, since Origenist metaphysics are based on a natural kinship between the divine and the intellectual:

Whenever we consider material substances, we come to the memory of their contemplation; and when we have received the contemplation, we go again further away from the material substances. But this is not what happens to us in relationship with the Holy Trinity; for it is only essential contemplation.... When the νοῦς shall receive the essential science, then it will also be called God, because it will also be able to found various worlds.[19]

God does not transcend the intellect; once purified, detached from matter and "simple" in its contemplation, the intellect sees God as he is, in his essence. Here Evagrius diverges from both the Cappadocians and Pseudo-Dionysius, who firmly maintain the notion of divine transcendence.[20]

Evagrius' doctrine on prayer became a classic in the Byzantine world. Taken out of the metaphysical context of its author, it was interpreted by whole generations as the expression of a spirituality inherited from the Cappadocians, in particular from Gregory of Nyssa. In the writings of the latter, the doctrine of the "spiritual senses" was based on the idea of the natural supremacy of the νοῦς over matter, but it implied neither the metaphysical independence of the mind from the body nor the immanence of God in the mind. As has already been said, Evagrius's Origenism taught the pre-existence of the minds (νόες) and their natural goodness and promised them a general apocatastasis. He considered Christ as merely a mind that had escaped materialization. According to Evagrius, "intellectual prayer" was the means of salvation that restored the mind to its original function. Neither the incarnation nor grace were necessary to that effect, and the outcome was an extreme form of Pelagianism. The danger was avoided only by the integration of Evagrius's doctrine of prayer (which became popular under the pseudonym of St. Nilus) into a Christian metaphysical system that altered its meaning. Yet the Origenist temptation remained extremely strong in Eastern monasticism throughout the fifth and sixth centuries. The most striking example is that of the Isochrist monks, who claimed that they became "equal to Christ" by the restoration of their minds in the contemplation of God, since Christ was only a mind that had not fallen.

The Origenist temptation was not overcome simply by the formal condemnation it incurred in 553. Among the monks another tendency, both spiritual and theological, enjoyed great influence: based upon a biblical conception of man that excluded the Platonic dualism between the "intellectual" and the "material," it saw man's way toward deification in a Christ-centered sacramental spirituality. Paradoxically, the most representative author of this group, an anonymous writer whose "spiritual homilies" were preserved under the name of St. Macarius of Egypt, is identified by some modern scholars with a Symeon of Mesopotamia, the main leader of the "Messalian" sect.[21] The implication of this identification, which is still anything but proved,[22] is that the entire tradition of Eastern Christan monastic spirituality, which is practically inseparable from the name and the writings of "Macarius the Great," is suspect of metaphysical dualism, Pelagianism and materialistic visionarism. We will not discuss the issue here, for it can be solved only on the basis of a clear definition of "Messalianism," which is still lacking, and an assumed agreement on what is "orthodox" in spirituality.

In the spiritual tradition of the Christian East, the various elements of Evagrian and Macarian asceticism must be understood in the light of general assumptions about the nature of sin, the original destiny of man and salvation conceived as deification, which have been mentioned at the beginning of this chapter. Evagrius's doctrine about the passions, once it had been integrated into the great Byzantine spiritual tradition, expressed the *corruption* of human nature; sin as a specific action is only the external manifestation of our "passionate" state, our corrupted and mortal state. Having become mortal through the sin of Adam, man, so to speak, attaches himself to the lower realms of material existence, gives way to the needs of the flesh and lets the "prince of this world" rule him. The struggle against the passions goes well beyond the simple negative commands that made up the essentials of the Old Testament law and were only concerned with *actions*. It supposes a return to the original balance between mind and matter, between man and the world, and finally between man and God. This balance is realized in Christ, the new Adam, in whom the Christian recovers his true existence. The conception of sin as above all the expression of a corresponding passion explains the role of the "spiritual father," the holy "elder" in the East. He is a charismatic guide and physician, rather than a judge with the power of the keys.

Moreover, many aspects of the ascetical tradition of the Christian East can present to the Western observer a Pelagian aspect. It was mentioned above that these are the grounds on which the so-called Messalianism of Macarius is usually condemned. In fact, Evagrius would fall under the same criterion even more easily if it were applied to him. For both of them the true vision of God is considered, on the one hand, as fundamentally identical with the kingdom of God and salvation; on the other hand, it depends on the human effort that consists of the *praxis* of asceticism and continual prayer. However, if one remembers the conception of the image of God as it prevails in the Greek Fathers, the problem of the relationship between grace and human freedom is on a different level from that which opposed Augustine to Pelagius in the West. Nature, and therefore true freedom, presuppose communion with God in grace. From there stems the concept of synergy in Gregory of Nyssa and in Macarius. It is not the blasphemous juxtaposition of divine grace and human effort but the concrete realization in Jesus Christ of man's primitive image. In the West this synergism was taxed with being semi-Pelagian in the person of Cassian, but the judgment was given in connection with categories foreign to Eastern patristic tradition. Gregory of Nyssa writes:

> If some necessity ruled human life, the image, on this point, would be a lie, having been altered by an element different from the model. How can something be called an image of the sovereign nature when it is subjected and enslaved to necessities? What has been made in all aspects in the image of the divinity must undoubtedly possess in its nature a free and independent will, in order that participation in the divine advantages should be the prize of virtue.[23]

Macarius develops the same idea in this characteristic passage:

Divine grace arranged things in such a way that

everyone participates in spiritual growth as he chooses, according to his own will, his own labor, and his own effort, in proportion to his faith and zeal. The more one loves, the more one gives oneself to the fight, in one's body and in one's soul, in order to accomplish the commandments, the greater the communion one achieves with the Spirit into the spiritual growth of the renewing of the mind; acquiring salvation by grace and divine gift, but receiving by faith, by love, and by the effort of free choice, progress and increase in the measure of the spiritual age. Thus eternal life will be inherited by grace, but also in all righteousness, since it is not only through the divine grace and power without human collaboration (συνεργεία) and effort that progress is made; nor is it only by one's own power, one's own effort and one's own strength, without the collaboration and help of the Holy Spirit, that the perfect accomplishment of the divine will and the full measure of all freedom and purity shall be reached.[24]

A passage like this can be understood only in a Pelagian or semi-Pelagian sense unless one accepts that human freedom and effort can only be achieved in *participation* with divine life, in the real *communion* with the Archetype of whom man is an image, in other words, in what the Christian East calls deification. Athanasius and Cyril respectively fought Arianism and Nestorianism primarily to defend the possibility and the reality of that communion with God in Christ: for them it was the very basis of the Gospel.

In order to guarantee and express the necessary collaboration of human freedom in the work of salvation, the Macarian tradition (perpetuated in various forms in Byzantium by Diadochus of Photike, Maximus the Confessor, Symeon the New Theologian, and many others) insisted on the conscious character of the participation of man in the divine life. There is no question here of a latent Messalianism, since Macarius and his disciples all assert the necessity of baptism as the first step to any life in Christ; they recognize, therefore, that divine grace is in no way tied to man's "consciousness"; the question is simply to maintain that once man reaches the age of consciousness in his collaboration in his own salvation he is implicated in a direct and personal meeting with God.

This meeting, whatever word is used for it—union, contemplation, vision, gnosis, deification—implies that the soul becomes *one with God,* since it cannot see him as long as it remains alone, left to its own resources. It even seems that all the misunderstandings concerning the supposed Messalianism of Macarius, or the semi-Pelagianism of the spirituality of the Greek Fathers, come from applying to them criteria that exclude the idea of communion with God and of participation in divine life. These are precisely the concepts that form the basis of that spirituality. Man is called to participate in God, without there ever being any confusion between his nature and that of God, without any diminution of his freedom; on the contrary, it is in this communion that he finds, "in a total feeling of certainty of the heart" (ἐν πάσῃ αἰσθήσει καὶ πληροφορίᾳ),[25] his own destiny, while continuing the fight against Satan, who retains his power until the day of judgment.

In a Macarian context, the perpetual prayer that Evagrius expressed in the framework of an Origenist metaphysical system acquired a definitely christocentric character: it became the prayer of the name of Jesus. The sacred character of the "name" of God is a well-known biblical concept. The name of Yahweh was pronounced only once a year in the Holy of Holies by the high priest of the Old Testament. But after the incarnation, that name—identified with the name of Jesus—must be constantly present in the mind of each faithful; for God has become immanent and can be partaken of. This specifically Christian character of the monk's prayer is expressed clearly by a remarkable spiritual doctor of the fifth century, Diadochus of Photike. Taking over the Evagrian idea of prayer as the mind's "proper occupation," he writes:

The mind demands of us, when we close all its

opening by the thought of God, a work to satisfy
its need of activity. It must, therefore, be given the
Lord Jesus as the only occupation corresponding
fully to its objective. *For no one,* as it is written,
*can say "Jesus is Lord" unless he is guided by the
Holy Spirit* [1 Cor 12:3]. . . . For all who meditate
without ceasing in the depth of their hearts on
this holy and glorious name, can also see at last
the light of their own minds. . . . Then in fact the
soul contains the very grace which meditates and
shouts with it, the *Lord Jesus,* as a mother teaches
her child the word father by repeating it with the
child until, instead of any other baby talk, she will
have accustomed it to calling distinctly its father,
even in its sleep.[26]

The practice of the Jesus prayer dominates Eastern
monasticism to our day: it is the essential element of Byzantine *hesychasm* (ἡσυχία: rest or contemplation). Based
on the synergy of human effort and grace, constant prayer
is the proper occupation for the mind freed from the passions.
Isaac of Nineveh writes:

When the Spirit establishes his dwelling in man,
the latter can no longer stop praying, for the Spirit
never ceases praying in him. Whether he sleeps
or stays awake, prayer is not separated from his
soul. While he eats, while he drinks, while he lies
in bed or is working, while he is plunged into sleep,
the perfume of prayer spontaneously exhales from
his soul. Henceforth he masters prayer not during
determined periods of time, but at all times.[27]

And John Climacus, the author of the *Ladder of Paradise,*
also describes the hesychast's prayer: "Hesychia is an uninter-
rupted cult and service of God. May the memory of Jesus
be one with your breathing and you shall understand the
usefulness of hesychia."[28]

The hesychast tradition took different forms down

through the centuries, but it remained unified in its fundamental inspiration: in Christ (ἐν Χριστῷ) man recovers his
original destiny, re-adapts his existence to the divine model,
rediscovers the true *freedom* that slavery to Satan made him
lose, and makes use of that freedom, with the collaboration
(συνεργεία) of the Holy Spirit, in order to love and know
God. He can then, by anticipation, participate in the kingdom
that Christ said was "within" us, and know by experience
what is the true divine light. Macarius writes:

> As the sun is altogether like itself, having no
> inferiors but being all resplendant with light, is all
> light and similar in all parts, or as in fire, the light
> of fire is totally similar to itself, having nothing
> primary or secondary, greater or smaller, in the
> same way the soul which has been fully illuminated
> by the ineffable beauty of the glory of the light
> of the face of Christ and filled with the Holy
> Spirit, worthy of becoming the dwelling and the
> temple of God, is all eye, all light, all face, all
> glory, and all spirit, Christ adorning it in this way,
> carrying it, directing it, supporting it, and decorating
> it with the spiritual beauty.[29]

This is deification (θέωσις), which the patristic tradition of the Christian East considers at the final aim of the
spiritual life, and which gives its mystical character to
Byzantine spirituality. In all modern Western languages,
however, the word "mysticism" evokes a subjectivist and
emotional religious context, which is in consequence unstable
and undemonstrable. This is not at all what is implied in
patristic literature. In fact, the union with God and the
vision of light of which the Fathers speak is a reality at
the same time fully objective, fully conscious, and fully
personal: the dilemma between grace and free will, between
divine action and human effort to which it corresponds and
which it causes, does not exist for them.

All things exist by participation in the Only Existing One,
but man has a particular way in which he participates in

God, different from that of all other beings. He communicates with him *freely,* because he carries in himself the image of the Creator. Deification is precisely this free and conscious participation in the divine life, which is proper to man only.[30] Because of that, the union with God mentioned by the Fathers never amounts to a disintegration of the human person into the divine infinite; but, on the contrary, it is the fulfillment of his free and personal destiny. Thence also springs the insistence of the Byzantine spiritual writers on the necessity of a personal encounter with Christ, the consequence of which is the deification of the whole man by the anticipation of the general resurrection of the bodies. Macarius says:

> The Kingdom of light and Jesus Christ, the heavenly image, illuminate the soul already today in secret, and reign in the souls of the saints; however, Christ is hidden from the eyes of men and is manifested truly only to the eyes of the soul, until the day of the resurrection, when the body itself shall be restored and glorified by the light of the Lord which already now is present in the soul.[31]

It is essentially this reality of a deification accessible to man in Christ that St. Athanasius wanted to defend when he proclaimed in opposition to Arius this great principle of patristic theology: "If God did not become man, man cannot become God." And the mysticism of the name of Jesus, that is, of the person or hypostasis of the incarnate Word assuming human nature and becoming in this way the new Adam, is itself intimately linked with the doctrines of the councils of Nicaea, Ephesus, Chalcedon, and Constantinople.

7.

The Cosmic Dimension of Salvation: Maximus the Confessor

Until the seventh century, Origen was the only author who had tried to construct a Christian system of metaphysics. However, although it had nourished patristic thought for several generations, Origenism as a system was rejected by the Church. Its very coherence and inner logic, based on the axioms of Platonism, rendered impossible assimilation by the Christian tradition. The successive condemnations of Origenism, the condemnation of 553 being the culminating point, resulted in just as many problems for Byzantine theologians. Were there any alternatives to the Origenist solution, and could Christian metaphysics be built into a different system?

During the age of Justinian the great Monophysite personality of Severus of Antioch so completely dominated the scene that the Chalcedonian theologians were reduced for the most part to the role of apologists. Not one first-class writer appeared among them. Only with Maximus the Confessor did there appear a theologian who not only was capable of going beyond the narrow horizons of the dispute (to which he devoted the major part of his life, and died a martyr for the authentic Chalcedonian faith), but also was able to provide a glimpse of a complete system of thought that answered in a new way the problems posed by Origenism.[1] In fact, Maximus can be called the real father of Byzantine theology. Only through his system, in which the valid traditions of the past found their legitimate place, were the ideas of Origen, Evagrius, the Cappadocians, Cyril, and Pseudo-Dionysius preserved within Eastern Christianity.[2]

However, although the various elements of Maximus' thought constitute an organic system, his thought falls far short of appearing as a system in his own writings. The Confessor's thought is scattered through a multitude of isolated "Chapters," in commentaries on difficult texts of Scripture or of the Fathers (*Ambigua*), or in small polemical writings. The existing publications of his works are defective and incomplete, and it is not surprising, therefore, that modern commentators on Maximus do not always succeed in clearly presenting his ideas. It remains impossible, however, to understand the whole of Byzantine theology without becoming aware of Maximus' synthesis.

The fundamental error of Origenism lay in its treatment of the problem of creation. Originally immutable and static, the eternal world of minds proceeded toward a diversified and material existence as a consequence of the fall. Only the free self-determination of the intellects made them enter the realm of time. As for divine actions, including creation, they are eternal (hence the de facto identification between the procession of the divine hypostases and the world's creation). St. Maximus designates the Origenist system by this triad: the immobile state (στάσις), movement (κίνη-σις), and genesis (γένεσις). The coming into existence of the visible world is not for Origen a true "beginning"; it is only the temporal and dynamic manifestation of an eternal and immovable existence. Maximus answers:

> The principle of all natural movement is the genesis of the beings set into motion; and the principle of the genesis of the beings set into motion is God as Creator (γενεσιουργός). The immobile state is the aim of the natural movement of created beings; this state comes from the Infinitude (ἀπειρία) when one goes beyond all that is finite: in it, for lack of space, all movements of the beings set naturally into motion ceases. . . God is the principle

(ἀρχή) and the end (τέλος) of all genesis and
of all movement of beings: from him they come,
towards him they move and in him they shall find
immobility.[3]

There will be further discussion later of this problem
of the "immobility" in God, which touches the Maximian
doctrine of deification. For the time being it is sufficient
to note that the Origenist triad is reversed by Maximus.
It becomes: genesis (γένεσις), movement (κίνησις), and
the immobile state (στάσις).

God is the Initiator and the end of all natural movement.
He is also, in an absolute way, the Creator, the Transcendent.
When Maximus is asked how the idea of immobility (στάσις) can apply to God, since it is preceded by no movement,
he answers that the divine Infinitude (ἀπειρία) that stops
all movement is only a reality "around God," who incom-
parably transcends it,[4] and that "Creator and the creature
are not the same thing."[5] Maximus writes:

> Some pretend that creatures coexist with God
> from all eternity, an impossible thing.... This is,
> however, the doctrine of the Greeks who teach us
> that God is in no way Creator of essences, but only
> of qualities. But we who know that God is almighty,
> we assert that he is Creator not only of qualities
> but also of created essences.[6]

In this way Origenism is outstripped on two accounts:
the absolute transcendence of the divine being, and the full
reality of creation in time are solidly established. The intellectualistic and monistic conception of Origen's world, which
assumed the pre-existence of minds in the eternal contemplation of the divine essence, is replaced by the biblical dualism
of Creator-creatures, God being the sole and absolutely free
origin of beings. Maximus, however, takes over some of
Origen's insights; he resurrects and exploits the Alexandrian
doctrine of the Logos; he keeps the notion that "being"
implies movement, but gives to that movement an opposite

direction; movement does not consist of fall, as in Origen, but of a *movement upward toward God;* he expresses it, like Pseudo-Dionysius, by a new triad: essence, power, energy; finally, he re-asserts the teaching on freedom, to which Origen gave such importance, but he fundamentally reinterprets it.

The Logos doctrine is developed in Maximus' refutation of Origenism. While he firmly holds his position on creation as a free act of God in time, he does not want to reject the doctrine according to which creation exists by participation (μετοχή) in God, who alone exists "by himself." A commentary on an ambiguous passage of St. Gregory Nazianzen, with Origenist overtones,[7] gives him the opportunity to develop a system of thought close to that of St. Irenaeus.

The divine Logos, *in whom* (Col 1:16) all things were created, contains in himself the diversity of creation. "By contemplating that diversity," writes Maximus, "who will not perceive that the single Logos is a multitude of *logoi* (τις...οὐχὶ πολλοὺς εἴσεται λόγους)...and that, conversely, the multitude is one in the universal return toward him?"[8] There is no question of an eternal pre-existence of the beings themselves in God; for all things visible and invisible were created from non-being (ἐκ τοῦ μὴ ὄντος) by the divine good-will (βουλήσει ἀγαθῇ) and at the right time (κατὰ τὸν δέοντα χρόνον); the reference is to the existence of their *logoi* within the single divine Logos.[9]

Maximus writes:

> We believe that the *logos* of the angels preceded their creation; [we believe] that the *logos* of each essence and of each power which constitute the world above, the *logos* of men, the *logos* of all that to which God gave being—and it is impossible to enumerate all things—is unspeakable and incomprehensible in its infinite transcendence, being greater than any creature and any created distinction and difference; but this same *logos* is manifested and multiplied in a way suitable to the Good, in all the beings who come from him according to the

> analogy of each, and he recapitulates (ἀνακεφα-
> λαιούμενον) all things in himself.... For all
> things participate in God by analogy, insofar as they
> come from God....[10]

Any object receives its very existence from the *logos* that is in it and makes it participate in God. Separated from its *logos*, a creature is but non-being (μὴ ὄν). This participation of beings in God allows Maximus to distinguish in Scripture "the letter from the spirit"; in creation, "the *logos* from the appearance"; and in man, "intellect from sensation," for God is to be found in the spirit of Scripture, in the *logos* of creation, and in man's mind.[11] This universal participation in God does not, however, endanger his transcendence; the divine *Logos,* as super-essential, is not participated in by anything.[12] Maximus will easily be recognized here as a disciple of Dionysius and not of Origen; God is both participated in and "unpartakable."

It was seen earlier that for Maximus the creation of beings implied the idea of their movement (κίνησις). The *logos* of each being implies also an "aim" or direction" (σκοπὸς) in conformity with that being.[13] H. Urs von Balthasar writes in this context: "Nature is a tendency, a plan (λόγος), a field, and a system of movement."[14] This is but a paraphrase of Maximus: "The definition of all nature is the *logos* of its essential activity."[15] One of the most stable principles of Maximus's thought is expressed by the triad of essence (οὐσία), power (δύναμις), and act (ἐνέργεια), which is a parallel to the triad of genesis, movement, and the immobile state, mentioned previously. "The natural power of each being," he writes, "is nothing but an indefectible movement from nature to action."[16]

This is the natural law (λόγος φύσεως) of creation, and it will soon be apparent how important this conception of energy as the essential manifestation of nature is, in Maximus's Christology.

The doctrine of "natural law," considered as the proper dynamism of nature, does not mean, however, that Maximus considers creation as an autonomous entity, as Western scholasticism was to do later. Natural movement itself requires participation in God. This participation flows from the very notion of *logos,* which is always conceived as an action of the divine Logos. One thus comes to the other three-part diagram of Maximus, expressing the relation between God and creation: "God is the principle, the center and the end, insofar as he *acts* without *being passive.* . . . He is the principle, as Creator; he is the center, as Providence; and he is the end, as a conclusion, for *All things come from him, by him and towards him* (Rom 11:15)."[17]

Created existence as such, in all the stages of its movement, requires God's collaboration and participation, although its movement always remains fully its own: such is its *nature,* which, far from being opposed to the notion of God's "grace," presupposes it. This becomes even clearer when Maximus' anthropology and his conception of freedom are taken into account. One of the chapters of Maximus' *Centuries on Charity* is particularly eloquent in this respect:

> By bringing into existence the reasonable and spiritual nature, God, by a supreme goodness, communicated to it four of the divine properties by which he maintains, keeps, and preserves beings: being, ever-being, goodness, and wisdom. Of these gifts, the first two were attributed to the essence; the two others, goodness and wisdom, to the free choice (τῇ γνωμικῇ ἐπιτηδειότητι) in order that what he himself is by essence his creature might be by participation. Therefore, it is said that a creature is made in the image and resemblance of God: first, in the image of his being, by the fact of being; secondly in the image of his ever-being, by the fact of being always, if not without beginning, at least without end; then in the resemblance, as being good, from him who is good, as being wise, from him who is wise, resembling thus by grace him who is good and wise by nature. In this way every reasonable nature is the *image* of

God; but in his *resemblance* are only those who are good and wise.[18]

This passage begins by asserting the principle mentioned above, according to which beings exist thanks to their participation in divine properties and not by themselves; subsequently Maximus develops a doctrine of the image and the resemblance that the patristic tradition knew before him[19] and that integrates perfectly with *genesis-movement;* God not only grants beings their existence, and in the case of man, an eternal existence; but he also assigns to them a goal to reach, and in the case of man this goal implies a *free* movement toward God.

In the passage from the *Centuries on Charity* just quoted, it may seem that the idea of freedom coincides in essentials with that of Origen, for whom it was merely a choice between good and evil. The *Centuries* constitutes, in fact, a work of Maximus' youth (written *c.* 626), and is a witness to an Origenist influence more pronounced than in his later works. Subsequently, Maximus covers the whole realm of man's movement toward God by the conceptions of will (θέλημα), energy (ἐνέργεια), free movement (αὐτε-ξούσιος κίνησις), and natural will (θέλημα φυσικόν), the idea of deliberative choice (γνώμη, θέλημα γνωμι-κὸν) appearing only as a consequence of sin. This distinction between the natural will and the deliberative will constitutes one of the most important contributions of the Confessor to the elaboration of Christian tradition.

In his *Dialogue with Pyrrhus,* Maximus develops the doctrine of the image, conceived not only as a reflection of the divine being but as a reflection of that being's freedom: "If man is the image of the divine nature and if the divine nature is free (αὐτεξούσιος), so is the image."[20]

As a result, man possesses a natural will (φύσει θελη-τικός),[21] and that will is a freedom of nature (ἡ κατὰ φύσιν αὐτεξουσιότης)[22] in conformity with divine freedom and unable to lead to anything but the Good. Created in paradise in the image and resemblance of God, man did not need to deliberate in order to acquire participation in the divine goodness and wisdom. He only had to follow the laws of his own nature, the *raison d'être* (λόγος τοῦ εἶναι) of his existence in order to have access to the "well-being" (λόγος τοῦ εὖ εἶναι) for which he was destined. Undoubtedly, this was a free movement, but this freedom did not reside in a permanent choice between several possible ways of realizing his destiny. Man's only true destiny was to conform to his nature, that is, to be in communion with God.

Maximus writes:

> Today man in his actions is possessed by the irrational imagination of the passions, deceived by concupiscence, or pre-occupied either by the contrivances of science because of his needs, or by the desire to learn the principles of nature according to its laws. None of these compulsions existed for man originally, since he was above everything. For thus man must have been in the beginning: in no way distracted by what was beneath him or around him or near him, and desiring perfection in nothing except irresistible movement, with all the strength of love towards the One who was above him, i.e., God.[23]

The natural movement of man toward God is not, however, conceived by Maximus as a flight from the world. On the contrary, man is inseparable from God, and since he thus possesses a particular relationship with the Logos, he reflects the latter's cosmic role. In this perspective, following Gregory of Nyssa, Maximus develops the idea of man as a microcosm who gathers into himself the various aspects of creation—mind, psyche, and matter[24]—and is called to reunify all things in himself. For the tangible world adapts to man's five senses; the five senses in turn are governed by five powers of the soul, of which they are the images, since Maximus considers that sight reflects intellect, hearing reflects reason, smell reflects the irascible power (θυμός), taste reflects the faculty of concupiscence (ἐπιθυμία), and touch reflects the faculty of life. By a right use of these powers, the soul not only accomplishes its own destiny but discovers God hidden in the secret of the universe and thus develops within itself virtues corresponding to each of these powers, and crowned by love (ἀγάπη), unifying and deifying virtue.[25] Man's natural movement toward God thus possesses a cosmic impact. Man finds God in the world and the world needs man in order to find its Creator again. Through the image the world recovers the Prototype.

This man-centered Maximian conception of the universe is further illustrated by his cosmological ideas, which discover in beings five fundamental dualities or divisions (διαίρεσις): created and uncreated, intelligible and tangible, heaven and earth, paradise and universe, and male and female. Within the framework of these divisions the history of salvation takes place, and man participates in his very being in each of these dualities, having received the task of overcoming them in his movement toward God. The Creator desires that "the multitude of beings, separated the ones from the others by their natures, should come to unity, converging the ones toward the others in the single nature of man, and that God himself should in this way become all in all."[26]

"This is the reason why man was the last to make his entrance among beings," writes Maximus. His role is to be "a natural link (σύνδεσμός τις φυσικὸς) between the extremities of creation," in order to unite all things in God. Such is "the great mystery of the divine plan."[27] Originally, man was called to overcome the sexual opposition by "impassibility,"[28] and to unite through holiness (ἁγιοπρεπὴς ἀγωγὴ) the universe and paradise, thus making one single and new earth. He was then to unite earth and heaven by virtue, in order to make one single, tangible creation, to unify the tangible and intelligible worlds by acquiring angelic gnosis (διὰ τὴν πρὸς ἀγγέλους κατὰ τὴν γνῶσιν ἰσότητα), so that creation might no longer be divided between those who know and those who do not know God. Finally, man was to reunite by love (ἀγάπη) the created and the uncreated, so that in his love for creation, God might become all in all.[29]

This is the sense of the movement ordered by God for man's nature. It is a re-establishment of the natural harmony of creation that constitutes the basis of spiritual life, described as follows by Maximus:

> The mind acts according to nature when it keeps the passions in submission, when it studies the *logoi* of the beings, and remains near God.... Do you want to be righteous? Give to each part which constitutes you what it deserves—I mean your soul, and your body.... To the reasonable part of the soul, give readings and contemplations and prayer, to the irascible part, spiritual love, the adversary of hatred; to the concupiscible part, chastity and temperance; to the flesh, food and clothing, which alone are indispensable.[30]

This natural movement determined by God was interrupted by the revolt of man against his Creator, and turned against man's proper nature. For man was "free" (αὐτε-ξούσιος) and preferred to become body and dust instead of being one Spirit with God.[31]

Maximus, following the whole patristic tradition, insists on this free self-determination as being the origin of evil. Evil has no proper nature; it possesses

> neither essence, nor nature, nor hypostasis, nor power, nor actuality in beings; it is neither quality nor quantity, nor relation, nor place, nor time, nor position, nor creation, nor movement, nor state, nor passion, which could be observed naturally in beings.... Evil is the defect which prevents the powers inherent in human nature from acting in conformity with their aims, and nothing else.[32]

This defect can come only from a personal choice, originally made by Satan, and later, by man. Giving way to the serpent's temptation, Adam abandoned what was proper to his nature—constantly to rise toward God—and gave himself up completely to his senses (μόνῃ τῇ αἰσθήσει), with the result that he did not even obtain the true enjoyment of the senses, "for he had taken over what belonged to God, outside of God, instead of God and not according to God."[33] In consequence, Adam's sin prevented the natural relationships between man and God as well as between man and creation.

In a long *Answer* to Thalassius, entirely devoted to the doctrine of sin and redemption, Maximus explains that human nature, as originally created, was made neither to enjoy nor to suffer through the senses. Enjoyment was guaranteed only when it elevated the intellect toward God. When man turned toward enjoyment of the senses (ἡδονή), he inevitably had to participate in suffering (ὀδύνη), and that implied death. Divine wisdom itself had foreseen this righteous means to make the human mind understand its folly; to seek the pleasure of the senses brings the destruction of man's nature. What is against nature cannot subsist, and death puts an end to it; for corrupted nature, suffering is a warning against any temptation to consider the enjoyment of the senses as normal for man, and death is a liberation and a grace.[34]

The transmission of original corruption to the descendants of Adam and Eve is also determined by the correlation "enjoyment-suffering." Maximus writes:

> Since after the fall, enjoyment preceded natural birth for all men, no one was naturally free from the passionate generation belonging to this enjoyment; all, by nature, had to render their due of sufferings, of which death is the conclusion; the way of freedom was completely impracticable for those who found themselves under the tyranny of unrighteous enjoyment and of just sufferings, and were naturally (φυσικῶς) subjected to the very just death.[35]

It was seen above[36] that Greek patristic tradition, in its conception of original sin, ignored the idea of a transmittable guilt. Adam's sin was conceived as the beginning of a corruption of human nature manifested first of all in hereditary mortality. The role Maximus gives to the pleasure of the senses or the enjoyment of the flesh was not found in the texts of Cyril and Theodoret quoted above. For Maximus, and for the monastic tradition he represented on that point, which continued to exercise a great influence on the spiritual literature of the Christian East, the enjoyment of the senses (originally designating all attachment to the visible world, which after sin replaced the only true enjoyment, that of God) is now more or less identified with the idea of sexual pleasure, and as such expresses what is corrupted in human nature from the moment of sin.[37]

The most direct consequence of sin was the fragmentation of human nature, originally created one, and the gradual opposition of people one to another in their opinions and attitudes (κατέτεμεν εἰς πολλὰς δόξας καὶ φαντασίας); for revolt against God was leading to ignorance of God; ignorance, in turn, was the origin of self-love (φιλαυτία) which finally made possible the replacement of love by tyranny as the norm of human relationships.[38] Man, who had been created to reign over the world by the grace of the Creator, misused the power allocated to him by turning it "against nature," and introduced into the world confusion and death.[39]

The fall of man, who had been placed by God at the center of creation and called to re-unify it, was a cosmic catastrophe that only the incarnation of the Word could repair.

Christ's work, for Maximus, is a "recapitulation" (ἀνακεφαλαίωσις);[40] his thought goes back to a conception used by St. Irenaeus against the Gnostics five centuries earlier. The Logos, by whom and in whom all things were originally created, gives a new orientation and integration to the whole of creation by assuming it after it had abandoned the movement assigned to it by God. The fundamental dualities (διαιρέσεις) of creation, which had become elements of disintegration and corruption because of sin, are overcome in him. By his virginal birth, Christ overcomes the opposition of the sexes—"In Christ," says Paul, "there is neither male nor female" (Gal 3:28). By his death and resurrection, Christ destroys the separation that existed since the fall between paradise and the universe. "Today you shall be with me in Paradise," says Christ to the good thief (Lk 23:43)—giving to the human race access to the forbidden garden, coming back himself on earth after his resurrection, and showing that in himself paradise and the universe are henceforth one. By his ascension he unites heaven and earth through the exaltation of the human body, co-natural and consubstantial with ours, which he had assumed. By going beyond the angelic orders with his human soul and body, he restores the unity between the worlds of sense and of mind, and establishes the harmony of the whole creation. Finally, as man, he accomplishes in all truth the true human destiny that he himself had predetermined as God, and from which man had turned: he unites man to God.[41]

The ultimate aim of the divine plan is thus man's deification:

> that whole people might participate in the whole God (Θεὸς ὅλος ὅλοις μετεχόμενος), and that in the same way in which the soul and the body are united, God should become partakable of by the soul, and, by the soul's intermediary, by the body, in order that the soul might receive an unchanging character (τὴν ἀτρεψίαν) and the body, immortality; and finally, that the whole man should become God, deified by the grace of God become man, becoming whole man, soul and body, by nature, and becoming whole God, soul and body, by grace.[42]

This essentially dynamic doctrine of salvation supposes a double movement: a divine movement toward man consisting of making God partakable of by creation, and a human movement toward God, willed from the beginning by the Creator and restored in Christ. The hypostatic union of these two movements in the incarnate Word constitutes the essence of Maximus' Christology: two natures imply two energies or wills meeting one another.

The notion of "energy," which lay at the center of the christological controversy in the seventh century,[43] had already been widely used in theology, especially in the controversy between the Cappadocians and Eunomius.

"God's energies descend to us," wrote St. Basil, "while his essence remains inaccessible."[44] With Gregory of Nyssa, the energy constantly designates what is partakable of in God: "He who is invisible by nature becomes visible in the energies."[45]

In his short treatise addressed to Ablabius and intended to refute the reproach of the "neo-Nicene" orthodox by the Sabellians, according to whom the doctrine of the three hypostases necessarily implied that there were "three gods," Gregory had recourse to the same distinction between an unknowable and unnameable essence, and the energies. All that we know of God is energy or movement (κίνησις) *ad extra,* and not his essence; but any divine operation or energy is always a trinitarian action, "from the Father, through the Son, in the Spirit." There is, therefore, only one God. There is also only one human nature, but human individuals act by themselves, and therefore each possesses his own energy: one must thus speak of men in the plural. But the manner of being of the divine hypostases within the unknowable and transcendent divine nature is such that the Father, the Son, and the Holy Spirit have only one energy; there is, therefore, only one God.[46] It was widely accepted, at the time of Maximus, that the divine energy depended on the common divine essence and that it was that which made it possible to see God and to share in the divine nature. It is not surprising that, after some hesitation, he convicted the monoenergistic or monothelite doctrine of being a crypto-Monophysitism. In his eyes, the Monothelites' argument (in Christ, energy and will depended on the hypostasis and therefore were one) could only destroy the whole of Gregory of Nyssa's argument, since in this case three divine hypostases would suppose three deities and three energies. For Maximus, however, in Christ two natures necessarily suppose two energies or wills.

This fundamental relationship between the essence and the energy is linked in Maximus with the distinction *logos-tropos,* which he applies very generally to his trinitarian doctrine, as well as to the economy:[47] every being possesses in himself a pre-existent and natural law (λόγος τῆς φύσεως), but concretely it exists only according to a "mode of existence" (τρόπος ὑπάρξεως) proper to it. The divine order of nature always remains transcendent and inaccessible to the creatures, although in his energies God reveals himself as Trinity, and in a sense the divine hypostases are particular "modes of existence." Man also possesses an order of nature pre-established by God and common to all men, but his tragedy is that after the fall his mode of existence is in opposition to his nature. The real mode of existence, the perfectly human mode of existence, is restored only in Christ.

Maximus has been criticized for promoting a completely abstract conception of essence or nature.[48] Indeed, concrete reality is for him *hypostatic.* Following Leontius of Byzantium, Maximus formally opposes the concept of essence as it exists "with the philosophers," where it is "a reality in itself necessitating nothing else in order to exist" (αὐθυπόστατον πρᾶγμα μὴ δεόμενον ἑτέρου πρὸς σύστασιν), to that of the Fathers who recognize in it "a natural entity (ὀντότης φυσικὴ) proper to numerous and different hypostases." This conception of hypostasis as the concrete source of existence is not a simple return to Aristotelianism, nor even less the reduction of the notion to a simple relationship, as in Leontius; the context shows clearly that Maximus has a personalistic concept of the hypostasis: "The hypostasis," he writes, "is, according to the philosophers, an essence with characteristics; for the Fathers, it is each man in particular as distinct from the other men."[49]

The vocabulary, inherited from Leontius of Byzantium,

is integrated here into a Christian ontology. In God, as within human nature, the hypostasis is, therefore, the center of every concrete reality that determines and qualifies the "mode of existence" (τρόποι ὑπάρξεως) or "movement" of the nature. We must remind ourselves that in the case of man, freedom—which the hypostasis alone can enjoy—has plunged mankind into a fallen state, without, however, being able to alter either the nature itself, or its fundamental unity. Maximus would be reducing nature to an abstraction if he conceived it in a static way; in fact, there is for him no nature without movement, without energy, without existence; without movement, it is not nature.[50] Energy is in this way the concrete manifestation of nature; and the hypostasis gives it its quality or manner of being; the triangle—hypostasis, nature, energy—is thus the key to the whole system of Maximus, and in particular to his Christology.

The recapitulation of human nature in Christ implies that the incarnate Word assumed human energy and restored it in conformity with the primitive divine plan. There are thus in Christ two energies or wills, the latter term having been largely used, even before Maximus, as a synonym of energy.

In pre-Maximian tradition, there were precedents of great weight in favor of this doctrine. St. Athanasius himself, in spite of the general tendency of his thought to consider Christ in his theandric unity, interpreted the Gethsemane prayer (Mt 26:19) in a formally dyothelite sense: "He manifests here two wills (δύο θελήματα): the human will, which belongs to the flesh; and the divine will, which belongs to God."[51]

Monothelitism seems to go back to such different and even opposite contexts as Apollinarius and Nestorius.[52] Maximus' doctrine of the two wills, on the contrary, takes up again and preserves the Chalcedonian definition that specified that each nature, within the union, maintained its own manner of being, and that the union itself was hypostatic. This is in opposition to the natural union of the Monophysites and the union "according to energy" or "according to the will" of the Nestorians.[53]

The restoration of fallen mankind takes place when human nature, created in the image of God and made to remain in conformity with it, is re-assumed by its Model—the divine Logos—who is henceforth the hypostasis determining its manner of being or will. Maximus writes:

> Christ, being God by nature, made use of a will which was naturally divine and paternal, for he had but one will with his Father (συνϑε-λητὴς τοῦ ἰδίου γεννήτορος); being himself man by nature, he also made use of a naturally human will which was in no way opposed to the Father's will, since he actions were foreign to all imagination; neither nature itself, nor anything natural, is opposed to the Origin of nature, not even free will (γνώμη) and what depends on it, insofar as it is in concordance with the natural law (τῷ λόγῳ συννεύει τῆς φύσεως)....[54]

> Christ restores nature in conformity with itself....
> Becoming man, he kept his free will (γνώμη) in impassibility and peace with nature.[55]

It is clear that, for Maximus, the notion of nature supposes communion with God and therefore movement toward the Good. The choice that led Adam to sin was made on the level of individual freedom and not of nature. Together with the conception of *gnome* that appears in the passage just quoted, one meets the chief notion that allows one to understand Maximus' anthropology and Christology. It also gives relief to the importance of the hypostatic existence at the level at which the *gnome* is placed.

Refuting a Monothelite adversary, Maximus asks him to define explicitly the significance of the "single will." Is it natural? In that case Christ would possess a particular "Christic" nature. Is it gnomic? In that case it would characterize neither nature "but only the hypostasis, for the gnomic element individualizes the person (πρόσωπον γὰρ ἀφοριστικὸν ὑπάρχει τὸ γνωμικόν), and Christ would have a will distinct from that of the Father and of the Spirit."[56] The doctrine of the single will appears thus to Maximus as a form of Nestorianism, for Nestorius interpreted the union of the two natures as a relative (σχετικὴ) union of two *gnomai* into a single "will" (θέλημα), which evidently would suppose in Christ the existence of two hypostases, "since," repeats Maximus, "*gnome* reflects the person or hypostasis."[57] The gnomic unity can only be conceived as relative between distinct hypostases. God and the saints are united in this way into "a single nature, a single *gnome* and a single will," when "love persuades free will to oppose nature no longer" and "when the law of nature is freely (γνωμικῶς) renewed by the law of grace."[58]

In the works of his youth, Maximus seems to use the term *gnome* in a sense almost synonymous with "will" or "energy," and some passages (for example, the one quoted) seem to admit the existence of a divine *gnome*.[59] Later, and very clearly, *gnome* becomes the main term to designate the free will of created hypostases, the seat of the *posse peccare* (potential sin).

Let us come back to the first triad: genesis, movement, and the immobile state, the importance of which we saw in Maximus' conception of creation. It corresponds, on the level of anthropology, to another triad: being, well-being, and ever-being, of which the first and last elements have God alone for cause. For he is the sole Creator who gives being and the sole Immortal who gives immortality. Nevertheless, to pass from the first to the third element supposes the participation of "our free will (*gnome*) and all our movement (γνώμης τε καὶ κινήσεως τῆς ἡμετέρας),"[60] and this passage indicates a personal and hypostatic choice. "The reasonable beings," he writes elsewhere, "move naturally by being pushed towards their goal according to their free will on account of their wellbeing (πρὸς τέλος κατὰ γνώμην διὰ τὸ εὖ εἶναι)."[61]

Free will (γνώμη), therefore, is on a level with movement, moral choice, which Maximus likes to associate with the idea of imitation of, or similitude with, God: "God alone is good by nature, and only God's imitator is good by his *gnome*."[62] This imitation and this choice presume collaboration between grace and human freedom: "The Spirit does not give birth to a stubborn will (γνώμην μὴ θέλουσαν), but if it so desires, he transforms and deifies it."[63] "Our salvation," writes Maximus, "depends on our will."[64]

Adam's sin was essentially a catastrophe of human freedom making a choice "against nature": "the single nature entered into conflict with itself (πρὸς ἑαυτήν)," and this conflict took place "according to free will" (κατὰ γνώμην).[65] Maximus always insisted that nature remained intact in spite of sin, and clearly opposes *physis* to *gnome*.[66] The direct consequence of sin was a sort of contamination of the nature's will, which until then could only will good; the contamination came through the *gnome*. Man acquired in this way a gnomic will, which chooses, hesitates, ignores the real good, inflicts pain because its decisions are taken blindfolded; it is "a kind of desire adhering to what is, or what he thinks is, a relative good."[67]

Gnome is intrinsically linked with hypostasis, or human person, as we have already seen. Sin is always a personal action that does not corrupt nature as such. This explains why the Word could fully assume human nature, *sin excepted.* Sin remains on the level of the *gnome,* of personal choice.[68] Christ possessed a natural human will, but since the subject of this being was the Logos himself, he could have no gnomic will, the only possible source of sin. According to Maximus, those who attribute to Christ a gnomic will "consider him as a mere man, possessing a will like our own, ignorant, hesitant, and in conflict with himself.... In the Lord's human nature, which possessed not a simple human hypostasis but a divine hypostasis, ... there could be no *gnome*."[69]

Spiritual life, life in Jesus Christ, the way of deification, essentially supposes the transformation of our gnomic will into a "divine and angelic *gnome*,"[70] for our nature's participation in the divine nature and God's condescension, which it presupposes, are not compatible with the inner conflict introduced into nature by the devil through the *gnome*.[71]

This transformation—the aim of asceticism and of all spiritual life—does not imply the acquisition of supernatural or extrinsic virtues but the re-integration of those virtues that were our own from the time of creation.[72] Maximus goes as far as to say that deification itself is in this sense natural to man since it was God's intention from the beginning: "Let us become gods through the Lord, because for this did man come to exist: God and Master by nature (φύσει ὢν Θεὸς καὶ δεσπότης)."[73]

It has been seen that our salvation, that is, our re-integration into the natural state, "depends on our will"; one could not conceive a system of thought more different from Western Augustinianism; and yet Maximus is in no way a Pelagian. His doctrine of salvation is based on the idea of participation and of communion that excludes neither grace nor freedom but supposes their union and collaboration, which were re-established once and for all in the incarnate Word and his two wills.

This conception of natural deification cannot help bringing out the question of Maximus' dependence on Origenism and in particular on Evagrius. If union with God is natural for man, is he not by nature a divine spirit that merely returns to its primitive state and in which God is immanent? The question deserves to be asked all the more in that the explicit dependence of Maximus' writings (in particular the *Centuries on Charity*) on Evagrius and also their belonging to the same spiritual tradition are established facts.[74]

The answer to this question is in Maximus' doctrine of ecstasy (ἔκστασις): to be united with God of whom he is the image, man must "freely go out of himself (ἐγχώρησις γνωμικὴ)" and abandon what is really or intelligibly natural to him and receive in this way the sovereign grace of the Spirit.[75]

The apparent contradiction between this statement, which seems to oppose nature and grace, and Maximus' statement elsewhere that it is natural for man to "become God" illustrates yet again his dynamic conception of nature. Because man is made in the image of the transcendent God, his very nature allows him to "go beyond" himself and communicate with his Archetype. This going beyond, or ecstasy, is produced because of the presence of the Spirit, who co-operates with the free choice and effort of man. However, even after this going beyond has taken place, man cannot communicate with the divine essence itself (τὰ κατ' αὐτὸν) but only with what is "around God" (τὰ περὶ Θεόν), and Maximus refers immediately to Gregory of Nyssa and to Dionysius.[76] "We know God," he writes, "not by his essence (ἐκ τῆς οὐσίας) but through his magnificence and his providence towards beings."[77]

The human ecstasy corresponds to an act of God, who also comes out of his transcendent essence to meet the creature. The meeting of the two movements was fully and hypostatically accomplished in the incarnate Word, but our gnomic acceptance of this meeting—it is the condition of our salvation and of our deification—remains the goal of the spiritual life, which receives in this way its necessary place in the economy of salvation.[78]

8.

An Effort at Systematization: St. John of Damascus

Origen, Pseudo-Dionysius, and Maximus, by exceeding the limits of mere polemics against heretics, had already produced "systems" of theological thought. St. John of Damascus' system is of a very different type. There is no new creation in it; it is essentially a school manual, and was used as such throughout the Byzantine Middle Ages. The *Fount of Wisdom*, the Damascene's main work, comprising a *Dialectic*, a catalogue of heresies, and an *Exact Exposition of the Orthodox Faith,* constitutes above all a handy summary of patristic theology. But once it is studied in the light of several minor works, sermons, short dogmatic treatises, and hymns, it represents more than a simple repetition of other people's ideas. By putting side by side the Cappadocians' trinitarian terminology, the Chalcedonian Christology, the clarifications brought to it in the sixth century, and the ideas and terminology of Dionysius and Maximus, John of Damascus discovers their inner coherence, and with the help of supplementary sources—such as the writings of pseudo-Cyril on the Trinity—arrives at his final synthesis.

The now-classical definitions of the terms used in trinitarian theology and in Christology constitute the most interesting element of the Damascene's *Dialectic*. Nevertheless, it is in their very application to the theological reasonings of the *Exact Exposition of the Orthodox Faith* that their Christian sense appears most clearly. For instance, he defines

153

"nature" (φύσις) as "a species which cannot be divided into other species," the "most special species" (εἰδικώτατον εἶδος).[1] The word "nature" therefore reflects above all the *difference,* and one will remember that Athanasius previously had made use of it in precisely this sense: created humanity and uncreated divinity are two different natures. Although it cannot be divided into species, a nature can nevertheless be composite; man, for instance, is formed of a body and a soul, and the human body itself is composed of different elements. This combination constitutes the nature common to all men, to all bodies, etc. . . .[2] However, for the union of distinct elements to be considered as a nature, their union must be permanent. In other words, the elements must really be *parts* of the single nature, and their union must be "natural" and not accidental or limited in time. Therefore, one cannot say that Christ has one nature, since, on the one hand, the divinity existed as a perfect nature before the union, and it is therefore not "a part" of Christ's nature,[3] and, on the other hand, the composite divinity-humanity is an absolutely unique and not a generic case: there is no "Christic nature."[4]

Yet John of Damascus was well aware that the Fathers, and in particular Cyril of Alexandria, spoke of "one incarnate nature" of the Word. He recognizes, therefore, that the word "nature" can mean also the concrete reality of an individual existence (ἐν ἀτόμῳ θεωρουμένη), and that in this sense it does not coincide with the concept of common nature distinguished "by contemplation" (ψιλῇ θεωρίᾳ) in beings of the same species.[5] John of Damascus admits, therefore, the full validity of Cyrillian theology with his insistence on the fact that the single nature is "incarnate": "We also confess," he writes, "*the single incarnate nature of the God-Word,* because we say: *incarnate,* and proclaim in this way the essence of the flesh."[6]

Cyril's faith, he asserts, is common to the Chalcedonians and the Monophysites:[7] it expresses the reality of the incarnation of the Word who assumed not an abstract human nature, common to all, but that of a concrete individual, hypostatized in the Son; in this sense the Christology of

Cyril keeps its full validity for John of Damascus.

Fully conscious of the Cyrillian interpretation of Chalcedon, as defined in 553, John nevertheless devotes a large part of his theological work to attacking the Severian Monophysites. While taking into account that they are orthodox in all things except their opposition to Chalcedon,[8] he does not recognize any difference between the Monophysitism of Eutyches and the Christology of Dioscorus and Severus. The fact that the latter rejected Chalcedon apparently constitutes for him sufficient proof of their belonging to Eutychianism.[9]

John's doctrine of the incarnation is based on the Chalcedonian definition, but the latter is framed in a system of terms and concepts that summarizes the results of the theological developments of the sixth and seventh centuries. First of all, he defines the notion of hypostasis as an existence "by itself" (τὸ καθ' ἑαυτὸ ἰδιοστάτως ὑφιστάμενον).[10] This is Leontius of Byzantium's definition, and from the same Leontius, John borrows the now-classical conception of the *enhypostaton,* a reality that does not exist by itself but "appears in the hypostases: as for example, the aspect or the nature of men does not appear in a hypostasis of its own, but in Peter or Paul." When *enhypostata* of different natures are "enhypostatized" into a single hypostasis, the latter becomes a composite hypostasis (ὑπόστασις σύνθετος), the most common example being the human hypostasis, composed of a body and a soul.[11]

Nevertheless, John very clearly rejects the Evagrian aspects of Leontius. The difference appears particularly in the use he makes of the anthropological example of soul-body. In Leontius, as we saw, man was made of two perfect entities, which theoretically could pre-exist as two separate hypostases, and which really became two hypostases after death in order to be united again at the resurrection.[12] Against this Origenist anthropology, and the Christology it represented, John clearly asserts that if, "at death, the soul is separated from the body, the hypostasis of both remains the same."[13] Similarly, Christ did not become "two hypostases" at the moment when his soul separated from his body, but "was hypostatically united by the Word."[14] For Christ, the hypostasis is not simply a "state" and a "relationship," as Leontius thought, but a much more fundamental reality; and the image soul-body, which John still refers to occasionally in his Christology, only appears to him as an analogy with a very limited significance.[15] What also separates John from Leontius is that, following Cyril of Alexandria and the council of 553, he considers the hypostasis of Christ as the pre-existent hypostasis of the Logos. Chalcedonian orthodox Christology does not conceive the hypostasis of Christ as having come into existence as a consequence of the union of two *enhypostata,* the divine and the human, but as the assumption by the Logos of the human nature in addition to the divine nature that he had possessed from all eternity. Orthodox dyophysitism does not believe in a symmetrical putting together of two natures but in their union into a single hypostasis that is divine from all eternity. The duality of the two natures, or *enhypostata,* is expressed never in terms of separation—for the incarnate Word is a unique being—but only in terms of intelligible distinction (κατ' ἐπίνοιαν).[16]

In order to realize the exact significance of this "asymmetrical" Christology, one must consider first of all its soteriological bearing. "The Word has the initiative in the work of the incarnation, and it is evident that the theory of enhypostasis, while asserting and underlying Christ's humanity, shows in an unequivocal way the primordial greatness of the divinity."[17]

Only God can be the Savior; he himself is the Author of salvation: flesh can but accept and cooperate with the divine action. "The Word himself became the hypostasis for the flesh," writes John of Damascus, "so that it was at the same time flesh, flesh of the Word of God and animated, rational, and intelligent flesh. This is why we do not speak of a divinized man, but of a God who became man."[18] "Remaining himself in the elevated state of his own divinity, he also accepts what is inferior, divinely creating in himself the human, and he mingles the Archetype with the image."[19] Man, created in the image of the divine Archetype, is thus restored to his original dignity by the fact that God himself becomes man.

Excluding all pre-existence of Christ's humanity before the incarnation ("the Word himself became hypostasis for the flesh"; the latter could not have existed before, since it had no hypostasis), John of Damascus conceived the "composition" of the incarnate Word's hypostasis in a sense that recalls the thought of Leontius of Jerusalem. The Logos' hypostasis, "which beforehand was simple, entered into composition: it did not become a composite nature, but the composite hypostasis made up of the divinity which pre-existed in it, and of the flesh which it assumed and which is animated by a reasonable and intellectual soul."[20] This assumption of humanity by the Archetype, in whose image it had been created, constitutes the hypostatic union; it does not amount to the junction of two parallel entities, since there can be no parallelism when the Creator meets his creature, but simply a relationship of dependency. As there never was a human nature of Jesus outside of, independent of, the Logos' hypostasis, Mary gave birth to that very hypostasis in its composite state: "The holy Theotokos engendered a hypostasis manifested in two natures."[21] Hence the importance of the term *Theotokos*: "This term summarizes all the mystery of the economy [of salvation], for if the mother is Theotokos, it is because her Son is surely God and surely man."[22] For the Word's hypostasis

does not exist as the hypostasis now of one nature, now of the other, but always without division or separation, as the hypostasis of both. Without being sundered or divided, . . . it belongs wholly to them both without division and totally. For the flesh of the Word of God did not have its own existence and did not become another hypostasis side by side with the hypostasis of the Word of God, but subsisting in that hypostasis it became enhypostatized and not an hypostasis having in itself its own existence. This is why it is not without an hypostasis, yet does not bring another hypostasis into the Trinity.[23]

The act of the incarnation thus has the Logos as its only subject: hence, a dissymmetric Christology conceived as a soteriological necessity. This dissymmetry, however, does not interefere with the fullness of Christ's humanity since there was in Christ a hypostatic union, not a fusion of natures. It is in the definition of the hypostatic union that the Greek Fathers, of whom the Damascene is an expression, illustrate what is characteristic to the conception of hypostasis, defined by its "particularities" (ἰδιώματα), different from those of nature.

It was seen earlier[24] how Leontius of Jerusalem, in attempting to define the composite hypostasis of Christ, described it as having acquired by the incarnation new characteristics (ἰδιώματα). His argument took as a starting point Basil's definition of the hypostasis as "a nature limited by particular characteristics"; in the case of Christ, the nature of the Logos would simply have become "more composite" than before the incarnation. Leontius' reasoning was insufficient in that it defined Christ's humanity as "an individual nature" and as a coherence of particular characteristics, without admitting that it was a hypostasis. John of Damascus' clearer conception of hypostasis, which rules out its reduction to the notion of individual nature, overcomes this difficulty.

John writes:

> The Word's hypostasis, previously simple, becomes composite, but preserves the particular and distinctive character of the divine filiation of the God-Word, by which it is distinguished from the Father and the Spirit; it also carries, according to the flesh, particular and distinctive characteristics distinguishing it from its mother and all other human beings; moreover, it possesses the characteristics of the divine nature, by which it is united with the Father and the Spirit, as well as the characteristics of human nature, by which it is united to its mother and to us.[25]

This passage shows that, according to John, the enhypostatization of human nature into the Logos can give that human nature a properly human or "carnal" principle of individuation; in other words, Jesus, even though he does not possess a human hypostasis, is individualized—in relationship to his mother and to us—*as man,* and not just as God, and that human individuation is based on his hypostatic existence, which is divine.

> The God-Word has not assumed nature as pure theory (this would not be the incarnation, but deceit, and the appearance of an incarnation), neither has he assumed that which is contemplated in the species (ἐν τῷ εἴδει), for he has not assumed all the hypostases, but an individual nature (τὴν ἐν ἀτόμῳ), which is the same as that of the species [but which] only came into existence through the [Logos'] hypostasis (ἐν τῇ αὐτοῦ ὑποστάσει ὑπάρξασαν).[26]

As the source of existence, and not the product of natural existence, the hypostasis thus represents the key notion of orthodox Chalcedonian soteriology: the incarnate hypostasis of the Word, by becoming for Jesus' human nature the source of a properly human existence, becomes precisely because of this the fount of salvation. In the light of this conception of hypostasis, the crucial Cyrillian formula acquires its exact value: "The Word suffered in the flesh." "Being God," writes John of Damascus, "[the Word] assumed passible flesh; being God, he became man in order that he might suffer."[27]

God, being impassible by nature, suffers hypostatically "in the flesh": it is evident, therefore, that the hypostasis remains in some way independent of the characteristics of its own nature; it can be liberated from it by assuming the characteristics of the flesh. However, the characteristics of the divine and the human natures make possible the fact and the consequences of the hypostatic union.

You may ask why do we say that the nature of the flesh was deified and suffered, while we do not attribute [deification and suffering] to all the hypostases of mankind? Why, then, do we say that the nature of the Word became incarnate, without attributing incarnation to the Father and the Spirit?[28] Because human nature in its totality can be modified by what is natural to it, as well as by what is foreign to it or is beyond it (δεκτικὴ ἐστι τῶν κατὰ φύσιν καὶ παρὰ φύσιν καὶ ὑπὲρ φύσιν), while the divine nature can receive neither modification nor addition. On the other hand, the [Word's] flesh constitutes the first fruits of our nature; it is not an individual hypostasis [of the human nature], ὑπόστασις ἰδιοσύστατος, but an enhypostatized nature, a part of Christ's composite hypostasis; it was united to the God-Word not for its own sake, but for the common salvation of our nature.[29]

The Logos' divine hypostasis in this way assumed a definite human nature, especially by the following distinctive marks. First, in contrast with divine nature, whose essential characteristic is to be unchangeable (ἄτρεπτος) and impassible (ἀπαθής), it was created like the whole human nature, *for the purpose of* being deified; its natural character is dynamic and its destiny is to participate supernaturally in divine life; we have already seen that for the Greek Fathers, the concepts of nature, grace, and the supernatural are not opposed to one another but are complementary.

Second, having no human hypostasis of its own, and being individualized (enhypostatized) by the Logos' hypostasis—the Archetype of all men—it constitutes or represents, in a sense, the whole of mankind (without losing, as we saw it, the individual human character of Jesus, son of Mary). Jesus is not *only* an individual within the human race, he is also the new Adam, "first fruits of our nature," the Christ and the Servant foretold by the prophets of the Old Testament, who summarizes in himself the destinies of the whole of Israel, Israel becoming his Body, the Church. Each one of us can in this way see in Jesus not only a fellow human being but also the Model in whose image we were created, the Father of those who practice righteousness (1 Jn 2:29), with whom we are joined by an infinitely more intimate link than with any other human being who is humanly hypostatized. In Christ is the very root of our existence. The biblical notion of the new creation is in this way characterized by the fact that the divine model is not exterior to the new creation that is enhypostatized in him.

These christological categories determine, in St. John of Damascus, the doctrines of salvation and of redemption.

In the beginning, man was created with a dynamic nature, destined to progress to divine communion: Adam was "in a state of deification, by participation in the divine enlightenment" (θεούμενον μετοχῇ τῆς θείας ἐλλάμψεως).[30] John thus ignores, as does the whole of the Greek patristic tradition, the notion of a static "pure nature." Hence, participation in God was what gave Adam immortality, for he was not immortal by nature, but by grace.[31] This dependence of man on God, however, is not considered as a reduction of man's dignity as such; on the contrary, man, precisely because he participates at the same time in God and in the realm of creation, is conceived as superior to the angels themselves,[32] and as king of the created universe: "Man is a microcosm; for he possesses a soul and a body, and is placed between spirit and matter; he is the place in which the visible and invisible creations, the tangible and intelligible creations, are linked together."[33] And man also received a mission. In John's words:

> God gave us the power to do what is good; but he also made us free (αὐτεξουσίους), in order that the good *might come both from him and from us;* for whoever chooses the good, receives God's collaboration to do the good, so that, having preserved what is natural to us, we might receive what is supernatural—incorruptibility and deification—by union with God, by becoming members of

> his household by the power of our will....For if
> our will does not submit to the divine will, but if
> our free intellect uses its passionate element to
> follow its own choice on its own initiative, it does
> evil.[34]

Original human nature, which participated in divine
life and glory, is thus "without sin by nature" and "free
in its will,"[35] or again, by the very fact of being created, it
is "susceptible to change" (τρεπτή),[36] God alone being by
nature unchangeable (ἄτρεπτος). The change, however,
only intervenes by the free choice of the person. Freedom,
of which the hypostasis is the acting agent, and not nature,
can become the seat of sin. "Sin is not in nature but rather
in the free choice," says John of Damascus.[37]

To designate this freedom of choice, he currently used
a terminology introduced by Maximus: *gnome* or *thelema
gnomikon*. He defines this gnomic will as a function of the
created hypostasis and therefore "susceptible to change,"[38]
in opposition to the natural will that is accomplished only
in conformity with the divine plan and will. By nature, as
a creature, man not only is "good," but he possesses the
dynamic faculty of communicating with God and of progressing toward the divine image: this is his *natural will*.
But there is also in him a faculty of discernment, a free will
that *chooses*, and therefore *hesitates*, and eventually can
revolt against God. This is the gnomic will, a function of
the created hypostasis.

Thus, in Adam, "the *gnome* desired what was contrary
to the divine will: this was the transgression."[39] And as the
hypostasis is the determining source of the natural dynamism,
the gnomic choice of Adam's hypostasis immediately inter-
fered with the dynamic faculties of nature itself. Turned
from its destiny, which was to draw from the inexhaustible
divine fount of life, reduced to an autonomous existence,
when it had been created to communicate with God, human
nature fell under the control of death. It has been seen that
the Greek Fathers conceived original sin as first of all
hereditary mortality that maintained mankind under the

devil's control. This cosmic and almost personalized conception of death, which is already found in St. Paul—"...death reigned from Adam to Moses even over those who had not sinned by a transgression similar to that of Adam...." (Rom 5:14)—is taken up again by St. John of Damascus. The consequence of Adam's sin was that the soul, made to control the body, because it was the reasonable and free element linking man with God,[40] submitted to the body, the seat of animals passions and of corruptibility.[41] And Adam was overcome by mortality (νέκρωσις or θνητότης),[42] of which physical death is but one manifestation, and which is essentially a spiritual state of separation from God and of submission to the devil. Man can no longer liberate himself by his own strength. He is in submission to the cosmic powers that the prince of this world temporarily controls; and he is deprived of that authentic freedom that resided in fulfilling the natural will in conformity with God's plan for creation.

This catastrophe suffered by Adam was not only his personal catastrophe but that of the whole of mankind. The means chosen by God to maintain man within creation was to give man himself a way of reproducing himself. The separation of the sexes and the creation of woman is envisaged by John as an act of God's mercy. Knowing before-hand that man would fail in his original task, God gave him a "help" (Gen 2:18): "Knowing in his foreknowledge that man would fall into transgression and would submit to corruption, God created woman that she might be a help by his side, similar to him, a help who might after the transgression maintain, through generation, the perpetuation of the human race...."[43]

This rather restricted view of the origin of the sexes should not be understood in an Augustinian sense. John does not consider that the mode of reproduction as such implies sin and that consequently woman can only be an instrument of corruption. On the contrary, the perpetuation of mankind, made possible by the separation of the sexes, is a providential grace allowing human nature partially to overcome the consequence of its ancestors' sin, to overcome mortality if not individually, at least as a race and to become the instrument of the history of salvation. For from a woman was to be born the savior Jesus.

In order to save man, God did not have recourse only to his omnipotence: he willed that man should participate himself in his salvation. By assuming human existence itself, by hypostatizing it in himself, the Word became the Savior.

> After man had been vanquished, God allowed him who had been enslaved to death by sin to vanquish the tyrant...: he gives him victory again and saves the same by the same (τῷ ὁμοίῳ τὸ ὅμοιον)... Conceived by the Holy Spirit and according to the first generation of Adam..., he became obedient to the Father, by curing from disobedience our nature which he assumed by borrowing it from us.[44]

"Christ's human nature," writes John, "must be totally human: With the whole of himself he assumes the whole of me; with the whole of himself he unites himself to the whole of me, in order to give salvation to the whole of myself...." John then cites St. Gregory Nazianzen: "What is not assumed is not healed."[45]

He uses this same quotation to illustrate against Apollinarius the orthodox conception of a human intellect in Christ. For the intellect is par excellence the image of God in man. There is no true human nature without intellect; the Word assumed this human nature, this image, to restore it.[46]

Christ's human nature, however, is not, as has been seen, an abstract human nature: it is *our* human nature, as it exists concretely with all the consequences of Adam's sin. For the Word "assumed man in his totality, the reasonable soul and the body, the characteristics (ἰδιώματα) of human nature, the natural and incorruptible passions."[47] We must note in this text the distinction established between the "characteristics" (ἰδιώματα) of the flesh, that is, all the manifestations of a created existence, and the "natural and incorruptible passions" (τὰ φυσικὰ καὶ ἀδιάβλητα πάθη).

The characteristics of human nature make a human being. They existed fully in Adam, before as after the fall; they exist also in all of us. As for the passions, John of Damascus defines them as "actions [or energies] contrary to nature,"[48] and therefore contrary to the Creator's will. In this sense original human existence was impassible par excellence. In it, everything was perfectly natural. The goal of the Christian's spiritual life consists precisely of the acquisition of impassibility (ἀπάθεια), which is a necessary condition for deification. From this comes monastic asceticism, which practically identifies itself with the struggle against the passions.

Nevertheless, in speaking of Christ, John specifies that he assumed "the incorruptible and natural passions." It is evident that the passions against which man has to struggle to acquire impassibility are the passions that imply sin, of which Christ was completely exempt. In this sense John asserts that the human nature of Jesus was that of Adam before the transgression.[49] But the ambiguity of the word "passion" in its patristic use leads John to assert also with strength that the Word really assumed the "incorruptible" passions, that is, the consequences of the sin of Adam, attached to fallen mankind, which he came to save by restoring its original impassibility. The Byzantine liturgy can thus speak of the passion of Christ that liberates us from our passions.[50] Thus the identification of the Word with our fallen humanity provides no problem for John: "He assumes the natural and incorruptible passions of man," he writes, "such as hunger, thirst, tiredness, toiling, tears, corruption, reticence before death, fright, anguish, which provokes sweat, drops of blood, the comfort brought by the angels to the weakness of the flesh, and all the rest which belongs by nature to all men."[51]

The condemnation of the Aphthartodocetae, who conceived the humanity of Christ not only as sinless but as having been completely alien to the consequences of the sin of Adam, is an absolute necessity for John of Damascus.

And yet these incorruptible passions, insofar as they express an hypostatized existence within the divine Word, do not lead in Jesus to consequences that would be normal among fallen mankind. Ascetic spirituality, perfectly familiar to John, is based on the fact that the passions are the source of sin: hunger, thirst, the weakness of the flesh, when the soul enslaves itself to them, lead it to actions and thoughts contrary to nature, and that is precisely the meaning of sin. And as there is at least one passion that the soul can never escape—death, and the anguish associated with it—sin, in one form or another, holds the soul prisoner.

There is thus a fundamental, although subtle, difference in the nature of the passions in Christ and in ourselves. John insists that Christ assumed *fully* the human condition and therefore suffered *like us*. This is how he defines the heresy of the Aphthartodocetae: ,

> They consider that the Lord's body was incorruptible (ἄφθαρτον) from the time of its formation; they also confess that the Lord suffered the passions (τὰ πάθη)—hunger, thirst, tiredness—but that he suffered them in a way different from our own: while we suffer them as a natural necessity, Christ, they say, suffered them freely (ἑκουσίως) and he was not subjected to the laws of nature.[52]

What then is the difference between orthodox and aphthartodocetic Christology? John himself writes in an-other place about Christ: "There is nothing in him by com-pulsion or necessity but everything is free; willingly (θέλων) he was hungry, willingly thirsty, willingly he was frightened and willingly he died."[53]

John therefore agrees with the Aphthartodocetae in saying that Christ suffered "freely," but he condemns them when, on the pretext of that *divine* freedom, they diminish the *human* reality of his suffering. The heresy of the Aphthartodocetae consisted of their conception of the hu-manity of Jesus as an ideal humanity, free from the con-sequences of sin, the passions being individual acts of con-descension and of "economy" that could or could not have been. For John, and for the whole orthodox tradition, the incarnate Word accepted, from his conception, the assumption of human nature in its fallen state. As God, hypostatically, he undoubtedly remained free from the passions and from human nature itself, but the economy of salvation implied that once and for all he should become Servant, that he should accept the necessities of human nature, but not of sin, in order to free himself from them "from within," and by doing just that, to open the way to freedom for the whole of mankind.

Precisely because in him the passions did not imply sin, that is, the "corruptible passions," they possessed a redemptive character. In Christ, the Christian acquires freedom. The passions did not overcome him, and insofar as we are in him, they have no dominion over us either. Neither hunger nor thirst nor fright nor death itself control any longer the saint, who, because he is in Christ, becomes also impassible, and possesses in himself the hope of acquiring, at the time of the resurrection, liberation from the incorruptible passions themselves. For Jesus, after his triumph over death, had no longer any passions: neither corruptibility, nor hunger, nor thirst, nor sleep, nor tiredness, nor anything similar.[54]

These same christological notions are also expressed in John, as in Maximus the Confessor, in the fact that the incarnate Word, while possessing the complete sum of human energies, the human will, was not, however, the active agent of a gnomic, hesitant, changing, and therefore unstable will, which is proper to created human hypostases. The divine and unique hypostasis could not hesitate between good and evil; and it was the only subject, the only agent in the actions, or energies, of Christ.[55] That is why his human will, the energies and the passions proper to the human nature, never received the imprint of a gnomic or fallen will. There was in them no element of sin. And yet they were fully human in the natural sense.

Is a true humanity possible when the origin of its actions and its very life is the divine hypostasis of the Logos? It has been seen in the preceding chapters that several modern authors reproach post-Chalcedonian Byzantine Christology for having a crypto-Monophysite leaning, and these re-

proaches are based on the modifications that enhypostatization would bring to the human existence of Jesus himself.
The problem is to know whether these modifications affect
the human nature as such, or simply its manifestations,
which are dependent on the state in which the human nature
exists.

Let us consider two examples of these modifications of
Jesus' human nature due to the actual fact of the hypostatic
union, as we find them in St. John of Damascus.

First, in enumerating the human energies of Christ, he
writes:

> [Christ, however,] did not have the spermatic and
> generative (τὸ γεννητικὸν) energy, for the char-
> acters of the divine hypostases are unchangeable
> and it is impossible that the Father or the Spirit
> should become Sons.... On the other hand, a
> hypostasis can only unite itself to another hypostasis
> of the same nature; but there is no other hypostasis
> which would be at the same time Son of God and
> Son of man.... Moreover, even if the natural
> [sexual] union is a fact in most men, it is not
> necessary to them, for it is possible for a man to
> live without practicing the [sexual] union, and
> many abstained from that passion.[56]

John, therefore, clearly considers "engendering" as an
action of the hypostasis, and that it is obvious that the Son
of God could not have a son; in addition, he considers it
as a phenomenon that is obviously a human energy but is
not necessary to human life as such. Jesus could thus be
fully man without becoming a father.

The second, and more difficult, problem also dealing
with anthropology is that of Jesus' ignorance. Like most
Byzantine authors, John of Damascus denies that Jesus could
have been ignorant and interprets passages like Mk 13:32
(ignorance of the day of Parousia) in a pedagogical sense:
Christ did not want to manifest his omniscience.... But
then, if he possessed omniscience, did Jesus really have a

human nature similar to ours? John of Damascus answers affirmatively, while maintaining also that *our* nature is ignorant. "One must know," he writes, "that the Word assumed *the ignorant and subjected nature* (ἀγνοούσαν καὶ δούλην)," but "thanks to the identity of the hypostasis and the indissoluble union, the Lord's soul was enriched with the knowledge of things to come and other divine signs; similarly, the flesh of human beings is not by nature life-giving, while the Lord's flesh, *without ceasing to be mortal by nature,* became life-giving, thanks to its hypostatic union with the Word."[57] Whether it be ignorance or mortality, the existential reality they represented in Christ depends on the point of view taken: the hypostatic, personal life, or the assumed nature. Nothing in the assumed nature could be opposed to the divine existence of the hypostasis, hence the impossibility of conceiving in Christ a "generative" energy: the rest of what is natural coexists with the hypostatic reality that assumes it.

This point is again illustrated by the manner in which John interprets the "progress in wisdom" of Christ (Lk 2:52); in the same text, he speaks of a simple manifestation of (divine) wisdom that the Word possesses in himself eternally, and "of the human theognosia and salvation," in which "he makes his own progress in assuming everywhere what is ours."[58]

There is no doubt that Byzantine Christology is little concerned with the preoccupation, so widespread in modern theology, of finding in Christ a "human psychology." It is probable, as we stated earlier,[59] that the Evagrian notion of gnosis that Leontius of Byzantium applied to Christology contributed to a certain obscurity in patristic thought on this point. Thus John of Damascus, after defining prayer in the manner of Evagrius as "an ascension of the intellect towards God," explains that in Christ, the "holy intellect did not have to elevate itself, since it was united once and for all to the God Logos."[60] Hence, of course, his omniscience.

These obscurities, however, are better explained by the fact that patristic thought ignores the notion of "pure nature," and that its conception of humanity is first of all placed in a theocentric and soteriological perspective; but salvation implies communion with God for the human nature, and its transfiguration, and exhaltation at the level of uncreated divine life. On the christological plane, this transfiguration of the flesh is based on the doctrine of *communicatio idiomatum.*

The unity of the hypostasis means that both divinity and humanity possess in Christ a single source of existence; their respective actions (or energies) have but one agent. This one and divine hypostasis communicates to the human nature characteristics that normally belong only to the divinity, and, reciprocally, the Word assumes a human mode of existence. Nevertheless, this is not an absolute reciprocity; for we have seen that there was a dissymmetry in Christ, due to the fact that the hypostasis is divine and that the Deity is unchangeable. This is why there is, in the incarnate Word, and through him, in the whole Body of which Christians are members, deification of the flesh, but not "carnification" of the Deity. The Son's hypostasis becomes incarnate but not the divine nature: Only the divine hypostasis, not the divine nature, receives and assumes.

"Christ is one," writes John, "therefore the glory which naturally comes from the divinity has become common [to both natures] thanks to the identity of hypostasis; and, through the flesh humility has also become common..., [but] it is the divinity which communicates its privileges to the body, remaining itself outside the passions of the flesh."[61] He writes elsewhere: "The nature of the flesh is deified, but the nature of the Logos does not become carnal."[62]

The *communicatio idiomatum* (ἀντίδοσις ἰδιωμάτων) implies, strictly speaking, the Logos's hypostasis and also the nature of the flesh. For it is the Word who became flesh, was born of the Virgin Theotokos, suffered, and died; it is to him as hypostasis that these characteristics, which normally belong to the flesh, must be attributed, while the *communicatio idiomatum* makes it possible to speak of the "deification of the flesh" as nature. It is precisely this that is the salvation of mankind and the supreme goal of creation.

In his famous homily on the transfiguration, John of Damascus defines this soteriological dimension of the deified flesh of Christ:

> Today has been seen that which is invisible to human eyes, an earthly body resplendent with divine splendor, a mortal body pouring out glory and divinity. For the Word was made flesh and the flesh Word, although the latter did not leave the divine nature. Oh miracle surpassing all intelligence! For the glory did not come towards the body from outside, but from within, from the supradivine divinity of the Word of God, united to the body according to the hypostasis, in an unspeakable way. How can things which cannot be mixed be mingled together and remain without confusion? How can the incompatibles concur into one, without leaving the conditions of their nature? This is the action of the union according to the hypostasis. Those united things are one. And they are one hypostasis, in an indivisible difference and a union without confusion, while the unity of the hypostasis is preserved and the duality of nature is maintained by the unchangeable incarnation of the Word and by the unchanged deification of mortal flesh, above all understanding. And the things human become those of God, and the divine those of man, by the mode of mutual communication, and the interpenetration without confusion of the one into the other, and of the extreme union according to the hypostasis. For he is one God. He who is eternally God, and who later became man.[63]

The glory of the divinity thus becomes the "glory of the body."[64]

This is exactly the conception of the incarnation that Gregory Palamas defended six centuries later against Barlaam of Calabria;[65] for by making divine his own human nature, Christ opened salvation by deification to all the human hypostases. God himself, in Christ, made for us the final choice, but each Christian is called to assume freely, hypostatically, what the incarnate Word did for human nature. In this free fulfillment resides the Christian's spiritual life, and the Spirit's activity is addressed above all to this free choice. For it is by him that our freedom assumes Christ's incarnate manhood. And, as seen in the spiritual doctrine of Macarius, the same Spirit assures, between grace and human freedom, the *collaboration* (συνεργεία) that makes us friends of God.

In this way orthodox Christology met, at the deepest level of spiritual experience, the ascetical doctrine of the desert Fathers and served as the ultimate criterion for the spirituality of the Christian East.

9.

Vision of the Invisible:
The Iconoclastic Crisis

The Byzantine East is the only geographical region of the Christian world where the problem of images created a theological debate lasting for more than a century. There are psychological and historical reasons for this phenomenon. The Christian piety of Greek-speaking countries was rooted in a tradition in which the religious image had a necessary cultic place, while the Syrian or Armenian Christian communities, without being always hostile toward images, did not have a natural tendency to make them the object of a cult, but considered them in their purely didactic aspect, as simple illustrations of the biblical text.

It is possible that both tendencies would have peacefully continued to coexist within the same Church if the decrees of the iconoclastic Emperors had not posed the problem in a radical manner, thus forcing theologians to elaborate the very principles of iconoclasm and of iconodulia. The christological dimension of the problem was apparent from the beginning of the debate, but only during the second half of the eighth century were the christological *formulas* implied by the iconoclasts' rejection of images to receive their final elaboration.

Historians are still arguing about the motives that induced the iconoclastic Emperors Leo III the Isaurian (717-741), Constantine V, Copronymos (741-775), and their successors, to fight against images. Their mere belonging to the Eastern, or Semitic, as distinct from the Hellenic, tradition, is not enough to explain the rigor and even the fanaticism with which they tried to destroy the best-established practices of the Greek Church. The war they were constantly waging against iconoclastic Islam; their sensitivity to the reproaches of idolatry thrown at the Byzantine Christians by the Muslims, who presented themselves as the representatives of a purer religion; and their radically "caesaropapist" pretensions, which led Leo III to initiate a radical reform of the Church[1] and drove his son Constantine to fight against monasticism, that core of Christian non-conformity, were certainly more important reasons for their opposition to images than considerations of a national or cultural order.[2]

Nor does it seem that they used from the start theological arguments in favor of iconoclasm. The formulation of a theology was forced upon them by the opposition they met. As there was no question of falling back on the theology of Islam, which was precisely the enemy to be fought, they had to draw on sources known to the Church. In addition to the Old Testament and its innumerable denunciations of idolatry, they had recourse, on the one hand, to the Origenist tradition, which in spite of the condemnation of 553 remained present in the minds of all those who continued to think in the categories of neo-Platonism, and on the other hand, to a Christology close to Severian Monophysitism. Once it had reached that theological stage, iconoclasm developed exclusively within the religious categories of Hellenism.[3]

In the first centuries of Christianity, the Old Testament prohibitions against idolatry violently clashed with the religious habits of the Greek world. The idols, considered as "demonic" by the Christian apologists, had become the very symbol of paganism. The anti-Christian polemicists had to find a metaphysical justification for them. Neo-Platonists like Porphyry, Celsus, or the Emperor Julian took up this task. Although they insisted on the didactic value of the cult of images, they had recourse to the notion of material symbols as an expression of eternal and spiritual realities.[4]

The polemic between Christians and pagans during the

first three centuries, however, put the neo-Platonists in a paradoxical position. It forced them to take the defence of *material* images, while their metaphysics considered *matter* as an essentially inferior state of existence. Hence came their *relative* conception of the image, as a means of access to the divine prototype, necessary as long as this prototype remained veiled by the material limits of our present existence. They did not fail, however, to counterattack by aiming at the Christian doctrine of the incarnation: "Do the Christians," they asked, "have the right to criticize idols, when they themselves venerate a God who became flesh?"

"The human flesh [of Jesus]," writes Celsus, "was more corruptible than gold, silver or stone; it was made out of the most impure mud."[5] Porphyry's thought is similar to that of Celsus: "If some Hellenes are light-headed enough to believe that the gods live inside idols, their thought remains much purer than that [of the Christians] who believe that the Divinity entered the Virgin Mary's womb, became a fetus, was engendered and wrapped in clothes, full of blood, membranes, gall and even more vile things."[6]

These third-century neo-Platonic texts touch the very basis of the problem of images, by showing the embarrassment of both parties. In the second and third centuries, one could find Platonists, whose metaphysics despised matter, defending the cult of images, and Christians, whose faith was based on the incarnation, opposing them. These positions obviously had to be adjusted in a more logical way. A recent historian thus wrote: "A moment came, between the third and the seventh century, when the Christians adopted the pagan arguments."[7] From the moment paganism ceased to represent a real danger for the Christian Church, numerous favorable references to images appeared in Christian literature.[8] Whatever in ancient Greek culture could validly be assumed by the new religion was taken over; and the new religion often gave new meaning to those elements of antiquity that it adopted. This was true particularly in the case of images.

Within the framework of biblical revelation, there was

no question of a formal reconciliation with idolatry. The image could not be identified with the prototype. Nevertheless, Christian theologians formed in the neo-Platonist school understood perfectly that the image-prototype relationship was not, for the neo-Platonists, an identification. The image was simply a material symbol of an intelligible reality destined to elevate the mind toward the divine. This doctrine of the image was adopted by the Origenist school and is found in the sixth century in Pseudo-Dionysius. It is applied first to the Logos himself, revealing image of the Father, and, as image, subordinated to the prototype. It is also applied to man, created in the image of God, to the images of the absolute that the human mind discovers within creation, and to the historical events related in the Bible and considered as allegories of the intelligible world. Material images and their veneration also receive their place, which remains very modest and ambiguous, within the hierarchical conception of the world that the Origenist and Dionysian schools inherited from neo-Platonism. These images represent at best a means of educating the soul as long as it is still on the lower steps of its ascension toward the divine, its ultimate destiny being, of course, to recover its original immaterial state of the contemplation of God. At worst, they are considered as material distractions that prevent the soul from going back to the immaterial prototype.

Thus in the concrete problems that divided orthodox and iconoclasts at the beginning of the eighth century, the Origenist position, heir to neo-Platonism and essentially ambiguous, could not provide decisive arguments either for the iconoclasts or for the orthodox.

The iconoclasts lacked patristic references directly condemning the veneration of images;[9] they had at their disposal only a series of fragments from Epiphanius, of dubious authenticity, and a letter of Eusebius of Caesarea to Constantia, Constantine's sister. The authenticity and the iconoclastic character of this letter are beyond doubt.[10] It contains a very clear exposition of Origen's doctrine of salvation. The "form of the servant" assumed by the Logos was no longer in the realm of realities. He undoubtedly assumed it, but in order to transform it into a divine reality; it is important, therefore, that the Christians, if they desire to anticipate the glory that is his, and to which they also aspire, should contemplate God in the purity of their hearts and not in artificial images of a historical past that is now over.[11] "The flesh of Christ has now been confused (ἀνακεκρᾶσθαι) with the divinity,"[12] writes Eusebius, using the very terms of the Christology that was to become known later as Monophysite, showing in this way that Origenism, with its denial of the proper value of the flesh and its indifference to the full reality of the incarnation, was ready to adopt the position of Eutyches.

It is thus apparent that the christological problem was implied in all the discussions about images. Writers such as Celsus or Porphyry already had accused the Christians of being illogical, since they both objected to images and believed in the incarnation. Origen's metaphysics spiritualized the conception of image precisely because the historical fact of the incarnation was pushed into the background. In the eighth century, it was inevitable that the attack started by the iconoclastic Emperors against sacred images should pose anew the christological problem. Both sides were to resort to the arguments of Origenism and Pseudo-Dionysius: the iconoclasts in order to justify a spiritualist outlook and Christology with Monophysite tendencies, and the orthodox in order to construct a theology of the image based on the *historical* reality of the incarnation, which the images were supposed to reflect. Origen and Dionysius thus underwent, in the history of the Church, a new phase of Christianization.

The christological dimensions of the problem of images had already been posed before the beginning of the iconoclastic quarrel, in the famous Canon 82 of the Quinisext Council (692):

> In certain reproductions of venerable images, the Precursor is figured indicating the Lamb with his finger. This representation had been adopted as a symbol of grace, but it was a hidden figure of that true lamb who is Christ our God, which was shown

to us according to the Law. Having thus welcomed these ancient figures and shadows as symbols of the truth transmitted to the Church, *we prefer today grace and truth themselves,* as a fulfillment of this law. In consequence, and in order to expose to the sight of all, even with the help of painting, what is perfect, we decide that henceforth *Christ our God must be represented in his human form* instead of the ancient lamb.[13]

The negative attitude of the Quinisext Council toward symbolism, and its emphasis on the concrete and historical reality of the incarnation as the authentic foundation of the art of images, made it inevitable that the debate started by the iconoclastic decree of the Emperor Leo III should immediately become a christological debate; the problem was already posed within the framework of a theology of the incarnation.

Even before the iconoclastic decrees, Germanus, who was patriarch of Constantinople under Leo III, established the basis of orthodox apologetics:

In eternal memory of the life in the flesh of our Lord Jesus Christ, of his passion, his saving death and the redemption for the world, which result from them, we have received the tradition of representing him in his human form, i.e., in his visible theophany, understanding that in this way we exalt the humiliation of God the Word.[14]

According to Germanus, it is possible to make an image of the "only Son who is in the bosom of the Father," because he "deigned to become man"; it is not an image of the "incomprehensible and immortal deity" that the Christian iconographer represents but one of his "human character," witnessing by this that God "really became man in all things, except sin which is sown in us by the enemy."[15] The images represent already for Germanus a confession of faith against docetism.[16]

The same idea is taken up with greater force by John of Damascus in the famous treatises in defense of images that he wrote during the reign of Leo III, protected, however, against prosecutions in far away Palestine, which was occupied by the Arabs. He begins his first treatise with the christological argument, and there is no doubt that he considers it the principal and decisive one: "I represent God, the Invisible One, not as invisible, but insofar as he has become visible for us by participation in flesh and blood."[17] "If we made an image of the invisible God, we would certainly be in error," John writes again at the beginning of his third treatise, "but we do nothing of the sort; for we are not in error if we make the image of the incarnate God, who appeared on earth in the flesh, and who, in his ineffable goodness, lived with human beings and assumed the nature, the thickness, the shape and the color of the flesh."[18]

The iconoclasts obviously had recourse to the severe condemnations of idolatry in the Old Testament, an argument that had been widely used also in the first centuries of the Church by the Christian authors in their polemic against paganism. John of Damascus, who on this point was followed by all later Orthodox authors, opposes to it the totally new situation of the relationship between Creator and creatures, God and men, Spirit and matter, which follows the reality of the incarnation:

> In former times, God, without body or form, could in no way be represented. But today, since God has appeared in the flesh and lived among men, I can represent what is visible in God (εἰκονίζω Θεοῦ τὸ ὁρώμενον). I do not venerate matter, but I venerate the Creator of matter, who became matter for my sake, who assumed life in the flesh and who, through matter, accomplished my salvation.[19]

The christological argument opposed to the iconoclasts by Germanus and John of Damascus required an answer. Yet we do not know much about the theology of the iconoclasts during the first decades of the eighth century. It seems probable that the direct and arbitrary tendency of the Emperor to "purify" religion received little support at that time among the theologians. The Origenist bishops of Asia Minor, whom we know from the correspondence of Germanus, seem to have been the only theological counselors of the Emperor. It was in the reign of Constantine V, Copronymos (741-775), that the iconoclastic party was given a theology that contemporaries attributed to the Emperor himself, and which some modern authors consider a work of genius.[20] Constantine's thought is well known to us through the decisions of the council of 754, reproduced in the Acts of the Second Council of Nicaea (787), which rejected them, and through the works of the orthodox Patriarch Nicephorus, who refuted the writings of Constantine after his deposition in 815 by Leo V the Armenian. The iconoclastic argument, as it is found in Constantine, is a christological argument. Together with the answer given to it by the orthodox authors Theodore the Studite and Nicephorus, it represents a very important stage in the development of thought in Byzantium. If there was really a danger in Byzantine Christology that, after the triumph of Cyrillism under Justinian, it should lose sight of the Christ-Man, the anti-iconoclastic polemic gave it the opportunity to free itself from this bias.

There was no question that Constantine V and the Iconoclast Council of 754 should formally renounce the doctrine of the six councils. The latter is reasserted in the Acts[21] and is even used as a criterion for the refutation of the christological arguments of Germanus and John of Damascus. The latter said that Christ could be represented in a material image because he had become real man. The iconoclasts replied with the following dilemma: if the image represents the humanity of Christ to the exclusion of his divinity, it implies a Nestorian Christology and separates in Christ God from man; if on the contrary, the iconographer pretends to represent Christ in the individual fullness of his divinity and his humanity, he assumes that the divinity itself can be circumscribed, which is absurd, or else that it lives in a state of confusion with the humanity; in the latter case he falls into the heresy of Dioscorus, Eutyches, and Severus.[22]

The argument did not lack force; it rested on the definition of Chalcedon that had asserted that the two natures
of Christ were united at the same time "without confusion"
and "without separation." The iconoclasts wanted to give a
full sense to the Chalcedonian apophaticism that had defined
the hypostatic union in negative terms. According to Constantine V, this negation and mystery disappeared once one
made of Christ a material image, implying a *positive* vision
of the incarnate Word, which brought about either the
confusion or the separation of the natures. In fact, however,
the Iconoclast Council of 754 rejected the concept of the
historical Christ whom the apostles "saw and touched,"
under the pretext that the humanity of Christ was also the
"humanity of the Logos,... completely assumed by the divine
nature and totally deified." The iconoclast assembly proclaimed that

> the divinity of the Son having assumed the nature
> of the flesh into its own hypostasis (ἐν τῇ ἰδίᾳ
> ὑποστάσει τὴν τῆς σαρκὸς φύσιν, προσλα-
> βούσης γὰρ τῆς τοῦ υἱοῦ θεότητος), the
> [human] soul [of Christ] became the intermediary
> between the divinity and the thickness of the flesh;
> therefore, the soul is also the soul of the God-Word.
> It is ambivalent, i.e., the soul having been deified,
> as well as the body, and divinity remaining insep-
> arable from the one as well as from the other,
> wherever the soul of Christ is, there is the divinity;
> and where the body of Christ is, there also is the
> divinity; [and this applies] even to the very moment
> when the soul [of Christ] separated itself from the
> body in the voluntary passion.[23]

The iconoclast Christology rests, therefore, on Chalcedonian apophaticism and on the theory of *communicatio
idiomatum* pushed to its extreme limit. Formally, it recognizes
the existence in Christ of two wills and two energies,[24] but
it seems to ignore completely the main assertion that Chalcedon had borrowed from the Tome of Leo: "each nature

preserves its own manner of being" and "meets the other
[nature] in the single hypostasis." Moreover it is characteristic that the iconoclasts, as seen for instance in the
text quoted above, speak of the divine nature assuming the
human nature "in its own hypostasis"—the hypostasis appearing as an expression of the natural existence and the nature
being treated as the true subject that assumed the human
nature. Iconoclast Christology, therefore, does not assimilate
the conception of a properly *hypostatic* union, implying a
real distinction between nature and hypostasis, and making
possible the preservation of the natural characteristics of the
divinity and of the humanity within a single or personal
hypostatic existence. It does, however, seem to indicate that
the deification of the humanity of Christ suppresses the
reality of the properly human natural character. Such a
notion of deification certainly contradicts the former tradition on the participation in God as a natural element of
humanity. It is not a priori surprising, therefore, that the
Monophysite Patriarch Michael the Syrian (twelfth century)
expresses his approval of Constantine V and speaks of him
as of a "cultured mind" who "sanely kept the mysteries of
the orthodox faith"; at the same time Michael accuses the
iconodule orthodox of "upholding the doctrine of Maximus,"
i.e., the Christology of the "two wills, or energies."[25] While
formally accepting the decisions of the councils of Chalcedon
and of Constantinople, iconoclastic Christology places itself
clearly on Monophysite or Monothelite positions, and therefore it is not surprising that Michael the Syrian should
approve of it.

The debate between orthodox and iconoclast concentrates
after the Iconoclast Council of 754 on two problems: that
of the *image* and that of the *prototype*. In the first case, the
question was to know under which form the reality represented can be found in the image. Is the image essentially
identical with the prototype, or is it but an inferior reflection
of it?

In order to justify their position, the iconoclasts were
obliged to defend as exclusive a notion of the image as
"consubstantial to the prototype," which post-Nicene theology

applied to the Logos, sole "image of the Father."[26] According to the iconoclasts, the blasphemy of orthodox iconodulia consisted in the fact itself that "images of God" were made or painted, because every image must necessarily be *identical* with the divine Model: an "image of God," fabricated or painted, is therefore essentially an *idol,* since it pretends to "be God." On this point, the orthodox could easily call on tradition, including Origenist tradition, to show that the concept of image could in no way be reduced to an identification with the Model. Only the Son and the Spirit are "natural images," consubstantial to the Father, their Model, although different through their hypostasis. Other types of images imply an essential difference. Therefore, a material image could in no way be considered as consubstantial with the divine.[27]

The council of 754 itself had admitted that image and Model were not necessarily identical; it had proposed a positive and very original doctrine of the image of the incarnate Word: that of the Eucharist conceived as image. But the orthodox had no difficulty in opposing to it the realist interpretation of the sacrament, which is not an image but "truth itself." The source of this iconoclastic doctrine of the Eucharist as image or symbol was none other than Pseudo-Dionysius,[28] and with its condemnation by the orthodox party, one witnesses a new stage in the Christianization of Dionysius' Hellenism by tradition.

These discussions on the concept of image illustrate above all the ambiguity of the Origenist tradition, to which both parties too often had recourse.[29] Their most concrete result was a precise orthodox definition of the cult of images at the Second Council of Nicaea, in the writings of John of Damascus and, especially, in the writings of Theodore the Studite. The image, essentially distinct from the original, is an object of *relative veneration* (προσκύνησις σχετικὴ)[30] or *honor* (τιμητικὴ προσκύνησις)[31] while worship (λατρεία, λατρευτικὴ προσκύνησις) is reserved for God alone and can in no way be addressed to images. The Theotokos and the saints themselves cannot be "worshipped, but only venerated."[32] Nevertheless, the actual veneration given to images does not have them for its ultimate object, since the image is only a relative connection with the represented object (πρός τι). The religious action is addressed to the prototype, and then becomes adoration. Thus the same action is veneration insofar as it concerns the image or the saints and adoration insofar as it is addressed to God.[33]

This subtle, yet very clear, distinction between worship and veneration, implying an essential distance between the Model and its image, represents an important safeguard against the animistic or fetishistic tendencies that could have found a justification in the cult of images in the East. The distinction was unfortunately lost in the bad Latin translation of the Acts of the council of 787. Charlemagne, on the basis of this translation, rejected the decree in his famous *Caroline Books,* and the distinction was never very well understood in the West. The misunderstanding can be illustrated by the fact that even after the council's acceptance by the Latins, St. Thomas Aquinas himself admitted a "relative adoration" (*latria*) of the images, and this provoked accusations of idolatry against the Latin Church by certain Orthodox[34] and later by the Reformers of the sixteenth century.

The discussion of the nature of the image cannot be separated from the other aspect of the iconoclastic controversy: that concerning the prototype, i.e., the Christological problem itself. The iconoclastic position, essentially opposed to the idea of making an image of God, was rejected by the orthodox because it ignored the fact that God became *man.* Both parties agreed on the impossibility of representing God in himself, but they were fundamentally divided over the problem of the reality, permanence and character of Jesus' humanity.

"If someone dares make an image of the immaterial and incorporal divinity, we repudiate him," writes St. John of Damascus.[35] The Logos himself, before the incarnation, could not be represented; he is the image of the Father, but that image cannot be materially reproduced.[36] "It is not only vain, but it is stupid, to limit spatially the unincarnate Word...: it is idolatry," writes Theodore.[37] Thus, as had been written by Germanus of Constantinople: "We do not reproduce an image, a portrait, a sketch or a form of the invisible divinity, but since the only son...deigned to become man, we make the image of his human form and of his human aspect according to the flesh,...thus showing that it is not in a purely imaginary way that he put on our nature."[38]

However, in this mystery according to which "the Invisible shows himself,"[39] the whole problem of the hypostatic union of the two natures is posed again. Is it the man Jesus, the son of Mary, who apart from his invisible divinity can be represented on the icons? But can one consider him "separately" without falling into Nestorianism? Or is divinity itself "co-circumscribed" (συμπεριγράφεσϑαι) on Christ's image?

As has been pointed out above, the orthodox polemic against iconoclasm insisted first on the fullness of the human nature in Christ, thus largely recovering the christological tradition of Antioch.

For example, in the thought of Theodore the Studite, all ambiguity about the individual character of Christ's humanity disappears. If, in the time of Justinian, someone like Leontius of Jerusalem could speak of that humanity simply as "a sum of individual characteristics" assumed by the Word, Theodore's conception is much more concrete: "Christ was certainly not a *mere man* (ψιλὸς ἄνϑρωπος)" he writes, "neither is it orthodox to say that he assumed *an individual among men* (τὸν τινα τῶν ἀνθρώπων), but the whole, the totality of the nature. It must be said, however, that this total nature was contemplated in an individual manner (ἐν ἀτόμῳ)—for otherwise how could it have been *seen*—in a way that made it visible and describable..., which allowed it to eat and drink...?"[40]

Refuting the iconoclasts' position, according to which the humanity of Christ would have been indescribable (ἀχαρακτήριστον) because he was "man in general" (καϑόλου ἄνϑρωπος, the new Adam), Theodore evokes Aristotle to deny all ideal existence of the human nature: "It only exists in Peter and Paul," he writes, otherwise Christ's human nature could only have been intellectually contemplated, and Thomas's experience, placing his finger into Jesus' wound, would have been impossible. "The very name of *Jesus* makes him distinct in his hypostatical characteristics, in relationship to other men."[41] "An indescribable Christ would also be an incorporal Christ; but Isaiah (8:3) describes him as a male being (ἄρσην τεχθείς), and only the forms of the body can make man and woman distinct from one another."[42]

Nicephorus also stressed the human reality of Jesus, his experience of tiredness, of hunger, of thirst,[43] and of human ignorance. The problem of Jesus' ignorance, which was discussed earlier[44] in the framework of neo-Chalcedonian Christology and the Evagrian assumptions, is thus placed by Patriarch Nicephorus in a simpler perspective: while admitting that the hypostatic union *could* suppress all human ignorance in Jesus, in virtue of the *communicatio idiomatum,* he maintains that the characteristics of the human nature as such had been fully preserved in Christ and that, therefore, he "acted, desired, ignored and suffered as man,"[45] willingly.

The position of the Tome of Leo and of the Council of Chalcedon on the permanence of the characteristics proper to each of the two natures in Christ was the main argument of the orthodox polemicists against iconoclasm.

> The Inconceivable is conceived in the womb of a Virgin, the Unmeasurable becomes three cubits high; the Unqualifiable acquires a quality; the Undefinable stands up, sits down and lies down; He who is everywhere is put into a crib; He who is above time gradually reaches the age of twelve; He who is formless appears with the shape of a man and the Incorporeal enters into a body..., therefore the Same is describable and indescribable.[46]

For the iconoclasts, to assert that Christ was describable (περιγραπτός) was the equivalent of making him a mere man (ψιλός), an individual; for Theodore, the fact of being indescribable is a characteristic of the divine nature; to admit that the humanity of Christ acquires this divine quality amounts to introducing in Christ a "mingling" of the natures (condemned at Chalcedon)[47] and to reducing the mystery of the incarnation to a product of imagination.[48]

For Christ is consubstantial with the Father and also with his mother; and his mother is certainly a fully describable human being.[49] To be logical with themselves, the iconoclasts had to assume, Nicephorus points out, that the Virgin Mary's womb was indescribable, as soon as it was touched by the presence of the Logos. This was a form of Aphthartodocetism that the patriarch named *agraptodocetism*.[50] The result is that "too much honor given to the Mother of God amounts to dishonoring her; for one would have to attribute to her incorruptibility, immortality, and impassibility, if what by nature belongs to the Logos must also by grace be attributed to her who engendered him."[51]

This insistence on the full reality of the historical Jesus leads the supporters of images to use expressions directly borrowed from the Christology of Antioch. Theodore the Studite speaks of natural συνάφεια (attachment) of the two natures of Christ[52]—a rather unfashionable term after the Council of Ephesus—and of a single person (πρόσωπον) in two natures, of which one only can be represented.[53] This does not mean that Theodore rejects Cyrillian Christology; on the contrary, he formally recognizes the orthodoxy of the famous formula: "one incarnate nature of the God-Word," interpreted in a Chalcedonian sense. But it is undeniable that the iconoclasts' implicit Monophysitism gives to the orthodox the opportunity to prove that their tradition remains based on Chalcedon, and faithful to what was fundamentally true in Antiochene Christology: the human reality of the historical Jesus.

Nicephorus seems to go even further than the limits of post-Chalcedonian orthodoxy. Some passages of his *Antirrhetics* appear as formal denials of the theopaschism proclaimed by Cyril and the fifth council: "One cannot assert," writes Nicephorus, "either that the Word suffered the passion, or that the flesh produced miracles.... One must attribute to each nature what is proper to it."[54] This passage seems to ignore the distinction established by Chalcedonian and post-Chalcedonian Christology between the Logos' hypostasis—subject of the passion in the flesh—and his nature. The same Nestorianizing confusion appears when Nicephorus writes that the Word "is not described when his body is described,"[55] and in his tendency to minimize the value of the *communicatio idiomatum,* which, for him, merely manipulates "words" (ψιλὰ ὀνόματα).[56]

This resurgence of a Nestorianizing Christology, treating Christ as two objects to one another, and arising certainly from the relative fashion enjoyed by the biblical commentaries of Theodore of Mopsuestia and of Theodoret, was in no way typical of the theology of all the advocates of images. Theodore the Studite, in particular, bases the whole of his theology of icons on the doctrine of the hypostatic union. For Theodore, the very hypostasis of Christ is describable (περιγραπτή), and it is represented on the image. The Byzantine tradition, representing Christ with the letters ὁ ῎Ων—"he who is," the translation of the tetragrammaton YHWH—inscribed in the cross-shaped halo around the face of Jesus, well indicates the intention to see in the image the very hypostasis of the Son of God, no doubt invisible in its divinity, but having become visible in the human nature it had assumed.[57] For Theodore the Studite, "every portrait is, in any case, the portrait of an hypostasis, and not of a nature":[58] for the hypostasis is the only concrete form of existence of the human nature and, therefore, the only reality that can be represented; and the human nature of Christ is precisely hypostatized in the Logos' hypostasis, and it is the latter that is represented in the image, for "the image and the similitude with the prototype can only refer to one hypostasis and not to two."[59] It would be false, therefore, according to Theodore, to inscribe on the icons of Christ terms such as "divinity," "worship," or "kingship," terms that designate the Trinity; only the inscription ὁ ῎Ων, "he who is," and not ὀντότης, "being," is suitable for the image of Christ, image of the *actual person* of the incarnate word.[60]

Thus it is only the personalism of patristic theology that makes it possible to overcome the essential dilemma of the iconoclastic controversy and provides a solid basis for the veneration of images.

The hypostatic union implies, however, the *communicatio idiomatum* and therefore the *deified* character of Christ's representable humanity. Yet in becoming incarnate, the Word assumed our fallen human nature in order to save it: "He did not possess a flesh other than our own, that which fell as a consequence of sin; he did not transform it [in assuming it], but he was made of the same nature as we, however without sin, and through that nature, he condemned sin and death."[61]

In his polemic against the Origenist conception of an annihilation of the body, illustrated by the letter of Eusebius to Constantia, Nicephorus takes the opportunity to proclaim that, even glorified, the body of Christ remains a fully human body, that is, a describable body. Contact with the divinity, participation in the divine life, do not destroy human nature, but bring it back to its original state, its fully natural state.[62] "What characterizes incorruptibility," he writes, "is not to corrupt and destroy, but to preserve, to save, to make better and eternally immovable."[63]

Thus transformed and glorified after his death and resurrection, the body of Christ became the *source* of deification: thus the image of the incarnate Word is considered, in eighth-century orthodox theology, as a witness to the deified human nature of Jesus, a central soteriological notion in earlier patristic theology. If this human nature is "indescribable" as the iconoclasts would have liked, it is also *inaccessible,* and therefore the salvation of *our* human nature is not achieved. "I venerate God," writes St. John of Damascus, but also "the purple of the body [of Christ], not only as clothing, nor as the fourth person [of the Trinity], but because it was made similar to God (ὁμόθεον) and has become unchangeably one with the unction it received."[64] The image of Christ, venerated by the Christians, bears witness to the reality of the Eucharist: "The angels," writes John of Damascus, "do not partake of the divine nature, but only of the energy and the grace; but men participate in it; they are in communion with the divine nature, at least those who are in communion with the holy body of Christ and receive his blood; for the body and blood of Christ are hypostatically united to the divinity, and in the body of Christ with which we are in communion, there are two natures inseparably united in the hypostasis. We are thus in communion with both natures—with the body, corporally, and with the divinity, spiritually, or rather with both in both ways—without there being any identification between our hypostasis and that of Christ, for we first receive the hypostasis within the order of creation, then we enter into union, by the mingling (κατὰ συνανάκρασιν) of the body and the blood."[65]

The notion of the body of Christ, deified but also historical and describable,[66] is thus identified with the Church, the community of the faithful. From here comes Theodore the Studite's argument: "If Christ, after the resurrection, is indescribable, we also, who form one body with Him (σύσσωμος αὐτῷ, cf. Eph 3:6), become indescribable."[67] Or else, since this does not happen to us, "we cease being members of Christ."[68] The Eucharist itself represents for us salvation precisely because it is "body" and "humanity": "We confess," writes Nicephorus, "that by the priest's invocation, by the coming of the Most Holy Spirit, the body and the blood of Christ are mystically and invisibly made present...," and there is salvation not "because the body ceases to be a body, but because it remains so and is preserved as body."[69]

The real theological dimensions of the iconoclastic controversy thus appear clearly: the image of Christ is the visible and necessary witness to the reality and humanity of Christ. If that witness is impossible, the Eucharist itself loses its reality. The theory of the Byzantine iconostasis, manifesting visibly "toward the exterior" the nature of the mystery accomplished within the sanctuary, was certainly conceived in the light of the theology just analyzed.[70]

This theology also gives a quasi-sacramental role to iconography. St. Theodore the Studite compares the Christian artist to God himself creating man in his image: "The fact that God made man in his image and resemblance shows that iconography is a divine action."[71]

The artist, like God in the beginning, in representing Christ makes an "image of God" by painting the deified humanity of Jesus, hypostatized in the Word himself. In so doing, according to St. John of Damascus, he witnesses to the fact that "matter is God's creation, and he confesses that it is *good*,"[72] and that it no longer brings death, but life: "From the moment the divinity united itself to our nature, our nature was glorified as by some life-giving and wholesome medicine, and received access to incorruptibility: this is why the death of the saints is celebrated, temples are built in their honor, and their images are painted and venerated...."[73]

The enthusiasm of St. John of Damascus about the problem of the "cult of matter" (τὴν ὕλην σέβω)[74] is somewhat moderated by Theodore the Studite, who was very conscious of the dangers of fetishism into which some forms of icon-veneration fell. While admitting that the veneration of the Gospel Book or of material images implies "the exaltation of matter because of the elevation of the intellect towards God,"[75] he specifies several times that it is not "the essence of the image which is venerated, but the form of the prototype represented by the image, ... for it is not matter which is the object of veneration."[76] It seems that the concept of the theology of icons retains, with Theodore, a more pronounced neo-Platonic character than with John of Damascus. In any case, as we have seen, the *personal* aspect of the image is the crux of Theodore's thought. The encounter with the Word's hypostasis is the real aim of icon-veneration, and this encounter can and must happen through the intermediary of a material image, a witness to the historical reality of the incarnation and of the deification with which *our* human nature has been glorified in Christ.

The theology of the iconoclastic period, rather neglected and often badly understood by historians of dogma, exercised a vast influence on doctrinal developments and spirituality in later times. The Christology of the Byzantine Church found remarkable witnesses in John of Damascus, in Theodore the Studite, and in Nicephorus. These three managed, in the face of the decidedly Monophysite tendencies of the iconoclasts, to fully recover the meaning of Christ's humanity, as Maximus had already done in the seventh century, without prejudice to the central inspiration of the soteriology of St. Cyril of Alexandria, based on the concept of deification. The importance given by someone like Theodore the Studite to the doctrine of the hypostatic union in the Orthodox theology of images illustrates that the development of christological thought in Byzantium from the fifth to the eight centuries constitutes an inseparable and integral whole. This inner logic of Byzantine Christology enabled it not only to preserve a doctrinal truth but also to inspire generations of artists, creators of the great religious achievement that Byzantine art constituted. It made of this art not only a great aesthetic accomplishment but also, in the words of a twentieth-century Russian philosopher, "a theology in color."[77]

10.

Christology in Late Byzantium

Byzantine theology from the ninth to the fifteenth century was never divorced from Christology. However, as the "triumph of Orthodoxy" in 843 was interpreted by many as a final fixation of dogma, discussions of the formulas adopted by the "seven councils" could no longer take place. In the schools, the synthesis of St. John of Damascus was used as a manual, and no new categories were accepted in theology. This formal conservatism widely dominated government circles and the hierarchy from the ninth century until the great theological crisis of the fourteenth century.

Nevertheless, behind that façade, the movement of thought remains easily discernible. The interest of the Byzantine humanists in ancient Greek philosophy provided an opportunity for some talented minds, dissatisfied with the ready-made answers of scholastic theology, to propound new solutions to the problem of existence. The resurgence of neo-Platonism, with Michael Psellos and John Italos in the eleventh century, was reminiscent of the Origenist crises of the sixth century. Within school theology itself, occasional controversies forced the official Church to take a stand on a particular theological problem. (The conclusions of such episodes occurring in the time of Alexis and Manuel Comneni, and which were directly linked with Christology, will be discussed later.) Finally, in monastic circles, the great current of the Fathers' spirituality continued not only to bring forth fruits of holiness but also to evoke theological problems dealing with salvation, which were at the roots of the great christological debates of preceding centuries.

At the same time, this monastic tradition was dominated by the monumental figure of Symeon the New Theologian (949-1022). It would be vain to look for a new theology of the incarnation in him. Symeon is the prophet of Christian *experience,* but this experience is, for him, that of Christ, the incarnate Word, and it implies the possibility here on earth for each Christian to be consciously in communion with the divine life. The very foundation of Christian experience is thus found in the person of Christ. As a prophet of experience, Symeon stands within the tradition of the "spiritual homilies" attributed to Macarius,[1] and as the interpreter of the idea of deification, he merely continues the tradition of St. Maximus the Confessor. The actual object of his prophecy and of his mysticism is the possibility received by man to be in communion with God. To deny this possibility is, for Symeon, to cease to be a Christian and to become the worst of heretics:

> Here are those of whom I am speaking and whom I call heretics; those who say there is no one in our time, among us, capable of observing the Gospel commandments or of conforming to the holy Fathers...or able to be illumined, by receiving the Holy Spirit, and by him perceiving the Son together with the Father. Those who pretend this is impossible have not fallen into a particular heresy, but, if I can express myself in this way, into all of them at once, for this heresy outstrips them all by its impiety and the excess of its blasphemy, and includes them all.... Those who speak in this way close the heaven which Christ opened for us and block the way which he himself has traced out for our return. Then he, being God above all, in the heavens, standing at the door of paradise, stoops down, and through the Holy Gospel, cries out these words to the faithful who see him: "Come unto me all that labor and are heavy laden, and I shall

refresh you." But these enemies of God, or better these Anti-Christs assert: "It is impossible, impossible!"[2]

The reality of deification, which is neither a subjective state nor a purely intellectual experience, but the very content of the Christian faith, such is Symeon's own message, which in fact set the pattern for all the original developments of Byzantine theology. For the positions taken by the Church in the eleventh to the thirteenth century, especially the definitions of the councils of the fourteenth century, only expressed and protected what Symeon had proclaimed as religious experience.

For example, the negative attitude of the Byzantine Church toward profane Hellenism, expressed by the council of 1076-77 against John Italos, attacked above all the efforts of some humanists to build a metaphysical system independent of the Christian revelations. Italos's doctrine on the knowledge of God and "illumination," conceived as a function of the naturally divine intellect, based on a neo-Platonist conception of the world and of man as independent of the incarnation, directly anticipated the doctrine of Barlaam of Calabria in the fourteenth century. But whereas in the fourteenth century the real dimensions of the problem, christological and soteriological, were brought to light by the genius of Palamas, the reaction in the eleventh century was limited to school theologians who were satisfied with condemning Hellenism as a whole. Insofar as Italos referred to the Platonist tradition, it was the dogmas of that tradition, classified at the time of the condemnation of Origen as heretical, which were anathematized in 1076, even though Italos had not confessed them all: transmigration of souls, eternity of ideas and of time, the pre-existence of souls.[3] The *Synodikon of Orthodoxy*[4] was furnished at that time with a supplement of anathemas against these "Hellenistic" doctrines, thus establishing by an annual commemoration the official position of the Byzantine Church in this regard: true communion with God is produced "in Christ," in the participation in the deified humanity of the historical Jesus, and can in no way be identified with neo-Platonist illumination.

The positive and negative values of Symeon's work, on the one hand, and Italos's condemnation on the other, thus maintained Byzantine thought within the framework of traditional patristic Christology. The christological problem itself was also evoked in relation to the opinions expressed, in the years immediately following Italos' trial, by the monk Nilus and by the learned Metropolitan Eustratius of Nicaea. Both were in contact with Italos, and were later engaged in discussions with the Armenian Monophysites. It does not seem that Italos can be held directly responsible for their errors.[5]

The monk Nilus was accused and condemned for his assertion, made during discussions with Armenians, that Christ's humanity was deified only "by adoption" (θέσει). The Armenians, of course, stood for deification "by nature" (φύσει). Nilus' position was condemned as essentially Nestorian and as implying that there was no difference between Jesus, as deified man, and those who are "in Christ," since there was deification by adoption in both cases. The synod, by issuing the condemnation, excluded as inaccurate both expressions—"deification by nature" and "deification by adoption"—if applied to Jesus. The humanity of Jesus was united to divinity in a unique, hypostatic way, which granted access to "deification by adoption" to all those "in Christ."[6]

As for Eustratius, Metropolitan of Nicaea, renowned theologian and counselor of the Emperor Alexis Comnenus, he was certainly a disciple of Italos; engaged around 1114 in a discussion with the Armenians, he applied to Christology a philosophy of being that a modern historian has qualified as "nominalist," and ended by considering the "reality assumed" (τὸ πρόσλημμα) by the Word as a separate entity; it is by essence in a position of "servitude" (οὐσιῶδες δουλεία) in relationship to God; it worships (λατρεύει) God; it is different from him in dignity (ἀξία); it is imperfect and receives from him its perfection; it is "purified" by the perfection of virtues. Alone (ἰδίᾳ), this human nature can be called "high-priest," for this human title does not suit the divinity.[7] These different assertions of Eustratius are found in the confession of faith that he had to present to the synod in 1117, when he recanted,[8] a Christology very close to that of Theodore of Mopsuestia. In his polemical ardor against the Armenians, and by an evident desire to safeguard, in Christ, a humanity real and fully distinct from the divinity, Eustratius had lost contact with the positive value of the hypostatic union. His condemnation implied that every action, whether human or divine, of Christ, is the effect of a single agent; it is to the single hypostasis that the adjectives "son," "heir," and "servant" must be attributed, because in it there are two natures, but one cannot say that one of the natures worships the other. As the work of Christ consists precisely in liberating human nature from servitude, to grant it the dignity of heirdom, how could its *own* human nature be "servant"? The adoption is communicated to all who believe in Christ, and this is possible because they participate in the glorified human nature of Jesus. This is the meaning of the synodal decree against Eustratius, who had to renounce all his expressions that "gave the impression" of admitting in Christ two hypostases, or the sinful "imperfect" character of his human nature. The distinction of the natures, according to the synod, must be conceived "with piety as a distinction of the mind," as the fifth council indicated.[9]

The problem of the hypostatic union was posed in a more complex manner under Manuel Comnenus, during the debates that took place at two synods in Constantinople (1156 and 1157) concerning the teaching of a patriarch-elect of Antioch, the deacon Soterichos Panteugenos, who was supported by an appreciable group of prelates and theologians.

The discussion dealt with the concept of the sacrifice of Christ. Was the sacrifice offered to the Father or to the Holy Trinity? The second alternative, according to Soterichos, implied Nestorianism, since it supposed that in Christ, the human nature "offered," while the divinity "received" the offering. There would thus be two hypostases in Christ, as subjects of these two contradictory actions.[10] Nevertheless, Soterichos was himself accused of confusing the conceptions of nature and hypostasis: if each "action" implied an hypostasis, one should also distinguish between the hypostases of Christ as priest and as victim.[11] And the council opposed to him the conclusion of the prayer addressed to Christ in the Byzantine liturgies of St. Basil and of St. John Chrysostom: "For it is Thou who offerest and art offered, who receivest and art Thyself received."[12]

According to the councils of 1156-57 and Nicholas of Methone, their spokesman, the single hypostasis of the incarnate Word, precisely as hypostasis, can and must be the only subject of human actions, especially the offering, and divine actions, especially the reception, of the work accomplished by Christ. In this line of thought, in which one recognizes the thought of Maximus and, beyond, that of Irenaeus, the soteriological value of the sacrifice of Christ consists precisely of the fact that the priest, the victim, and the God who receives the offering are one. The sacrifice is not therefore offered to the Father alone, but to the Trinity, for the Son, having become man, and assumed the position of priest and victim, does not thereby abandon his seat at the right hand of the Father.

Soterichos had justified his position, "the sacrifice is offered to the Father alone," by asserting that the facts of offering and receiving respectively constituted hypostatical characteristics of the Son and the Father. In this principle, Nicholas of Methone discovered a major error: the confusion of the "hypostatic characters" of the persons of the Trinity with the energies or divine actions on the level of economy.[13] For all the actions of God *ad extra* are actions in which the three persons participate, the Father, the Son and the Holy Spirit; their participation remains, no doubt, personal, but the action is essentially one.

The Logos alone "becomes flesh," but the Father and the Spirit participate in the economy of salvation. One could therefore not imagine that the receiving of the offering could be a hypostatic characteristic of the Father alone, in which the Son would not participate: this reception is our very salvation accomplished by the one God, Father, Son and Holy Spirit.

It is, therefore, not surprising that Soterichos, in order

to be logical with himself, imagined salvation itself as *two* successive acts of reconciliation. According to him, a first reconciliation took place at the moment of the incarnation, between divinity and humanity, by the union of the two nature in Christ. This first reconciliation made the second possible, that is, the one that the Son as mediator accomplished on the cross by his sacrifice offered to the Father alone.[14] Nicholas of Methone and the councils of 1156-57 had little difficulty in showing that such a distribution of the actions or energies between the divine persons leads to an untenable position equivalent to tritheism. But their reaction against Soterichos led to a positive conclusion on the nature of salvation itself. The work of Christ, as Nicholas of Methone had shown, could not be reduced to a juridical notion of sacrifice, conceived as an exchange (ἀνταλλαγή or ἀντάλλαγμα). It is really a reconciliation (καταλλαγή), an action of divine forgiveness. God "did not have to receive anything from us," and "we did not go to him (to make an offering), but he condescended toward us and assumed our nature, not as a condition of reconciliation, but in order to meet us openly in the flesh."[15]

This extension of the debates to the dimensions of soteriology was the most positive conclusion of the controversy that arose over the ideas of Soterichos. The properly "sacrificial" element, in the ritual and juridical sense, as well as the Pauline idea of the redemption, "buying back" accomplished by Christ, only constitute particular aspects of the work of salvation, and could in no way be accomplished in isolation. Christ, as the *Synodikon* proclaims, "reconciled us to himself by means of *the whole mystery of the economy,* and by himself and in himself, reconciled us also to his God and Father and, of course, to the most holy and life-giving Spirit."[16] Christ's sacrifice is truly unique because it is not an isolated action but the culminating point of an "economy" that includes the Old Testament preparation, the incarnation, the death, the resurrection and the presence of the Holy Spirit, and because the Same "offers and is offered, receives and is received." This "economy" is essentially a Trinitarian action that also introduces human nature into the circle of divine love.

The fact that the discussion in the twelfth century revolved around liturgical formulas is not an accidental fact. For the sacrifice of Christ is made present in the Eucharist, and the debate could not help mentioning the meaning of the Lord's Supper as it is celebrated by the Church. The sacrifice of the Eucharist, as Nicholas of Methone and the anathematisms of the *Synodikon* proclaim, is offered to the Holy Trinity; this sacrifice is not only an "image" of the sacrifice of Christ, but it *is* that sacrifice.[17] In consequence, in the Eucharist, the notion of "exchange" is also overcome: the things offered belong to God before they are offered (τὰ σὰ ἐκ τῶν σῶν, "thine own of thine own"—formula of the Byzantine liturgy), because Christ "offers and is offered," while being also the one who "receives," and the Eucharist is not simply a repetition of Calvary. It is the realization, at the moment in which we partake of it, of the whole economy of salvation and with all its elements made really present: the incarnation of the Logos, his death, his resurrection, and his second coming. He is the one who is offered, but also "he sanctifies himself" (Jn 17:19)[18] in his human nature, in our human nature gathered round the eucharistic table: this is the mystery of the Church.

The twelfth-century discussion on Christology ended with a reaffirmation of full humanity in Christ, entirely "ours," even in the hypostatic union. This reaffirmation took place at the councils of 1166 and 1170, in the context of a controversy over the meaning of Jn 14:18: "My Father is greater than I." Active intellectual contacts with the West during the reign of Manuel I Comnenus may have originated the discussion. Contemporary debates among Latin theologians on comparing the "glory" of the Father and of the Son are well known.[19]

Byzantine theologians found no difficulty in applying Jn 14:18 to trinitarian relations. They agreed that the Father is "greater" than the Son, because he is the Origin of Godhead hypostatically. But whether the Johannine text had also a christological dimension was for them a more difficult issue. The Metropolitan of Corfu, Constantine, and the abbot John Eirenikos were maintaining that Christ's humanity, since it was deified (ὁμόθεον) and thus was to be venerated together with his divinity (ὁμότιμον), could not be "inferior" to the Father. They were ready to accept this "inferiority" only by virtue of an intellectual distinction (κατ' ἐπίνοιαν), when Jesus' humanity is viewed abstractly "as if it were not united" to the Logos.

Constantine and John Eirenikos were condemned, and their condemnation was included in the *Synodikon*. The text of the decision reaffirms the reality in Christ of a humanity, which is indeed "inferior" to God, precisely as *humanity*. The purely conceptual distinction that considers Jesus as simple man, separately from God, is necessary only when one envisages his "servitude," or his "ignorance," which are not natural properties of humanity in the Maximian sense but expressions of man's fallen state. Between true divinity and true humanity in Christ, there is union, but not one that excludes "natural" difference: divinity remains "greater" than humanity.[20]

A balanced Chalcedonian view of Christ was thus clearly restated, without prejudice to the idea of deification, which is, according to Maximus the Confessor, the truly natural state of man. One wonders, however, if the rather scholastic and academic character of the decisions of 1170 does justice to the full meaning of "servitude" and "ignorance" in Jesus, which certainly had, in several earlier writers, more than an abstract existence.

From the iconoclastic period until the fourteenth century, no inner theological movement stirred the masses of Byzantine Christians. The controversies just discussed concerned only isolated individuals and were fairly rapidly resolved by the Permanent Synod of Constantinople. This does not mean, however, that during that time the Byzantines as a whole were indifferent to theological problems. The passion with which they debated, mainly at the end of the thirteenth century, the problem of union with Rome proves the contrary. Nevertheless, only with the fourteenth-century debates was the Eastern Church called upon to take up once more a position on an essential soteriological problem, and the christological question returned to the foreground.

The elements of the debate between Gregory Palamas (1296-1359) and the Calabrian "philosopher" Barlaam are now well known.[21] In attacking first of all the possibility of "demonstrating" anything in theology, and later in refuting the pretention of the hesychast monks to "see God," Barlaam put himself in opposition not only to one of the most deeply rooted traditions of monasticism, that of which Symeon the New Theologian had become the spokesman, but also to the concept of participation in God. For him, the knowledge of God is either a mystical experience, individual and incommunicable, or a rational syllogism, constructed from revealed premises. In the latter case, knowledge has a purely dialectical nature, since it implies no real experience. Moreover, there is no trace in Barlaam of the patristic concept (which has been constantly emphasized in this book), that considers man as a creature made to participate in God, in whom he finds truth, life, and finally his own nature.[22] In his polemic against Barlaam, Gregory Palamas defends first of all the knowledge of God as a *fact of experience,* proper not only to some mystics but also to all those who enjoy the fullness of their human nature. This enjoyment, corrupted by sin, is restored in Jesus Christ. In Christ, therefore, and there alone, that is, in the fullness of the Church and sacramental life, personalized by asceticism and prayer, is also the fullness of knowledge.

The christological dimension of the issue thus posed by the controversy between Barlaam and Palamas contributed to neutralizing even further the influence that those Christian pillars of neo-Platonism, Evagrius and Pseudo-Dionysius, were so far exercising within Byzantine theology. On the level of spirituality and anthropology, Macarius' tradition of prayer and the experience of objective reality, given in baptism, present in the Eucharist, and destined to full realization in the resurrection of the bodies, finally christianized the notion of intellectual prayer; for the Atho-nite monks of the fourteenth century, and for all the Byzantine Christians, the "pure prayer" was no longer only communion with the divine in general but the "prayer of Jesus." In another connection, Palamas, while continuing to borrow from Pseudo-Dionysius his apophatic vocabulary, and interpreting it in the sense of the absolute and essential transcendence of God, liberated himself quite radically from the Dionysian conception of hierarchies in reference to Christology. Since the incarnation, the hierarchical orders no longer have to accomplish their role as intermediaries between God and man; for Christ is the only mediator. His coming among men, and the assumption by the Logos of human nature, are produced by a direct action of the divine almighty power and love: "Before God appeared in the flesh," writes Palamas, "nothing similar was taught us by the angels...and now that [grace] has appeared, it is no longer necessary that everything should be accomplished by intermediaries."[23]

The Dionysian hierarchies are thus fully real only within the framework of a fallen world; in Christ "the smallest become the greatest," heaven and earth are reunited.

This Palamite christocentrism, in direct dependence on St. Maximus, implies, as does also the thought of the Confessor, the doctrine of the energies. It is only within the perspective of the Maximian doctrine of the two energies or wills of Christ that it is possible to understand the terminology of St. Gregory Palamas. Moreover, the council of 1351 presents the Palamite doctrine of the energies as a development (ἀνάπτυξις) of the decrees of the Sixth Ecumenical Council of 680.[24]

The incarnate Word, having hypostatized human nature, acts in accordance with the divine and human wills or energies; in virtue of this hypostatic union, there is also *communicatio idiomatum,* and the humanity of Christ is penetrated by divine energies. In connection with the Christology of Maximus the Confessor, Palamas defines three modes of existence: the essence (or nature), the hypostasis, and the energy. To each of these modes of existence corresponds a mode of union. The union according to the essence is proper to the three Persons of the Trinity; it is inaccessible to creatures, for if God could be communicated by essence, he would become multi-hypostatic;[25] but created human nature can never enter in essential or natural union with God. The union according to the hypostasis was realized in Christ. The human nature of Jesus is therefore one hypostatically with the Logos, and in it the divine energies that have the Logos as their source penetrate created nature and deify it. This union "according to the energy" becomes in this way accessible to all those who are in Christ.[26]

For Palamas, the union "according to the energy" (or "by grace,") is a union with God himself. This union *with God* is what he seeks to preserve when he insists that the partakable divine energies are *uncreated*. For God is not limited by the concept of essence, transcendent and absolutely inaccessible: he acts, reveals himself and communicates himself; and man, as the patristic tradition unanimously asserts, was created in the beginning in order to participate in God, without, however, becoming "God by essence."

After the condemnation of Barlaam and his departure from Byzantium, Palamas met the opposition of several Greek theologians who refused to admit the real distinction between essence and energy. Thus Gregory Akindynos could write: "According to the divine Fathers, the essential and natural characteristics are, in God, essence and nature, since form, essence and nature are on the divine plane identical, and since essence means the same thing as energy."[27] "God is one," he writes elsewhere, "by the identity of essence, nature, divinity, power, energy, form, glory, kingship, and lordship."[28]

This attitude of Akindynos necessarily led him to deny the reality of deification and to interpret as periphrasis the patristic texts that assert it: "It is clear," he writes, "that the divinity which certain men possess is a divinity proportionate to themselves (κατάλληλον ἑαυτοῖς θεότητα)...and not a divinity proportionate to God (κατάλληλον τῷ Θεῷ)."[29]

Throughout his treatises against Palamas, Akindynos denies the possibility of any participation between the created and the uncreated: When St. Paul describes the new life in Christ, does he not speak of a "new creation"?[30] The "divinity proportionate to man," the vision of God enjoyed by the saints, the mystics' experience, imply no participation whatsoever in the divine life; they are but manifestations of "created grace (κτιστὴ χάρις)."[31] The parallel between this position and Thomism is evident.[32]

We shall not analyze further the thought of Akindynos, except to indicate its christological implications. In a manner reminiscent of Theodore of Mopsuestia, he looks upon the two natures of Christ as juxtaposed one against the other, each persevering in its own characteristics. He sees no positive value in the *communicatio idiomatum* and ignores the Cyrillian idea of "appropriation" of the flesh by the Logos.[33] It is evident that Akindynos does not deny these doctrines, yet his opposition to the Palamite notion of deification leads him to a "closed" conception of nature, which puts him at variance with the tradition of the Greek Fathers. Palamas, however, following St. Maximus, admits that participation in the divine is always a participation in the uncreated, and therefore that there is no "created grace," that the human nature of Christ, created by nature, is "uncreated by participation," and that it becomes in this way the "source of deification" and of "uncreated life." Akindynos accused him of Monophysitism, for according to him, any "participation by the energy" was necessarily a confusion of the natures.[34] He interpreted, however, in a rather curious way, the Eucharistic communion as a communion with the divine essence itself and accused Palamas of Nestorianism because he conceived the Eucharist as a participation in the *deified human nature* of Christ and, in it, in the uncreated energies of God.[35]

The defeat of the anti-Palamites in Byzantium in the fourteenth century was thus the triumph of a theology of the incarnation which was already that of the Church in the fifth, sixth, and seventh centuries. Gregory Palamas may have used, here and there, new technical expressions. His polemic against Barlaam and Akindynos may sometimes have led him to extreme positions, but the essence of his thought is best expressed in this passage from the *Triads,*

directly inspired by the homily on the transfiguration by
St. John Damascene:

> Since the Son of God, in his incomparable love
> for men, did not only unite his divine hypostasis
> to our nature by putting on an animated body and
> a soul endowed with intelligence,[36] in order to
> appear on earth and live among men,[37] but since
> he also united himself to the human hypostases
> themselves, in mingling himself with each faithful
> by communion with his holy body, and since he
> becomes one body with us (σύσσωμος ἡμῖν
> γίνεται)[38] and makes us a temple of the whole
> divinity—for in the very body of Christ *dwells*
> *corporally all the fullness of the divinity* (Col
> 2:9)—, how should he not illuminate those who
> worthily communicate with the divine ray of his
> body which is within us, lightening their soul, as
> he illumined the very bodies of the disciples on
> Thabor? For then that body, source of the light of
> grace, was not yet united to our bodies; it illumined
> from without those who worthily approached it
> and sent the illumination to the soul by the inter-
> mediary of the eyes of the senses; but today since
> it is mingled with us and exists in us, it illuminates
> the soul from within.[39]

In this passage, one sees the true problem of the argument about the "Light of Thabor" between Palamas and
his adversaries. For the latter, it was but a "corporal aspect"
(εἶδος σωματικόν), therefore a created aspect, of Christ's
divinity,[40] and the patristic and liturgical usage of calling
that light itself "divinity" was but a figure of speech.[41]
On the contrary, for Palamas, when St. Gregory Nazianzen
speaks of the "...divinity which appeared to the disciples
on the Mount,"[42] or when the hymns of the Byzantine
liturgy proclaim, "In thy light which today appeared on
Thabor we have seen the Father as Light and also the
Spirit as Light," for "Thou didst reveal to us a brightness

which cannot be distinguished from divinity,"[43] what is brought out is not only the real experience of God by a few mystics but human destiny itself, the experience of Christian faith as such. Jesus' manhood, assumed into the hypostasis of the Logos, becomes the inalienable "place" where the participation of man in the divine life is forever realized. The whole of mankind is called to partake in this divine life within the Church—the Body of Christ. God, however, remains in himself, in his essence, transcendent and free: all participation in his being remains thus a gift, a grace, and the human response can only be a thanksgiving or a "collaboration" (synergy), never a "possession" or a "merit."

The trend of thought favored in the last years of Byzantium by the triumph of the Palamite ideas led the most authentic representatives of orthodox spirituality to insist on the sacramental life, on the personal experience of Christ and the Spirit, and on the concept of participation in God. This theocentricism was not, however, prejudicial to the properly *human* functions of the "new humanity."

"Our Lord," wrote Nicholas Cabasilas, "not only assumed our body, but also the soul, the intelligence, the will, all that is proper to human nature, in order to be able to unite himself with the whole of our being, and penetrate our entire being.... Between him and men, everything is common, except sin.... This is the virtue and the grace of the Eucharistic meal for those who draw near it with a clean heart, and who keep themselves from all evil afterwards; with those who are thus prepared and well disposed, nothing prevents Christ from uniting himself intimately. 'Great is this mystery,' writes St. Paul, in order to exalt this union; for this is the celebrated wedding, during which the divine Bridegroom unites himself with his Church as with his virgin bride."[44]

Conclusion

This book has been fundamentally conceived as a *historical* study. Its goal was to provide the reader with information about the mainstreams of christological thought in Byzantium. Historical analysis, however, could not avoid touching upon controversial issues that recently have been widely discussed—especially among Roman Catholic theologians and historians of dogma—and taking a stand, explicitly or implicitly, on certain basic problems.

Thus, an attempt has been made to sustain the view that the so-called neo-Chalcedonian Christology, proclaimed as official orthodoxy during the reign of Justinian and symbolized by the condemnation of the "Three Chapters" at the council of 553, was not a simple concession to Monophysitism but a fundamental option, rooted in basic theological and anthropological presuppositions. Modern debates on the "orthodoxy" of Theodore of Mopsuestia, Nestorius, and the other representatives of Antiochene Christology, and on the supposed Monophysitism of Cyril of Alexandria and, consequently, of the Fifth Ecumenical Council, must take into account the fundamental concepts of God and man for which these respective authors stood.

Theodore of Mopsuestia, for example, seems to have had a concept of God that identified the divine essence with the philosophical concept of immutability and yet excluded any existence of divine ("uncreated") life *ad extra*. It is this concept of God that made impossible, in Theodore's thought, any form of real union between divinity and humanity, allowing only a juxtaposition of the two natures. An interesting parallel was recently drawn, on this point, between Theodore

209

and Augustine, on the level of their respective doctrines of God.[1]

What is involved in this particular issue—and also therefore in the whole result of the Fifth Ecumenical Council, which condemned Theodore—is the whole Greek patristic notion of "participation in divine life," of deification, as the real content of soteriology, which the Christologies of both Athanasius and Cyril meant to preserve. The hypostatic, or in Cyril's vocabulary the natural, union of divinity and humanity in Christ, as distinct from Theodore's notion of union according to the will or energy, presupposes an interpenetration of divine and human life. This interpenetration, however, at least in orthodox Chalcedonian thought, excludes confusion or total absorption of the human by the divine. On the contrary, as Maximus the Confessor shows it best, communion with the Logos is precisely the *natural state* (λόγος φυσικὸς) of true humanity.

Man is truly man when he participates in divine life and realizes in himself the image and likeness of God, and this participation in no way diminishes his authentically human existence, human energy and will.

Now this notion of participation presupposes that God is not only an immutable and imparticipable essence but also a living and acting person. By assuming humanity hypostatically, the Logos "becomes" what he was not before and even "suffers in the flesh." This "openness" of a hypostatic or personal God to the creature implies that the creature, and especially man, is a *reality,* even in respect to God, since, in a sense, it "modifies" God's personal existence. It excludes all Docetism or Monophysitism and affirms that the salvation of man was a matter serious enough to bring the son of God to the cross. It finally implies that, first, in Christ's humanity and, then, in his entire "body," God is present in "energy." Thus, we are led directly to the real distinction (which later Byzantine theology will take for granted) between three elements of divine existence: the imparticipable divine essence, the hypostasis, and the energy. This distinction is based not on philosophical considerations but upon the

Chalcedonian, post-Chalcedonian, and Maximian understanding of salvation.

The problem can also be approached "from below." The notion of participation implies not only openness in the divine being but also a dynamic, open and teleological concept of man. Since Gregory of Nyssa, the destiny of man is viewed, in Greek patristic thought, as an ascent in the knowledge of God through communion into divine life. Man, therefore, is not conceived as an autonomous and closed entity: his very life is in God, "who alone has immortality," while sin consists precisely in a self-affirmation of man in an illusory independence.

This approach "from below" to the mystery of Christ is the point where the post-Chalcedonian Byzantine thought meets the modern christological concerns. "Human being," writes Karl Rahner, "is a reality absolutely open upwards; a reality which reaches its highest (though indeed 'un-exacted') perfection, the realization of the highest possibility of man's being, when in it the Logos himself becomes existent in the world."[2]

Rahner defines man as "at once a concretely corporeal and historical entity on earth and an absolutely transcendent one"; he affirms that "man is continually kept in movement by the existential need to possess God concretely, to 'have to' possess him," and that "without such a deduction, and unless it is brought home to man as something really achieved, the historical message concerning Jesus the Son of God is always in danger of being dismissed as a mere piece of mythology."[3] This concept of man is precisely in the line of Greek patristic tradition, although expressed in terms of modern existential philosophy. It coincides with E. Schille-beeckx's definition of grace as "an interpersonal communion with God, an undeserved yet real qualification of man's being."[4]

By basing christological thinking on anthropology, one is necessarily led to the other major conclusions of Greek patristics: man does not disappear in contact with God but, on the contrary, becomes more truly and more freely man,[5] not only in his similarity to God, but also in what makes him radically different from his Creator. And this is the very meaning of the hypostatic union of divinity and humanity in Christ. According to Rahner:

> ...if what makes the human nature "ek-sistent" as something diverse from God, and what unites this nature with the Logos, are *strictly* the same, then we have a unity which (a) cannot, as uniting unity (*einende Einheit*), be confused with the united unity (*geeinte Einheit*)—this is not permissible—the Chalcedonian distinction between hypostasis and physis—(b) which unites precisely by making existent, and in this way is grasped in a fullness of content without any relapse into the empty assertion of the united unity—each nature keeps its property according to Chalcedon and the *Tome* of Leo—, and finally (c) which does not make the *asyngkhytos* (unconfusedly) look like a sort of external counter-balance to the unity, always threatening to dissolve it again—as Antiochene Christology would do—but shows precisely how it enters into the constitution of the united unity as an intrinsic factor, in such a way that unity and distinction become mutually conditioning and intensifying characteristics, not competing ones.[6]

The real basis of Nestorianism was precisely the idea of competition and mutual exclusion of divinity and humanity. The overcoming of that Nestorian tendency—which was at the root of all the criticism directed against the neo-Chalcedonism of the fifth council—thus leads inevitably to recovering the importance of considering the Logos as the hypostasis, the "uniting unity" and the source of Christ's human existence. And, in turn, this "open" understanding of hypostasis—as the person who, while pre-existing in divinity, *assumes* also humanity as his own, without making it less human—challenges the old Thomistic notion of God's immutability,[7] and also leads to the real distinction in trinitarian theology between essence and hypostasis: for immutability, if the hypostatic union is taken seriously, can be the property of the nature, or essence, of God but not of his hypostatic existence, which did change when the Son of God "became flesh." Thus Karl Rahner arrives at challenging the Latin idea that the persons of the Trinity are internal relations in the divine essence, for, indeed, if such were the case, the divine hypostasis of the Logos could neither be the subject of change and passion, nor be seen as the existential center of his human nature. A sound Christology implies, for Rahner, the return to a pre-Augustinian concept of God, where the three hypostases were seen first of all in their personal, irreducible functions,[8] as Father-God, Son-Logos, and the Spirit of God, and not only as expressions of the unique immutable essence.

For if one identifies the being of God with the essence *only*—as it was done in the West since Augustine—this essence loses its absolute transcendence, incomprehensibility, and immutability. Meanwhile, the distinction between the transcendent essence, the personal or hypostatic existence and the life *ad extra* of God, makes it possible to give a full meaning to apophatic theology, which the Greek Fathers cherished so much. "In the [immediate] vision," writes Rahner, "being in God himself and not any more in the infinite poverty of our transcendence, we will discover that he is incomprehensible."[9]

It is quite evident, therefore, that Karl Rahner's thought implies not only a return to pre-Augustinism but also a return to the basic presuppositions of the christological thought analyzed throughout this book. This coincidence cannot be explained only by a reference to Rahner's own patristic formation; it also shows the astonishing relevance, for our own time, of the patristic view of the Christian message. It is by facing the challenge of modern thought that contemporary Western Christian theology, in the persons of its best representatives, may discover its authentic roots. The ecumenical significance of this discovery is incalculable.

Abbreviations

ACO   E. Schwartz, ed., *Acta Conciliorum Oecumenicorum* (Strasbourg, 1914ff).

DACL   F. Cabrol and H. Leclercq, eds., *Dictionnaire d'Archéologie Chrétienne et de Liturgie* (Paris, 1907ff).

DOP   *Dumbarton Oaks Papers* (Washington, D.C., 1950ff).

DTC   A. Vacant and E. Mangenot, *Dictionnaire de Théologie Catholique* (Paris, 1909ff).

JTS   *The Journal of Theological Studies* (London-Oxford, 1900ff).

Mansi J. D. Mansi, *Sacrorum Conciliorum Nova et Amplissima Collectio* (Florence, 1759ff).

NF   *Neue Folge*

OCA   *Orientalia Christiana Analecta* (Rome, 1935ff).

OCP   *Orientalia Christiana Periodica* (Rome, 1934ff).

PG   J. P. Migne, *Patrologiae Cursus Completus, Series Graeca* (Paris, 1857ff).

PO   R. Graffin and F. Nau, eds., *Patrologia Orientalis* (Paris, 1903ff).

REB   *Revue des Études Byzantines* (Paris, 1943ff).

RHE   *Revue d'Histoire Ecclésiastique* (Louvain, 1900ff).

RSPT   *Revue des Sciences Philosophiques et Théologiques* (Paris, 1907ff).

RSR   *Revue des Sciences Religieuses* (Strasbourg-Paris, 1920ff).

TU   O. V. Gebhardt and A. V. Harnack, eds., *Texte und Untersuchungen zur Geschichte der altchristliche Literatur* (Leipzig, 1882ff).

Notes

NOTES TO CHAPTER 1

[1]See C. V. Sellers, *The Council of Chalcedon* (London, 1953), xvii.

[2]*Ep. 101 ad Cledonium, PG,* 37, col. 181 c-184 a.

[3]For this analysis of Apollinarianism, see mainly A. Grillmeier, *Christ in Christian Tradition from the Apostolic Age to Chalcedon* (London, 1965), 220-223. The author exaggerates, however, the value of what he calls "*Logos-sarx* Christology," which he considers as the primitive error of almost all the christological heresies of the fourth and fifth centuries. Useful as a working hypothesis, Grillmeier's position loses some of its convincing power as the author goes on to apply it in a general way to all the heresies of the time. His book, however, represents today the best introduction to the study of the christological debates of the fifth century.

[4]See, for instance, his letter 83 to Dioscorus of Alexandria, Schwartz, *ACO,* II, 1, 2, pp. 50-51 (*PG,* 83, col. 1272).

[5]'Ανάλογόν τε τῇ οἰκείᾳ προθέσει καὶ τὴν τοῦ Θεοῦ Λόγου συνέργειαν δεχόμενος, *De Incarnatione,* fragm. published in H. B. Swete's *Theodore of Mopsuestia on the Minor Epistles of St. Paul* (Cambridge, 1882), Appendix A, II, 296.

[6]Grillmeier, *op. cit.,* 373-388.

[7]On the debate concerning Nestorius' "orthodoxy," see the relevant bibliography in Grillmeier, *op. cit.,* 496-505; add to it the two diametrically opposed points of view of M. V. Anastos, "Nestorius was Orthodox," in *DOP,* 16 (1962), 119-140, and G. S. Bebis, Συμβολαὶ εἰς τὴν περὶ τοῦ Νεστορίου ἔρευναν (Athens, 1964).

[8]"Pour atteindre la christologie de Cyrille [il faut] la considérer comme l'infrastructure indispensable de sa sotériologie et montrer au passage que tout autre fondement serait insuffisant ou ruineux," G. M. de Durand, ed., *Cyrille d'Alexandrie, Deux Dialogues,* in the collection Sources chrétiennes, 97 (Paris, 1964), Introduction, 84-85.

[9]Ἡ τοῦ Λόγου φύσις ἤγουν ὑπόστασις, ὅ ἐστιν αὐτὸς ὁ Λόγος, *Apol. adv. Theod.* II, ed. P. E. Pusey, VI, 404.

[10]Apollinarius, *Ad Jovianum,* in H. Lietzmann, *Apollinaris von Laodicea und seine Schule* (Tübingen, 1904), 250-251; Apollinarius' text is quoted *in extenso,* with its attribution to Athanasius, in Cyril's *De recta fide ad reginas, PG,* 86, col. 1212-1213.

[11]All these passages in *Ep. 45, PG,* 87, col. 232; cf. *Ep. 46, ibid.,* col. 244: "How could we not accept that two natures exist inseparably (ὑφιστάναι ἀδιαιρέτως) after the union?"

[12]For a comparison between Cyril and Apollinarius, see Grillmeier, *op. cit.*, 401ff.

[13]M. Richard, "L'introduction du mot hypostase dans la théologie de l'incarnation," in *Mélanges de sciences religieuses*, 2 (1945), 12-17.

[14]*Second Letter to Cyril, PG*, 77, col. 52 b.

[15]*Ibid.*, col. 53 a.

[16]See H. M. Diepen, *Les Trois Chapitres au Concile de Chalcédoine* (Oosterhout, 1953), 50-57; R. V. Sellers, *The Council of Chalcedon*, 67-68.

[17]*Tome to Flavian*, in *ACO*, II, 2, 1, 27-29.

[18]*ACO*, II, 1, 2, 82-83.

[19]Cyril is mentioned by name in almost every vote, *ibid.*, 94-109.

[20]V. V. Bolotov, *Lektsii po istorii drevrei Tserkvi*, IV, 3 (Petrograd, 1918), 317.

[21]This formula σωζομένης τῆς ἰδιότητος ἑκατέρας φύσεως is the Greek equivalent of the *agit utraque forma quod proprium est* of St. Leo.

[22]Cyril, after having refused, in the fourth anathematism against Nestorius (*ACO*, I, 1, 1, 41), the method of exegesis that consisted in attributing some texts of the New Testament to the man Jesus, and some to the God-Word, eventually admitted the inevitability of that in his letter to Acacius of Melitene (*ACO*, I, 1, 4, 27: αἱ μὲν γὰρ τῶν φωνῶν ὅτι μάλιστα θεοπρεπεῖς, αἱ δὲ πάλιν ἀνθρωποπρεπεῖς) and in the formula of union of 433.

[23]Ἐγὼ γὰρ ἕνα εἰδώς τε καὶ διδαχθεὶς εὐσεβῶς υἱόν, μίαν ὁμολογῶ τὴν τοῦ σαρκωθέντος Θεοῦ Λόγου ὑπόστασιν (*ACO*, IV, 2, 191, lines 20-21). Proclus does not formally go beyond the limits of Cyrillian terminology, since for Cyril ὑπόστασις and φύσις are synonymous (see *supra*, p. 19); he corrects Cyril, however, by omitting φύσις.

[24]J. Pelikan, *The Christian Tradition. 1. The Emergence of the Catholic Tradition* [*100-600*] (Chicago, 1971), pp. 265-266.

NOTES TO CHAPTER 2

[1]See mainly R. Devreesse, "Essai sur Théodore de Mopsueste," *Studi e testi,* 141 (Vatican City, 1948).

[2]This is the thesis of R. Devreesse, upheld on this point by M. Richard, "La tradition des fragments du traité de Théodore de Mopsueste," *Le Muséon,* 56 (1943), 55-75; for a complete bibliography on the question, see J. Quasten, *Patrology,* III (Westminster, Md., 1960), 401-423.

[3]The best-documented and most brilliant presentation of this thesis is by C. Moeller, "Le Chalcédonisme et le Néo-Chalcédonisme en Orient de 451 à la fin du VIᵉ siècle," in Grillmeier-Bacht, *Das Konzil von Chalkedon,* I (Würzburg, 1951), 637-720. The group we call "strict dyophysites" are, for Moeller, "strict Chalcedonians." It is evident that the christological position of each author influences the terms he uses to designate the different groups.

[4]See mainly J. F. Bethune-Baker, *Nestorius and His Teaching* (Cambridge, 1908).

[5]See mainly H. M. Diepen, *Les Trois Chapitres au Concile de*

Chalcédoine (Oosterhout, 1953); F. A. Sullivan, *The Christology of Theodore of Mopsuestia, Analecta Gregoriana,* 82 (Rome, 1956). For an analysis of the controversy, see also J. S. Romanides, "Highlights in the Debate over Theodore of Mopsuestia's Christology and Some Suggestions for a Fresh Approach," in the *Greek Orthodox Theological Review,* 2, 2 (Winter 1959-60), 140-185.

[6]See E. Honigman, "Patristic Studies," *Studi e testi,* 173 (Vatican City, 1953), 174-184.

[7]See M. Richard, "Notes sur l'évolution doctrinale de Théodoret," in *RSR,* 25 (1936), 459-481; H. M. Diepen, *Les Trois Chapitres,* 75-90.

[8]See N. Glubokovskii, *Blazhennyi Theodorit,* 2 (Moscow, 1890), 339-342.

[9]*Haer. Fab. Compendium,* 15, *PG,* 83, col. 504-505 a; the structure of Theodoret's thought remains identical with his refutations of Cyril's *Anathematisms,* where there was also a reference to the soul's immortality (see *PG,* 76, col. 404 c, 449 b, etc.).

[10]Φύσει πεπονθέναι τὴν σάρκα, τοῦ δὲ Θεοῦ Λόγου ὠκειῶσθαι τὸ πάθος ὡς ἰδίας σαρκός, *Demonst. per Syll.,* III, 10, *PG,* 83, col. 332 d; on this aspect of Theodoret's thought, see N. Glubokovskii, *op. cit.,* vol. 1, 171-177.

[11]Theodoret, *Letter to John of Aegea,* Syrian fragment and translation, in F. Nau "Documents pour servir l'histoire de l'église nestorienne," in *PO,* 13 (Paris, 1919), 190-191; see M. Richard, "La lettre de Théodoret à Jean d'Égée," in *RSPT,* 30 (1941-42), 415-423.

[12]*Livre d'Héraclide de Damas,* ed. F. Nau (Paris, 1910), 327.

[13]Fr. Diekamp, ed., *Analecta Patristica, OCA,* 117 (Rome, 1938), 77-78.

[14]Large extracts of his commentaries on the Pauline epistles have been published by K. Staab, *Paulus Kommentare aus der griechischen Kirche* (Münster, 1933), 352-422.

[15]This fact is admitted by contemporaries like Ephrem of Amida, Chalcedonian successor to Peter the Fuller in the See of Antioch (526-544). In a book addressed to the Severian Zenobius of Emesa and analyzed by Photius, he showed that "the Easterners addressed this hymn to our Lord Jesus Christ, while the Byzantines and the Westerners linked the doxology to the consubstantial Trinity" (*Bibliotheca,* 228, *PG,* 103, col. 957 bc).

[16]On this collection, see E. Schwartz, *ACO,* III, 11-14.

[17]Εἷς γὰρ τῆς Τριάδος ἐστὶν ἐνανθρωπήσας Ἰησοῦς ὁ Χριστός, ὁ δὲ σταυρὸς περὶ τὸ ἀνθρώπινον τοῦ Χριστοῦ γεγένηται. Text published by E. Schwartz: "Publizistische Sammlungen zum Acacianischen Schisma" in *Abhandlungen der Bayer. Akad. der Wiss., Phil. Hist. Abt., NF,* 10 (1934), 125; and *ACO,* III, 217.

[18]Mansi, VIII, col. 795-799; see J. Pargoire, *Acémètes,* in *DACL,* 1 col. 307-321.

[19]Mansi, *ibid.,* col. 806 de.

[20]*Bibliotheca,* 107, ed. R. Henry, 2 (Paris, 1960), 78. C. Moeller, who otherwise considers the whole group of Antiochene theologians as strict Chalcedonians, is therefore wrong in classifying Basil among the Nestorians ("Le Chalcédonisme et le Néo-Chalcédonisme," 656). As he was a priest in Antioch under Bishop Flavian (498-512), he could be nothing but formally Chalcedonian.

[21]Leontius of Byzantium accuses the supporters of Theodore of Mopsuestia, who for him are Nestorians, "of calling upon the Great Council in front of simple people, while hiding their machinations," *Contra Nest.*

et Eut., III, *PG*, 86, I, col. 1361 a; also col. 1364 a. (The Nestorians, posing as supporters of the council, infiltrated the clergy.)

[22]I. B. Chabot, "Documenta ad origines monophysitarum illustrandas," *Corp. Script. Christ. Orient.*, *Scriptores Syri*, II, 37, *Versio* (Louvain, 1933), 182.

[23]Joseph Lebon, *Le Monophysitisme séverien; étude historique, littéraire et théologique sur la résistance monophysite au concile de Chalcédoine jusqu'à la constitution de l'Église jacobite* (Louvain, 1909), xxi. The minutes of the two successive consultations between Chalcedonians and non-Chalcedonians were published in *The Greek Orthodox Theological Review*, 10, 2, (Winter 1964-65), and 13, 1 (1968).

[24]On Monophysite theology, side by side with J. Lebon's work on Severus, one must mainly quote, by the same author, "La christologie du monophysitisme syrien," in Grillmeier-Bacht, *Chalkedon*, I, 425-580; see also R. V. Sellers, *The Council of Chalcedon* (London, 1953), 256-273.

[25]Ἡ δὲ ὑπόστασις οὐσία ἐστὶ καὶ οὐδὲν ἄλλο σημαινόμενον ἔχει ἢ τὸ αὐτὸ ὄν... Ἡ γὰρ ὑπόστασις καὶ ἡ οὐσία ὕπαρξίς ἐστιν, *Ad Afros*, 4, *PG*, 26, col. 1036 b. The identification obviously also covers φύσις in Athanasius.

[26]*Against Chalcedon*, ed. and tr. F. Nau, *PO*, 13, 2, 228-229.

[27]*Three Letters of Philoxenus*, ed. A. Vaschalde (Rome, 1902), 149.

[28]*Ibid.*, 133.

[29]*Ep.* 44, *PG*, 77, col. 225; cf. *Ep.* 40, *ibid.*, col. 192 d.

[30]*Against Nestorius*, XI, ed. and Engl. tr. by E. A. W. Budge, vol. 2 (London, 1894), xlii.

[31]According to Cyril, the Word became man "by the condescension of economy" (σύμβασις οἰκονομικὴ) and thus became one nature with the flesh (*Letter to Acacius*, PG, 77, 192 c, 198 a).

[32]Philoxenus, *De Trinitate et Incarn.*, ed. A. Vaschalde, *Corp. Script. Christ. Orient, Scriptores Syri*, II, 27 (Paris and Rome, 1907), 46, tr. J. Lebon, "La christologie," 440.

[33]*Ed. cit.*, 113-114 (tr. Lebon, *ibid.*, 443).

[34]*Letter to Œcumenius*, ed. E. W. Brooks, *PO*, 12, 2, 176-177.

[35]*Letter to Sergius*, ed. J. Lebon, *Corp. Script. Christ. Orient. Scriptores Syri*, IV, 7 (Louvain, 1949), 94.

[36]J. Lebon, "La christologie," 472-477.

[37]For a study of this Severian terminology, see J. Lebon, *ibid.*, 454-467.

[38]See Severus, quoted by Leontius of Byzantium, *PG*, 86, col. 908 a, 921 a, etc.

[39]Νοῦ μόνη φαντασίᾳ καὶ λεπτῇ θεωρίᾳ καὶ ἐπινοίᾳ, *ibid.*, 1921 a.

[40]Ἐν ψιλαῖς διελόντες ἐννοίαις, καὶ ὡς ἐν ἰχναῖς θεωρίαις, ἤτοι νοῦ φαντασίαις τὴν διαφορὰν δεξάμενοι, οὐκ ἀνὰ μέρος τίθεμεν τὰς φύσεις, *Ep.* 46, *Ad Succensum*, *PG*, 77, col. 245 a.

[41]*Letter to Sergius*, ed. Lebon, 60. Several monoenergist passages of Severus are preserved in the Acts of the Lateran Council (649); see Mansi, X, col. 1116-17.

[42]*Against Eunomius IV*, *PG* 29, col. 689 c; see J. Lebon, *Monophysitisme séverien*, 445-446.

[43]See Mansi, X, col. 1124 a.

[44]Ἐν συνθέσει δὲ ὑφισταμέναις ταῖς φύσεσιν ἐξ ὧν ὁ εἷς Χριστός, quoted by Eustathius, *PG*, 86, 1, col. 908 a. See an excellent

analysis on this point in V. V. Bolotov, *Lektsii po istorii drevnei Tserkvi*, IV, 3 (Petrograd, 1918), 338-340.

[45]See the brilliant article of A. H. M. Jones, "Were Ancient Heresies National or Social Movements in Disguise?" in JTS, New Series, 10 (1959), 297-298. For a general history of the emergence of Monophysitism, see W. H. C. Frend, *The Rise of the Monophysite Movement* (Cambridge, 1972).

NOTES TO CHAPTER 3

[1]The principal source on these events is the *Vita Sabae*, written by a contemporary, Cyril of Scythopolis (ed. E. Schwartz, in *TU*, 49, 4 [Leipzig, 1939], 85-229); see F. Diekamp, *Die origenistischen Streitigkeiten in sechsten Jahrhundert und das fünfte allgemeine Konzil* (Münster-in-W., 1899).

[2]Theophilus' synodal letter was preserved in the Latin text of St. Jerome, among the latter's letters; see Jerome, *Lettres*, IV, ed. J. Labourt, "Les Belles Lettres" (Paris, 1954), 154, and other texts by Theophilus on Origenist Christology, *ibid.*, V, 45-53.

[3]*Ibid.*, 221, 194, 175, 179.

[4]*Origène et la fonction révélatrice du Verbe incarné* (Paris, 1958), 103-120; see also C. Tresmontant, *La Métaphysique du Christianisme* (Paris, 1961), 395-518.

[5]*Ibid.*, 367.

[6]See V. V. Bolotov, *Uchenie Origena o Sv. Troitse* (St. Petersburg, 1879), 428, 434.

[7]*PG*, 86, col. 892-896.

[8]G. Florovsky, "The anthropomorphites in the Egyptian desert," in *Akten des XI. internationalen Byzantinistenkongresses. München, 1958* (Munich, 1960), 154-159.

[9]A. Guillaumont, "Évagre et les anathématismes antiorigénistes de 553," *Studia Patristica*, III, *TU*, 78 (Berlin, 1961), 219-226; by the same author, *Les Kephalaia Gnostica d'Évagre le Pontique et l'histoire de l'origénisme chez les Grecs et les Syriens* (Paris, 1962), 124-170; see also F. Refoulé, "La christologie d'Évagre et l'origénisme," *OCP*, 27 (1961), 221-226.

[10]See in particular *Vita Sabae*, ed. cit., 119; other witnesses assembled by F. Diekamp, *op. cit.*, 98-120. Diekamp's demonstration leaves no doubt on the condemnation of Origen, Evagrius, and Didymus at the council of 553. Some more recent authors (in particular L. Bréhier and Leclercq), motivated by the desire to protect Origen's memory, doubt the validity of this condemnation. According to them, it took place without the presence of Pope Vigilius, and was not officially confirmed by the Roman pontiff. However, both contemporary and medieval witnesses, including the popes, in particular Nicholas I in 886 (Diekamp, *op. cit.*, 118), considered that Vigilius had confirmed the decisions of 553 as a whole, concerning both the "Three Chapters" and Origen.

[11]Schwartz, ed., *ACO*, III, 189-214 (see also Mansi, IX, 524-539; *PG*, 86, col. 945-989); large extracts translated by C. Tresmontant, *op. cit.*, 504-509.

222   *Christ in Eastern Christian Thought*

[12]Text critically edited in F. Diekamp, *op. cit.*, 90-97 (cf. *PG*, 86, col. 989-993); Fr. tr. in G. Fritz, "Origénisme," in *DTC*, XI, 2, col. 1580-88.

[13]Schwartz, ed., *op. cit.*, 190.

[14]V. Bolotov, *Uchenie Origena...*, 206, 222-224, 229.

[15]J. Hefele-Leclerq, *Histoire des Conciles*, vol. 2, pt. 2 (Paris, 1908), 1191-96.

[16]See, for instance, *De princ.* III, 5, 3, ed. Koetschau, 272-273.

[17]*Ibid.*, II, 9, 6, *ed. cit.*, 169-170.

[18]*Ibid.*, I, 5, 3, *ed. cit.*, 71-73; I, 7, 3, 87-89; etc.; cf. C. Tresmontant, *op. cit.*, 405-411.

[19]It is the main Origenist heresy mentioned by Barsanuphius (*PG*, 86, col. 892 b) and by Cyril of Scythopolis (*Vita Euthymii*, ed. Schwartz, *TU*, 49, 2 [Leipzig, 1939], 39; *Vita Sabae, ibid.*, 124, 199).

[20]See I, 6, 2, *ed. cit.*, 79-80; II, 1, 3, 109; III, 5, 4, 273.

[21]*De princ.* III, 6, 5, *ed. cit.*, 286-287.

[22]See also Origen's condemnation by Theophilus of Alexandria, in *Doctrina Patrum*, ed. Diekamp, 180.

[23]*De princ.*, II, 3, 3, *ed. cit.*, 117-118.

[24]The hagiographic sources confirm that this belief was widespread among Origenist monks, Cyril of Scythopolis, *Vita Cyriaci*, ed. Schwartz, *TU*, 49, 2, 230.

[25]*Gnostic Centuries*, IV, 18, ed. and tr. Antoine Guillaumont, *PO*, 28 (Paris, 1959), 142.

[26]*Gnost. Cent.*, V, 81, *ed. cit.*, 211; for other parallels with the Anathematisms of 553, see *Gnost. Cent.*, I, 77; II, 43, 89; IV, 14, 80; cf. A. Guillaumont, *Les Kephalaia gnostica*, 151-159.

[27]Cyril of Scythopolis, *Vita Cyriaci, ed. cit.*, 230, line 10; cf. *Vita Sabae, ed. cit.*, 197.

[28]Several authors, among whom are Anastasius the Sinaite (*PG*, 89, col. 101 b) and the Patriarch Tarasius (*PG*, 98, col. 1465 d), as well as the Seventh Council itself (Mansi, XIII, col. 377 b), completely forget the episode of the "Three Chapters": for them, the council of 553 is the one that condemned Origen, Evagrius, and Didymus.

[29]*Le Christ et le temps* (Neuchâtel-Paris, 1947), 36.

[30]*Letter to Menas*, ed. Schwartz, III, 191; *PG*, 86, col. 949 bc.

[31]*Ibid.*, 205; *PG*, 86, col. 974 c.

[32]*Ibid.*, 192; *PG*, 86, col. 953 a.

[33]*Ibid.*

[34]*Ibid.*, 193; *PG*, 86, col. 953 d-955 a.

[35]Restitution to Evagrius and French translation by I. Hausherr, "Le traité de l'oraison d'Évagre le Pontique," in *Revue d'ascétique et de mystique*, 15 (1934), 34-93, 113-170.

[36]*PG*, 86, col. 893 c, 897 a.

[37]On these two poles of Eastern spirituality, see P. Minin, "The Major Tendencies of Mysticism in the Ancient Church" (in Russian), *Bogoslovskii Vestnik* (Dec. 1911), 823-838; (May 1913), 151-172; (June 1914), 304-326; and A. Guillaumont, "Le cœur chez les spirituels grecs à l'époque ancienne," in the article "Cor et cordis affectus," in the *Dictionnaire de Spiritualité*, II, 2 (Paris, 1932), col. 2281-88.

[38]This is how I. Hausherr presents it in his early article on "Les grands courants de la spiritualité orientale," in *OCP*, 1 (1935), 123-124; cf. a recent and much more balanced article by the same author, "L'hésychasme,

étude de spiritualité," in *OCP,* 22 (1956), 5-40, 247-285.

[39]See M. Richard, "Le traité *De sectis* et Léonce de Byzance," in *RHE,* 35 (1939), 695-723; "Léonce de Byzance et Léonce de Jérusalem," in *Mélanges de sciences religieuses,* 1 (1944), 35-38. Earlier publications on this subject are quoted in M. Richard's articles.

[40]See in particular Cyril of Scythopolis, *Vita Cyriaci, ed. cit.,* 230.

[41]My interpretation of Leontius owes much to D. Evans, *Leontius of Byzantium: An Origenist Christology,* Dumbarton Oaks Studies, 13 (Washington, D.C., 1969).

[42]*PG,* 86, col. 1276 a; Nonnus' name does not appear in the text, but he is identified in a marginal scholion; see M. Richard, "Léonce de Byzance était-il origéniste?" in *REB,* 5 (1947), 31-66.

[43]See, for instance, references to Philoxenus of Mabbug quoted by J. Lebon, *Le Monophysitisme sévérien,* 221-229.

[44]*Contra Eutych. et Nest.,* I, *PG,* 86, col. 1281 b.

[45]*Epilysis, PG* 86, col. 1944 c; cf. 1941 d-1944 a; see the analysis of these passages by M. Richard, "Léonce de Byzance," in *REB,* 5 (1947), 58-60.

[46]This is Leontius' main argument against the aphthartodocetae, who believed that the body of Christ was incorruptible from the moment of the incarnation (see, in particular, *PG,* 86, col. 1348 bd).

[47]See, for instance, *Contra Nest. et Eut.,* col. 1297 d, 1300 ab, 1301 bd, etc.; *Epilysis,* col. 1941 ab, etc.

[48]M. Richard, "Le traité *De sectis* et Léonce de Byzance," in *RHE,* 35 (1939), 710.

[49]Ὁ ἐκ Παρθένου πεφηνὸς Θεός τε ἐκλήθη καὶ Υἱὸς Θεοῦ ἐν τῷ Λόγῳ καὶ κατὰ τὸν Λόγον, *Contra Nest. et Eut.,* col. 1301 a (in Migne's text, Λόγος is printed with a small "λ" and this makes the sense of the sentence obscure).

[50]*Contra Nest. et Eut.,* col. 1332 a.

[51]*Ibid.,* col. 1332 d-1333 a.

[52]Cf. *supra,* p. 17.

[53]*Contra Nest. et Eut.,* col. 1357 c.

[54]Εἰ γὰρ οὐσίαν ἁπλῶς ὁριζόμενοι εἴπομεν τὴν τινος ὕπαρξιν δηλοῦν . . . , οὐ τὸ τί ἢ τὸ πῶς, *Epilysis,* col. 1921 c.

[55]*Epilysis,* col. 1945 c; cf. *ibid.,* col. 1920 d-1921 a.

[56]See *Contra Nest. et Eut.,* col. 1305 c; *Epilysis,* col. 1921 a, 1928 b, etc.

[57]*Contra Nest. et Eut.,* col. 1277 d.

[58]*Ibid.,* col. 1280 ab.

[59]*Epilysis,* col. 1941 d-1944 a.

[60]*Epilysis,* col. 1933 a.

[61]*Contra Nest. et Eut.,* col. 1292 a.

[62]*Ibid.,* col. 1289 a.

[63]"Léonce de Byzance," *DTC,* IX, 1 (1926), col. 412, summarizing a very abstract passage of the *Contra Nest. et Eut.* (col. 1238-89); see also A. Theodorou, "Χριστολογικὴ ὁρολογία καὶ διδασκαλία Λεοντίου τοῦ Βυζαντίου," in Θεολογία, 26 (1955), 212-222, 421-435, 584-592; 27 (1956), 32-44.

[64]*Contra Nest. et Eut.,* col. 1296 ac.

[65]*Ibid.,* col. 1289 bc.

[66]*Contra Nest. et Eut.,* col. 1277 cd.

[67]Does he not refer to St. Cyril himself, from whose theology his own is as remote as from that of the Nestorians?
[68]See mainly G. L. Prestige, *God in Patristic Thought* (London, 1952), 242ff.
[69]*Poem. dogm.*, XX, 3, *PG*, 37, col. 414 a; *Orat.* 39, 11, *PG*, 36, col. 345 d.

NOTES TO CHAPTER 4

[1]This point has been clearly noticed by Werner Elert, *Der Ausgang der altkirchlichen Christologie* (Berlin, 1957), 121-122.
[2]See *supra*.
[3]Moeller, "Le Chalcédonisme," 676; M. Richard, "Proclus de Constantinople et le théopaschisme," in *RHE*, 38 (1942), 329. See also W. H. C. Frend, *The Rise of the Monophysite Movement: Chapters in the History of the Church in the Fifth and Sixth Centuries* (Cambridge, 1972), pp. 266-267.
[4]Πάθος τοῦ Θεοῦ, Ignatius of Antioch, *Rom.*, VI, 3.
[5]*Hom.* 45, 28, *PG*, 36, col. 661 c; cf. τοῖς τοῦ 'Απαθοῦς πάθεσι, *Hom.* 30, 5, col. 709 a.
[6]*Hom.* 45, 19, 22, 28, col. 649 c; 653 a; 661 d.
[7]It is worthwhile noticing the radical difference that separates the positive appreciation of the work of John Maxentius by Orthodox authors such as M. Oksiuk (Archbishop Macarius), "Theopaskhitskie spory," in *Trudy Kievskoi Dukhovnoi Akademii*, 1 (1913), 529-559, and G. Florovsky, *Vizantiiskie ottsy*, 129, and the attitude of recent historians of neo-Chalcedonism for whom John Maxentius is but a blind fanatic, and his work "unbearable" to read, such as C. Moeller, "Le Chalcédonisme," 678-679; such a view is also curiously found in the Russian historian V. V. Bolotov, *Lektsii po istorii Tserkvi*, 4 (Petrograd, 1918), 366-369. Evidently the very essence of Christology is at stake here. On this problem, see also G. Glaiselle, *Justinien, sa doctrine christologique* (Lyon, 1905), 20-32, and particularly, A. Grillmeier, *Der Logos am Kreuz. Zur christologischen Symbolik der älteren Kreuzigungsdarstellung* (Munich, 1956).
[8]Besides Cyril himself, this aspect of the problem has been well remarked by Proclus of Constantinople (434-447), who in his *Tome to the Armenians* refutes the objection that the Word could not have suffered since his divinity is impassible. He obviously did not suffer "according to the divinity" (οὐδὲ γὰρ φάσκοντες αὐτὸν πεπονθέναι τῷ λόγῳ τῆς Θεότητος φαμὲν αὐτὸν πεπονθέναι) but according to the flesh. He, therefore, clearly defends Cyrillian theopaschism. Only his prudence and his perfectly justifiable reservations (accepted by Cyril himself) could lead M. Richard to believe that Proclus objected to theopaschism ("Proclus de Constantinople et le Théopaschisme," *RHE*, 38 [1942], 305-331). In fact, on that major point, Proclus is indubitably on the side of Cyril and not of Theodoret.
[9]See the analysis of John's system in C. Moeller, "Un représentant de la christologie néo-chalcédonienne au début du sixième siècle en Orient: Néphalius d'Alexandrie," *RHE*, 40 (1944-45), 122-128.

[10]The writings of Leontius of Jerusalem come within the framework of the anti-Origenist campaign in Constantinople that followed the Palestinian troubles. In his treatise entitled *Adversus Nestorianos* in Migne's edition, but which in fact was addressed against "those who say that there are two hypostases in Christ" (see *PG*, 86, col. 1399-1400), i.e., both the Nestorians and the Origenists, he names his adversary several times as being "an Egyptian" (Αἰγύπτιος, V, 7, 19, col. 1732 c, 1741 b). One might wonder whether the reference is not directly to Evagrius, monk of Skete.

[11]*Adv. Nest.* V, 28, *PG*, 86, col. 1748 d; cf. XII, 2, col. 1761 b; VII, 4, col. 1768 a.

[12]*Ὁ ἐπὶ Χριστοῦ λεγόμενος ἄνθρωπος μὴ καθ' ἡμᾶς ἰδιάζουσαν ἔχων καὶ διακεκριμένην πάσης ὁμοειδοῦς καὶ ἑτεροειδοῦς φύσεως τὴν ἑαυτοῦ ἀνθρωπείαν ὑπόστασιν, ἀλλὰ κοινὴν καὶ ἀδιαίρετον τῆς τε ἑαυτοῦ καὶ τῆς ὑπὲρ αὐτὸν φύσεως οὖσαν τοῦ Λόγου τὴν ὑπόστασιν, Adv. Nest.*, V, 29, col. 1749 bc.

[13]*Ibid.*, V, 30, col. 1749 d.

[14]*Ibid.*, col. 1749 d-1752 a.

[15]This understanding of "flesh" is obviously borrowed from St. Cyril; see in particular J. Liébart, *La doctrine christologique de St. Cyrille d'Alexandrie avant la querelle nestorienne* (Lille, France, 1951), 175-176.

[16]See especially R. Leys, *L'image de Dieu chez S. Grégoire de Nysse* (Brussels-Paris, 1951), 78-92.

[17]See *De Adoratione in Sp. et ver.* 2, *PG*, 68, col. 244-245.

[18]*Comm. on John*, 9, 1, ed. Pusey, II, 486.

[19]*Adv. Nest.* V, 28, col. 1748 d, 14; V, 29, col. 1749 c, 8; etc.

[20]See the relevant criticism of this interpretation of Cyril by W. J. Burghardt, *The Image of God in Man According to Cyril of Alexandria*, in the collection Studies in Christian Antiquity, 14 (Woodstock, Md., 1957), 108-111.

[21]*Adv. Nest.* V, 32, col. 1752 bc.

[22]*Ibid.*, I, 20, col. 1485 d, 2.

[23]*Ibid.*, col. 1485 b, 5.

[24]*Ibid.*, 1485 d, 6; see the correction made to the text by C. Moeller, "Textes 'monophysites' de Léonce de Jérusalem," *Ephemerides Theologicae Lovanienses*, 27 (1951), 474, n. 18.

[25]This last position is that of C. Moeller in the whole of his studies on neo-Chalcedonism. One should notice the trinitarian problem implicitly posed when the christological debates of the fifth and sixth centuries are analyzed. The same problem, linked with a different notion of hypostasis, came up later between East and West in relation to the *Filioque* problem.

[26]Cf. *supra*, pp. 67-68.

[27]See especially *Adv. Nest.*, VII. 6, col. 1768 d, bd.

[28]*Adv. Nest.* VII, 9, col. 1768 a.

[29]Leontius of Jerusalem strongly objected to the notion of "union according to the essence," and on this point one can reasonably detect in him a direct polemic against Leontius of Byzantium and Evagrian Origenism. (See, for instance, *Adv. Nest.* VII, 5, col. 1768 a, cd.)

[30]*Adv. Nest.* III, 8, col. 1629 a, c.

[31]*Adv. Nest.* I, 18, col. 1468 bc.

[32]The condemnation of the theologians of neo-Chalcedonism for the absence in them of the notion of "created grace" is, therefore, based on a misunderstanding; see an example of such a criticism in C. Moeller,

"Textes 'monophysites' de Léonce de Jerusalem," *Ephemerides Theologicae Lovanienses,* 27 (1951), 476; "Le Chalcédonisme," 708-717.

[33]The important work of Ephrem of Amida, Patriarch of Antioch (526-544), certainly had an influence on Justinian and on the decisions of the fifth council. His christological position, essentially similar to that of Leontius of Jerusalem, is known to us only through the detailed analysis of it given by Photius (*Bibliotheca,* 228-229; *PG,* 103, col. 957-1924; see J. Lebon's monograph, "Ephrem d'Amida," *Mélanges Ch. Moeller,* 1 [Louvain, 1914], 197-214).

[34]E. Schwartz, ed., "Drei dogmatische Schriften Justinians," *Abhandlungen der Münch. Akad. d. Wiss., NF,* 18 (Munich, 1939), 72-111 (*PG,* 86, col. 993-1035).

[35]See Severus objecting to any "number" in Christ, in J. Lebon, *Monophysitisme,* 259-260.

[36]*Ibid.,* 88.

[37]*Ibid.,* 86.

[38]*Ibid.,* 80-82.

[39]*Ibid.,* 82, line 20.

[40]J. Lebon, *Monophysitisme,* 345-368.

[41]*Ibid.,* 78, lines 5-10.

[42]C. Moeller, "Le Chalcédonisme," 661.

[43]Several recent Catholic historians formally restrict the authority of the fifth council to the limits within which it was approved by Pope Vigilius. As is known, approval was given after the end of the council, in a letter to Eutyches of Constantinople dated from Dec. 8, 553 (Mansi, IX, col. 413-417), and in the *Second Constitutum* of Feb. 23, 554 (*ibid.,* col. 455-488). These documents in fact limit themselves to a condemnation of the "Three Chapters" in the very terms used by the last three anathematisms of 553, but mention neither the council itself nor the previous anathematisms (see especially E. Amann, "Trois-Chapitres," *DTC,* XV, 1, col. 687-689). But can it be said, unless one adopts a modern Roman notion of the ecumenical council, that the council's decisions are valid in this restricted sense only? There is no consensus on this matter among all contemporary Catholic theologians (see in particular H. M. Diepen, *Les Trois-Chapitres au Concile de Chalcédoine* [Oesterhout, 1953], 119-123). For centuries, in any case, East and West agreed in recognizing that Vigilius had confirmed all the decisions of 553. Is it possible to go back on so unanimous an agreement of tradition? Besides, even if it were admitted that Vigilius consciously avoided confirming the council's decisions, with the exception of the last three anathematisms, the essence of the *theological* problem does not change. In the text concerning Theodoret, the Pope formally specifies that he condemns all that was written against Ephesus, against Cyril, and, he states more precisely, *against Cyril's Twelve Chapters.* The twelve chapters are, therefore, accepted by the Pope as a criterion of orthodoxy, and this is what "neo-Chalcedonism" consists of. Obviously the West's hand must have been forced to accept the decision, and its resistance played a positive role in the sense that it prevented the East from floundering into real Monophysitism. It is also evident that the fierce opposition of a part of the Western episcopate led the Popes, in particular Pelagius and St. Gregory the Great, to equivocate on the meaning of Vigilius' actions (see P. Galtier, "Le néochalcédonisme et l'Occident," *Gregorianum,* 40 [1959], 54-74). Yet one would wish that, at least today, the agree-

ment reached in 553 (by means one could have wished to be more peaceful) could remain beyond question.

[44]C. Moeller, "Le Chalcédonisme," 716.

[45]This attribution is today recognized as impossible (S. Rees, "The *De Sectis*, a treatise attributed to Leontius of Byzantium," *JTS*, 50 [1939], 346-556; M. Richard, "Le traité *De Sectis* et Léonce de Byzance," *RHE*, 35 [1939], 695-723; both these authors tend to attribute the treatise to Theodore of Raïthu).

[46]*PG*, 86, col. 1264 ab.

[47]*Adv. Incorrupticolas et Nest.*, *PG*, 86, col. 1373 b.

[48]See H. M. Diepen, *Aux Origines de l'anthropologie de S. Cyrille d'Alexandrie* (Bruges, 1957).

[49]*Dial de Trin.*, VI, *PG*, 75, col. 1064 a.

[50]The problem of Christ's ignorance as expressed by Cyril brought about lively arguments centered around the notion of "economy" (see in particular A. M. Dubarle, "L'ignorance du Christ chez S. Cyrille d'Alexandrie," *Ephemerides Theologicae Lovanienses*, 16 [1939], 111-120; J. Liébart, *La doctrine christologique de S. Cyrille d'Alexandrie avant la querelle nestorienne* [Lille, France, 1951], 88-111). Some Cyrillian expressions linked with this problem must be understood within the framework of the general ambiguity of his christological terminology. The human nature, for instance, is never designated as the Word's "proper nature" but as the nature which he "made his own," through the "economy" of salvation. Ignorance, a characteristic of mankind, is also therefore assumed in the framework of "economy." The desire to preserve the divine nature, which he does not distinguish from the Word's hypostasis, from any "passion" leads Cyril to use terms like "economy" or "appearance" when he speaks of the human consciousness of Christ. Chalcedonian theopaschism, distinguishing nature and hypostasis, goes beyond those ambiguities, since it can without danger speak of the "death" or the "ignorance" of the Word "according to the flesh" without any prejudice to the impassibility of the divine nature.

[51]*Julien d'Halicarnasse et sa controverse avec Sévère d'Antioche sur l'incorruptibilité du corps du Christ* (Louvain, 1924), 99.

[52]Cf. *supra*, pp. 79 and 86.

[53]"The sin of those who engendered us, viz. the sin of Adam and Eve, is not naturally (κατὰ φύσιν) mixed with our substance (οὐσία), as the evil and impious opinion of the Messalians, in other words the Manichees, claims, but because they (Adam and Eve) had lost the grace of immortality the judgment and the sentence reach down to us, when, following a natural disposition, we are born mortal insofar as [we are born] of mortal parents, but not sinners insofar [as we are of sinful parents]. For it is not true that sin is a nature (φύσις) and that it naturally passes from parents to their children," Severus as quoted by Draguet, *op. cit.*, pp. 130-131.

[54]See J. Meyendorff "Justinian, the Empire and the Church," *DOP*, 22 (1968), pp. 45-60.

NOTES TO CHAPTER 5

[1]On the similarities between Dionysius and Stephen Bar Soudaili, a Monophysite Evagrian Origenist, author of the *Book of Hierotheos,* an almost-contemporary work inspired by Dionysius, see A. Guillaumont, *Kephalaia Gnostica,* 302-332.

[2]See E. von Ivanka, "La Signification du Corpus Areopagiticum," *RSR,* 36 (1949), 5-24.

[3]This system has been depicted in a masterly way by R. Roques, *L'univers dionysien.* Structure *hiérarchique du monde selon le Pseudo-Denys* (Paris, 1954); for the properly theological side of Dionysian thought, see the introduction, by the same author, in the edition of *La hiérarchie céleste,* in the collection Sources Chrétiennes, 58 (Paris, 1958), xix-xcv; see also V. Lossky, "La théologie négative dans la doctrine de Denys l'Aréopagite," *RSTP,* 28 (1939), 204-221; *Théologie mystique de l'Église d'Orient* (Paris, 1944), 21-24; J. Vanneste, *Le mystère de Dieu. Essai sur la structure rationelle de la doctrine mystique du Pseudo-Denys L'Aréopagite* (Bruges, 1959).

[4]Ὁ τῇ φύσει ἀόρατος ὁρατὸς ταῖς ἐνεργείαις γίνεται ἔν τισι τοῖς περὶ αὐτὸν καθορώμενος, Hom. *VI on the Beatitudes, PG,* 44, col. 1269 a.

[5]*Letter 234, PG* 32, col. 869 b; see an excellent study of this doctrine of the Cappadocians in V. Lossky's *The Vision of God* (London, 1963), 61-74.

[6]*Divine Names,* I, 1, *PG,* 3, col. 588 b.

[7]Καὶ ἔστιν αὖθις ἡ θειοτάτη τοῦ Θεοῦ γνῶσις..., ὅταν ὁ νοῦς τῶν ὄντων πάντων ἀποστάς, ἔπειτα καὶ ἑαυτὸν ἀφείς, ἑνωθῇ ταῖς ὑπερφαέσιν ἀκτῖσιν, *Divine Names,* VIII, 3, col. 872 ab.

[8]*Theol. myst.,* col. 1001 a.

[9]*Hier. cel.* VII, 1-3, col. 205 b-209 d (ed. Sources Chrétiennes, 105-116).

[10]*Divine Names,* XIII, 3, col. 980 d-981.

[11]For this meaning of ἀναλογία in Dionysius, see V. Lossky, "La notion des analogies chez Denys le Pseudo-Aréopagite," *Archives d'histoire doctrinale et littéraire du moyen-âge,* 5 (1930), 279-309.

[12]*Divine Names,* II, 4, col. 640 d; πολλαπλασιάζεται, *ibid.,* 9, col. 649 b.

[13]*Divine Names,* II, 3, col. 640 b.

[14]A good commentary on this particular point is V. Lossky, *Vision of God* (London, 1963), 100-102.

[15]*Divine Names,* II, 5, col. 644 ab.

[16]*Divine Names,* I, 4, col. 592 bc.

[17]*Divine Names,* XIII, 3, col. 980 d-981 a.

[18]*Letter 7, to Polycarp,* 2, col. 1080 a.

[19]*Tu Solus Sanctus* (Paris, 1948), 115; see J. Vanneste, *Le Mystère de Dieu,* 7.

[20]J. Vanneste, "La théologie mystique du Pseudo-Denys," *Studia Patristica,* 5, *TU,* 80 (Berlin, 1962), pp. 403-407.

[21]*Ecclesiastical Hierarchy,* II, 3, 1, col. 397 bc.

[22]*Histoire de la Philosophie,* vol. 1, pt. 2 (Paris, 1948), 474-475.

[23]The most recent and complete analysis of the Neo-Platonist sources of Pseudo-Dionysius is to be found in R. Roques, *op. cit.,* 67ff.

[24]R. Roques, *op. cit.*, 135.

[25]*Celestial Hierarchy*, V, 6, col. 201 a; ed. Heil, in the collection Sources Chrétiennes, 58 (Paris, 1958), 104-105.

[26]Cyril of Jerusalem, *Catech. Hom.*, 23, 6, *PG*, 33, col. 1113 b; John Chrysostom, *Hom. on Genesis*, 4, 5, *PG*, 53-54, col. 44; *Apost. Const.*, VIII, 12, 27, ed. Funk, 504; cf. R. Roques, *Hier. Cel.*, *ed. cit.*, introd., lix.

[27]See in particular *Eccl. Hier.*, V, 2, col. 501 c.

[28]*Ibid.*

[29]*Cel. Hier.*, *ed. cit.*, 241 c, 127-128.

[30]This illogicality of Dionysius was corrected by one of his Byzantine commentators of the eleventh century, Nicetas Stethatos, who re-established the balance between the two hierarchies. According to Nicetas, the ecclesiastical hierarchy also possesses nine orders, divided into three triads: patriarchs-metropolitans-archbishops; bishops-priests-deacons; subdeacons-readers monks (ed. J. Darrouzès, in the collection Sources Chrétiennes, 81 [Paris, 1961], 327). Nicetas' imagination reaches absurdities, but the method is essentially identical with that of Dionysius.

[31]*Eccl. Hier.*, I, 3, col. 373 c.

[32]*Ibid.*, V, 7, col. 513 c, 516 a.

[33]See R. Roques, *L'univers dionysien*, 176, n. 1.

[34]*Eccl. Hier.*, III, 3, 1-2, col. 428 ac.

[35]*Eccl. Hier.*, III, 13, col. 444 c.

[36]*Eccl. Hier.*, III, 9, col. 437 c.

[37]*L'univers dionysien*, 267, 269. The references to Cyril of Jerusalem and to Theodore of Mopsuestia, where they speak of a "spiritual participation" in Christ in the Eucharist, and which R. Roques considers as respectable antecedents of Dionysius' sacramental theology, do not seem to justify the latter; the biblical opposition between πνεῦμα and σάρξ, which these authors apply in a legitimate way to the Eucharist, has nothing to do with the platonic opposition νοῦς-ὕλη, which dominates Dionysian thought.

[38]The best general outline given of this influence is to be found in the article "Denys" in *Dictionnaire de spiritualité*, III (1954), col. 287-430.

[39]*Cel. Hier.*, III, 1, col. 164 d.

[40]See the texts assembled by P. Chevallier, *Jésus-Christ dans les œuvres du Pseudo-Aréopagite* (Paris, 1951).

[41]*Eccl. Hier.*, I, 1, col. 372 a.

[42]*Eccl. Hier.*, IV, 4, col. 181 c.

[43]*Eccl. Hier.*, III, 2, col. 428, c; IV, 12, col. 484 c; V, 5, col. 512 c; V, 5, col. 505 b.

[44]See J. Vanneste, *Le Mystère de Dieu*, 34-35.

[45]*De la théarchie*, V., ed. J. Darrouzès, in the collection Sources Chrétiennes, 81 (Paris, 1961), 335-345.

[46]*Op. cit.*, 6.

[47]See S. L. Epifanovich, *Prepodobnyi Maksim Ispovednik i Vizantiiskoe Bogoslovie* (Kiev, 1915), 22.

[48]See, for example, G. Dix, *The Shape of the Liturgy*, 2d ed. (London, 1947), 304ff.

NOTES TO CHAPTER 6

NOTES TO CHAPTER 6

[1]Γέγονε ἄνθρωπος, ἵν'ἡμᾶς ἐν ἑαυτῷ θεοποιήσῃ, *Ad Adelphium*, 4, *PG*, 26, col. 1077 a; cf. *De Incarn.* 54, *PG*, 25, col. 192 b.

[2]Τὸ γὰρ ἀπρόσληπτον ἀθεράπευτον ὃ δὲ ἥνωται τῷ Θεῷ, τοῦτο καὶ σώζεται, *Ep.* 101, *Ad Cledonium*, *PG*, 37, col. 181 c-184 a.

[3]See W. J. Burghardt, *The Image of God in Man According to Cyril of Alexandria* (Woodstock, Md.), 25ff.

[4]*Commentary on John*, 1, 9, ed. Pusey, I, 111. The same relationship between "image," "participation," and "grace" is found in Athanasius (*De Incarn.*, 11, *PG*, 25, col. 113-116); according to St. Basil, the "natural state" before the fall was "the company of God and contact with him in love" (ἡ προσεδρεία τοῦ Θεοῦ καὶ ἡ διὰ τῆς ἀγάπης συνάφεια, *PG*, 31, col. 344 b).

[5]Ἡ φύσις τῆς ἀνθρωπότητος, ἐὰν καθ' ἑαυτὴν γυμνὴ ἀπομείνῃ καὶ μὴ λάβῃ τὴν μίξιν καὶ τὴν κοινωνίαν τῆς ἐπουρανίου φύσεως, οὐδὲν διωρθώσῃ, *Hom.* 32, 6, *PG*, 34, col. 737 b.

[6]*L'image de Dieu chez St. Grégoire de Nysse* (Brussels-Paris, 1951), 97-98.

[7]W. J. Burghardt, *op. cit.*, 38.

[8]*Glaphyra ad Gen. 1*, *PG*, 69, col. 24 c; see *Comm. on John*, 9, 1, ed. Pusey, II, 485. A great number of patristic references to that problem are to be found in S. Zarin, *Asketizm po pravoslavno-khristianskomu ucheniu* (St. Petersburg, 1907), 78-85.

[9]*Hom. quod Deus non est auctor malorum*, 6, *PG*, 31, col. 344 b. See the identical doctrine of St. Gregory of Nyssa in J. Gaïth, *La conception de la liberté chez Grégoire de Nysse* (Paris, 1953), 40-66.

[10]*In Rom.*, *PG*, 74, col. 789 ab.

[11]For other texts that show very well that this conception was general in the East, see J. Romanides. Τὸ προπατορικὸν ἁμάρτημα (Athens, 1957); J. Meyendorff, "'Εφ' ᾧ chez Cyrille d'Alexandrie et Theodoret," *Studia Patristica*, 4, *TU*, 79 (Berlin, 1961), 157-161; see also the articles that S. Lyonnet has dedicated to this subject in *Biblica*, 46 (1955), 436-456, and in *RSR*, 44 (1956), 63-84, and J. N. D. Kelly, *Early Christian Doctrines*, 2d ed. (London, 1960), 348-352.

[12]Cyril, *In Rom.*, *PG*, 74, col. 784 c.

[13]*De Incarn.* 20, *PG*, 25, col. 132 b (tr. Camelot [Paris, 1946], 245).

[14]*On the Eight Thoughts*, 7, *PG*, 40, col. 1273 bc (tr. L. Bouyer, *The Spirituality of the New Testament and the Fathers* [New York, 1960], 385).

[15]*De Oratione*, 34a, 35, 52, 84, *PG*, 79, col. 1173 d-1185 b. The treatise *On Prayer* was attributed, during the Byzantine Middle Ages, to St. Nilus of Sinai. Modern criticism restored it to Evagrius. It is still under the name of St. Nilus in Migne's *Patrologia*. A French translation by I. Hausherr was published in *Revue d'ascétique et de mystique*, 15 (1934), 34-93, 113-168.

[16]*Ibid.*, 85, col. 1185 b.

[17]*Ibid.*, 66, col. 1181 a.

[18]*Vision of God*, 88.

[19]*Centuries*, V, 61, 81, ed. A. Guillaumont, *PO*, 28, 1 (Paris, 1958), 203-211.

[20]See I. Hausherr, "Ignorance infinie," *OCP*, 2 (1936).

[21]Hermann Dörries, *Symeon von Mesopotamien. Die Überlieferung der Messalianischen "Makarios"-Schriften, TU,* 55, 1 (Leipzig, 1941); see also E. Klostermann and H. Berthold, *Neue Homilien des Makarius-Symeon, TU,* 72 (Berlin, 1961), with new texts and important analysis of manuscript tradition; H. Dörries, E. Klostermann, and M. Kroeger, *Die 50 geistlichen Homilien des Makarios* (Berlin, 1964), critical edition of the "50 homilies."

[22]See mainly W. Jaeger, *Two rediscovered works of ancient Christian literature: Gregory of Nyssa and Macarius* (Leiden, 1954); for full bibliography see J. Quasten, *Patrology,* III (Leiden, 1961); also J. Meyendorff "Messalianism or Anti-Messalianism? A fresh look at the 'Macarian' problem," *Kyriakon. Festschrift Johannes Quasten* (Münster Westf., 1972), pp. 585-590.

[23]*Orat. Catech.,* V, 10, ed. J. H. Srawley (Cambridge, 1903), 26-27.

[24]*Epistola magna,* ed. Jaeger, 238; a parallel passage in Gregory of Nyssa, *De Instituto Christiano,* ed. Jaeger, 46.

[25]This is a favorite expression of Diadochus of Photike (mid-fifth century), borrowed from Macarius; see *Chapters* 40, ed. des Places, in the collection Sources chrétiennes, 5 bis (Paris, 1955), 108.

[26]*Chapters,* 59, 61, ed. and Fr. tr. des Places, 111-121.

[27]*Treatises,* Eng. tr. A. J. Wensinck, *Verhandelingen der Koninklijke Akademie van Wetenschappen,* Nieuwe Reeks, 23, 1 (Amsterdam, 1923), 174. Isaac was the Nestorian Bishop of Nineveh in the seventh century. His mystical treatises, written in Syriac, translated into Greek in the ninth century, were widely circulated in the Byzantine world.

[28]*Scala,* XXVII, *PG,* 88, col. 1112 c.

[29]*Hom.* I, 2, ed. H. Dörries, 2 (*PG,* 34, col. 451 ab; tr. Bouyer, *op. cit.,* 448).

[30]See on that subject I. Popov, "Ideia obozheniia v drevne-vostochnoi tserkvi," *Voprosi filosofii i psikhologii,* 97 (1909), 185.

[31]*Hom.* II, 5, ed. H. Dörries, 19-20 (*PG,* 34, col. 468 ab).

NOTES TO CHAPTER 7

[1]The most complete and best-documented study on Maximus remains that of S. L. Epifanovich, *Prepodobnyi Maksim Ispovednik i vizantiiskoe bogoslovie* (Kiev, 1915). The more recent works of H. Urs von Balthasar, I. Hausherr, P. Sherwood, and L. Thunberg are quoted below.

[2]The study of Maximus within the framework of Byzantine tradition— which was really his own—constitutes the great merit of Epifanovich's book. Cf., on this matter, the pertinent remarks made by P. Sherwood, who, without knowing the works of the Russian theologian, arrived at similar conclusions, and gives a very just criticism of the recent works that ignore that perspective ("Survey of recent work on St. Maximus the Confessor," *Traditio,* 20 [1964], 428-437).

[3]*Amb., PG,* 91, col. 1217 cd.

[4]Περὶ Θεὸν γὰρ, ἀλλ' οὐ Θεὸς ἡ ἀπειρία, ὅστις καὶ ταύτης ἀσυγκρίτως ὑπέρκειται, *Amb., PG,* 91, col. 1220 c.

[5]Οὐ ταὐτὸν κτίστης καὶ κτίσις, *ibid.,* col. 1221 a; see also *De Char.* IV, 3-5, *PG,* 90, col. 1048 cd.

[6]*De Char.*, IV, 6, *PG*, 90, col. 1049 a; tr. P. Sherwood, in Ancient Christian Writers, 21 (Westminster, Md., and London, 1955).

[7]Gregory wrote that "we are a part of God (μοῖρα Θεοῦ) and we come from above" (*Or.* 14, 7, *PG*, 35, col. 865 b).

[8]*Amb.*, col. 1077 c; cf. 1081 c.

[9]See Lars Thunberg, *Microcosm and Mediator: The Theological Anthropology of Maximus the Confessor* (Lund, 1965), 80-81.

[10]*Amb.*, col. 1080 ab.

[11]*Ad. Thal.*, 32, *PG*, 90, col. 372 c.

[12]*Amb.*, col. 1081 b.

[13]See *Ad Thal.* 60, *PG*, col. 621 a; the final λόγος of the beings is evidently realized in the Incarnate Word.

[14]*Liturgie cosmique* (Paris, 1947), 98.

[15]Πάσης φύσεως ὅρος ὁ τῆς οὐσιώδους αὐτῆς ἐνεργείας καθέστηκε λόγος, *Amb.*, 1057 b.

[16]*Amb.*, *PG*, 91, col. 1237 b.

[17]*Cap. gnost.* I, 10, *PG*, 91, col. 1085 d-1088 a.

[18]*De Char.*, III, 25, *PG*, 91, col. 1024 bc.

[19]See L. Thunberg, *op. cit.*, 120-140.

[20]*PG*, 91, col. 324 d; see also *supra* p. 115.

[21]*Ibid.*, col. 304 d.

[22]*Ibid.*, col. 324 d.

[23]*Amb.*, col. 1353 c.

[24]*Myst.* 6, *PG*, 685 ac; Fr. tr., *Irénikon*, 14 (1937), 283-284; man as "microcosm" in Maximus is the main theme in the recent monograph by L. Thunberg, *op. cit.*

[25]*Amb.*, col. 1248 a-1249 b.

[26]*Ibid.*, col. 1092 c.

[27]*Ibid.*, col. 1305 bc.

[28]The "mode of existence" of Adam and Eve before the fall excluded, according to Maximus, sexual relations as such, which are a consequence of sin (see *Quaest. et dubia*, 3, *PG*, 90, col. 788 b; *PG*, 91, col. 1305 c, 1309 a, 1401 b): if man had remained in his original innocence, God would have provided him with another way of reproducing himself. As for the distinction between man and woman, manifestly established before the fall, it only exists—if one is to believe some very obscure passages of Maximus (in partic. *Amb.*, col. 1305 c)—in *pre-vision* of sin. This conception, very close to that of St. Gregory of Nyssa, seems to imagine for fallen mankind only one way of overcoming sexuality and restoring God's original plan for human nature: monastic celibacy. For celibacy alone can make life in Christ fully accessible, since there is in him "neither male nor female." If one excludes, however, Maximus' speculations about the unreal situation "if the fall had not happened," and if one holds on to the philosophical system that is at the basis of his thought—the overcoming in man of the *dualities* inherent in created nature—the Pauline doctrine of the single marriage in the image of Christ and the Church could have received in the light of Maximus' thought an exceptional relief. The absence in Maximus and in patristic tradition generally of a positive theology of marriage is probably due both to their monastic training and to their instinctive opposition to the sexual cults that characterized ancient culture. On the psychological and practical level, Maximus was on this point very close to the Augustinian position on sin and concupiscence, but one would

seek in vain in him for a detailed elaboration or a metaphysical foundation of that attitude.

²⁹*Amb.*, col. 1305-1308.
³⁰*De Charit.* IV, 44, 45, *PG,* 90, col. 1057 bc.
³¹*Amb.*, col. 1092 d.
³²Τὸ κακὸν τῆς πρὸς τὸ τέλος τῶν ἐγκειμένων τῇ φύσει δυνάμεων ἐνεργείας ἐστὶν ἔλλειψις, καὶ ἄλλο καθάπαξ οὐδέν, *Ad Thalas.*, Prologue, *PG,* 90, col. 253 ab.
³³*Amb.*, col. 1156 c.
³⁴*Ad Thalas.*, 61, *PG,* 90, col. 628 ac.
³⁵*Ibid.*, col. 628 cd.
³⁶Cf. *supra,* p. 88.
³⁷See also *Amb.*, col. 1348 a; Christ's virginal birth is the proof that he takes on our nature, "except for sin" (*Amb.*, 1309 a, 1317 a; *Ad Thalas.*, 61, col. 633 d).
³⁸*Ep.* 2, *PG,* 91, col. 396 d-397 b; see *Quaest. ad Thal., PG,* 90, col. 256 b.
³⁹*Ep.* 10, col. 449 b.
⁴⁰*Amb.*, col. 1308 d, 1312 a.
⁴¹See *Amb.*, col. 1308 d-1309 d.
⁴²*Amb.*, 1088 c.
⁴³On this controversy, the most recent work is that of W. Elert, *Der Ausgang der altkirchlichen Christologie: Eine Untersuchung über Theodore von Pharan und seine Zeit als Einführung in die alte Dogmengeschichte* (Berlin, 1957).
⁴⁴*Ep.* 234, *PG,* 32, col. 869 ab.
⁴⁵*De beat.* VI, *PG,* 44, col. 1269 a.
⁴⁶"Quod non sint tres dii," ed. W. Jaeger, *Gregorii Nysseni Opera,* vol. 3, pt. 1 (Leiden, 1958), 37-57.
⁴⁷P. Sherwood, "The Earlier Ambigua of Saint Maximus," *Studia Anselmiana,* 36 (Rome, 1955), 164-177.
⁴⁸G. L. Prestige, *God in Patristic Thought* (London, 1952), 278-279.
⁴⁹*Opusc. theol. et pol., PG,* 91, col. 276 ab.
⁵⁰*Amb.*, col. 1052 b.
⁵¹*De Incar. et contra Ar.*, 21, *PG,* 26, 1021 b.
⁵²Apollinarius, frag. 50, *Doctrina Patrum* 41, ed. Diekamp, 232; for Nestorius, the unity of the person of Christ was based on the one will of the Logos and of the *homo assumptus* (cf. Maximus, *Opusc. theol. et pol., PG,* 91, col. 192 c); on Maximus' Christology, see Lars Thunberg, *op. cit.*, 41-50.
⁵³On the true meaning of "inhabitation" κατ᾽ εὐδοκίαν in Theodore of Mopsuestia, see F. A. Sullivan, *The Christology of Theodore of Mopsuestia* (Rome, 1956), 244-247, and R. A. Norris, *Manhood and Christ. A Study in the Christology of Theodore of Mopsuestia* (Oxford, 1963), 218-220.
⁵⁴*Opusc. theol. et pol., PG,* 91, col. 77 d-80 a.
⁵⁵*Expositio orat. dom., PG,* 90, col. 877 d.
⁵⁶*Opusc.*, col. 53 c.
⁵⁷*Opusc.*, col. 192 c; cf. col. 40-45, 152 c, 268 b; *Disp. cum Pyrrho,* col. 329 d, 313 b.
⁵⁸*Ep.* 2, *PG,* 91, col. 396 c.
⁵⁹In his sixth letter Maximus, speaking of the divine characteristics,

defines them as τὰ μὲν διὰ τὴν οὐσίαν, τὰ δὲ διὰ τὴν κίνησιν, ἤτοι γνώμην καὶ διάθεσιν (col. 428 d).

[60]*Amb.*, col. 1116 b.

[61]*Amb.*, 1073 c.

[62]Φύσει ἀγαθὸς μόνος ὁ Θεὸς καὶ γνώμῃ ἀγαθὸς μόνος ὁ θεομίμητος, *De Charit.* IV, 90, col. 1069 c.

[63]*Ad Thal.*, col. 280 cd.

[64]Ἐν τῷ θελήματι ἡμῶν ἐστι λοιπὸν ἡ σωτηρία ἡμῶν, *Liber Asceticus*, col. 953 b.

[65]*De or. dom.*, col. 893 b.

[66]Γνωμικῶς, οὐ φυσικῶς, *ibid.*, col. 905 a.

[67]*Disp. cum Pyrrho*, col. 308 c.

[68]See *Op. theol. et pol.*, col. 192 a.

[69]Ἐπὶ τοῦ ἀνθρωπίνου τοῦ Κυρίου οὐ ψιλῶς καθ' ἡμᾶς ὑποστάντος, ἀλλὰ θεϊκῶς..., γνώμῃ λέγεσθαι οὐ δύναται, *Disp. cum Pyrrho*, col. 308 d.

[70]*De Char.* III, 80, col. 1041 b.

[71]*De or. dom.*, col. 901 c, 905 a.

[72]Οὐ πρὸς τὸ ἔξωθεν προσφάτως ἐπεισαγαγεῖν τὰς ἀρετάς, ἔγκειται γὰρ ἡμῖν ἐκ δημιουργίας, *Disp. cum Pyrrho*, col. 309 c.

[73]*Liber Asceticus*, col. 953 b.

[74]See mainly M. Viller, "Aux sources de la spiritualité de St. Maxime: les œuvres d'Évagre le Pontique," *Revue d'ascétique et de mystique*, 11 (1930), 154-184, 239-268, 331-336. The modern editors of the *Centuries on Charity* point out parallels all along Maximus' text: see in particular the editions of J. Pégon in the collection Sources Chrétiennes, 9 (Paris, 1943), and of P. Sherwood in Ancient Christian Writers, 21 (Westminster, Md., and London, 1955).

[75]Τῇ ἐκστάσει τῶν φυσικῶς ἐπ' αὐτῆς καὶ ὄντων καὶ νοουμένων, διὰ τὴν ἐκνικήσασαν αὐτὴν χάριν τοῦ Πνεύματος, *Amb.*, col. 1076 bc; on that aspect of Maximus' thought, in which the Confessor separates himself clearly from Evagrius, see I. Hausherr, "Ignorance infinie," *OCP*, 2 (1936), 351-362.

[76]*De char.* I, 100, col. 984 a; cf. II, 27, col. 992 cd.

[77]*Ibid.*, I, 96, col. 981 c.

[78]On Maximus' ascetical and spiritual doctrine, see mainly S. L. Epifanovich, *op. cit.*, 83-110; I. H. Dalmais, "La doctrine ascétique de St. Maxime le Confesseur," *Irénikon*, 26 (1953), 17-39; I. Hausherr, *Philautie: De la tendresse pour soi à la charité selon St. Maxime le Confesseur*, OCA, 137 (Rome, 1952); and, above all, W. Völker, *Maximus Confessor als Meister des geistlichen Lebens* (Wiesbaden, 1965).

NOTES TO CHAPTER 8

[1]*Dial.*, 5, PG, 94, col. 593 a; 10, col. 569.

[2]*Dial.*, 66, col. 668 a-669 b.

[3]*Dial.*, 66, col. 669 b; *De duabus vol.*, PG, 95, col. 113 a.

[4]*De fide orth.*, III, 3, col. 992 ab; 16, col. 1065 a.

[5]*Ibid.*, III, 11, col. 1021 d-1024 a.

[6]*Ibid.*, III, 7, col. 1012 b; cf. 11, col. 1024 c-1025 b; *De natura composita*, *PG*, 95, col. 117 a.

[7]*De recta sent.*, col. 1460 c.

[8]*De haer.*, 83, col. 741 a.

[9]See in particular *De fide orth.*, III, 3, col. 992 c.

[10]*Dial.*, col. 616 b.

[11]*Dial.*, col. 616 ab.

[12]Cf. *supra*, pp. 62-63.

[13]*Dial.*, col. 668 a; it is self-evident that John Damascene refutes the Evagrian Christology as it was condemned in 553 (*De fide orth.*, IV, 6, col. 1112 a-113 b), but it is doubtful whether he recognized the Evagrian background of Leontius.

[14]*De fide orth.*, III, 27, col. 1097 b.

[15]See his criticism of images in *De recta sent.*, *PG*, 94 col. 1465 bc.

[16]*De fide orth.*, IV, 18, col. 1188 b; cf. Justinian, *supra*.

[17]Keetie Rozemond, *La christologie de Saint Jean Damascène* (Ettal, 1959), 26.

[18]*De fide orth.*, III, 2, col. 988 a.

[19]*Hom. in transf.*, 4, *PG*, 96, col. 552 c (cf. Fr. tr. in K. Rozemond, *op. cit.*, 97).

[20]*Adversus Nest.*, *PG*, 95, col. 189 c.

[21]*De fide orth.*, IV, 7, col. 1113 c.

[22]*Ibid.*, III, 12, col. 1029 c.

[23]*De fide orth.*, III, 9, col. 1017 ab.

[24]Cf. *supra*, p. 76.

[26]*De fide orth.*, III, 7, col. 1009 ab.

[26]*De fide orth.*, III, 11, col. 1024 a.

[27]*Adv. Nest.*, *PG*, 95, col. 200 b.

[28]Τὴν δὲ φύσιν τοῦ Λόγου σεσαρκῶσθαι λέγοντες (οὐκ) ἐπὶ τὸν Πατέρα καὶ τὸ Πνεῦμα τὴν σάρκωσιν ἀναφέρομεν, we have corrected here the manifestly corrupt text given in Migne, by adding the negation οὐκ.

[29]*De recta sententia*, *PG*, 94, col. 1464 bc.

[30]*De fide orth.* II, 12, col. 924 a.

[31]'Αθάνατος οὐ φύσει, ἀλλὰ χάριτι, *ibid.*, II, 3, col. 868 b.

[32]*De duabus vol.*, *PG*, 95, col. 145 a; the patristic idea of man's superiority over the angels is particularly brought out by Kiprian Kern, *Anthropologiia sv. Grigoriia Palamy* (Paris, 1950).

[33]*De duabus vol.*, col. 194 b.

[34]*Ibid.*, col. 149 bc.

[35]*De fide orth.* II, col. 924 a.

[36]*De duabus vol.*, col. 161 b.

[37]*De fide orth.*, II, 12, col. 924 a.

[38]See, for example, *De duabus vol.*, col. 180 b.

[39]*Ibid.*

[40]*De fide orth.* II, 25, col. 956-957.

[41]*Ibid.*, 29, col. 977, b; cf. IV, 14, col. 1041 c.

[42]*Ibid.*, III, 1, col. 981 a.

[43]*De fide orth.*, II, 30, col. 976 b.

[44]*Ibid.*, III, 1, col. 984 ac.

[45]*Ibid.*, III, 6, col. 1005 b; cf. Greg. Naz., *Ep. 101, ad Cledonium, PG,* 37, col. 181 c-184 a.

[46]*Ibid.*, III, 18, col. 1072 c.

[47]*Ibid.*, I, 11, col. 84 b.

[48]*Ibid.*, II, 22, col. 948 a.

[49]*In dorm.*, I, 3, *PG,* 96, col. 704 c.

[50]Saturday Vespers, tone 1, *Apostikha.*

[51]*De fide orth.*, III, 20, col. 1081 ab.

[52]*De haer.*, 84, col. 156 a.

[53]*De fide orth.*, IV, 1, col. 1101 a.

[54]*Ibid.*, IV, 1, col. 1101 d.

[55]Εἷς γάρ ἐστι... θέλων καὶ ἐνεργῶν, *ibid.*, III, 15, col. 1052 b; cf. III, 18, col. 1076 d.

[56]*De duabus vol.*, *PG,* 95, col. 176 cd.

[57]*De fide orth.*, III, 21, col. 1084 b-1085 a.

[58]Τὴν τῶν ἀνθρώπων θεογνωσίαν τε καὶ σωτηρίαν οἰκείαν προκοπὴν ποιούμενος καὶ οἰκειούμενος πανταχοῦ τὸ ἡμέτερον, *ibid.,* III, 22, col. 1088 a.

[59]Cf. *supra*, p. 87.

[60]*Ibid.*, III, 24, col. 1089 cd.

[61]*Ibid.*, III, 15, col. 1057 bc.

[62]*De recta sent.*, col. 1461 c; cf. *De fide orth.*, III, 4, col. 1000 a; III, 7, col. 1012 c; IV, 18, col. 1184 cd.

[63]*In transf.*, 2, *PG,* 96, col. 548 c-549 a.

[64]*Ibid.*, 12, col. 564 bc; see K. Rozemond, *op. cit.*, 48.

[65]See for instance Palamas, *Triades pour la défense des saints hésychastes,* I, 3, 38, ed. J. Meyendorff, vol. 1, in Spicilegium Sacrum Lovaniense, 30 (Louvain, 1959), 190-193; see also my *Introduction à l'étude de Grégoire Palamas* (Paris, 1959), 223-256 (Eng. tr. [London, 1964], 157-184).

NOTES TO CHAPTER 9

[1]It should be noted, however, that the letters to Pope Gregory II, which attributed to Leo a claim to "priesthood," have recently been shown to be apocryphal (J. Gouillard "Aux origines de l'iconoclasme," *Travaux et Mémoires,* 3 [Paris, 1968], pp. 243-307).

[2]The historical origins of iconoclasm are discussed at length by L. Bréhier, *La querelle des images* (Paris, 1904); G. Ostrogorsky, *Studien zur Geschichte des byzantinischen Bilderstreites* (Breslau, 1929); G. B. Ladner, "Origin and Significance of the Byzantine Iconoclastic Controversy," *Medieval Studies,* 2 (1940), 127-149; A. Grabar, *L'iconoclasme byzantin: Dossier Archéologique* (Paris, 1957); for a recent and sympathetic view, see S. Gero, *Byzantine Iconoclasm During the Reign of Leo III* (CSCO, 346, *Subsidia* 41), Louvain, 1973.

[3]G. Florovsky, "Origen, Eusebius, and the iconoclastic controversy," *Church History,* 19 (1950), 77-96; P. J. Alexander, *The Patriarch Nicephorus* (Oxford, 1958), 9.

[4]See C. Clerc, *Les théories relatives au culte des images chez les auteurs*

grecs du II⁰ siècle après Jésus-Christ (Paris, 1915); also P. J. Alexander, *Patriarch Nicephorus*, 24-30.

[5]*True Discourse*, II, 3, 36, ed. C. Glockner, *Kleine Texte... herausgegeben von H. Lietzmann*, III (Bonn, 1924), III, 42, 18.

[6]*Against the Christians*, fragment 77, ed. A. Harnack, in *Abhandlungen der Königliche Preussische Akademie der Wiss.* (Berlin, 1916), 93.

[7]J. Alexander, *op. cit.*, 33.

[8]Ernst Kitzinger, "The cult of images in the age before iconoclasm," *DOP*, 8 (1954), 83-150.

[9]On the patristic anthologies used by the iconoclastic councils of 754 and 815, see M. V. Anastos, "The argument for iconoclasm as presented by the iconoclastic council of 754," *Late Classical and Medieval Studies in Honor of A. M. Friend, Jr.* (Princeton, 1955), 177-188; "The ethical theory of images formulated by the iconoclasts in 754 and 815," *DOP*, 8 (1954), 153-160; P. J. Alexander, "The iconoclastic Council of St. Sophia (815) and its definition," *DOP*, 7 (1953), 37-66.

[10]Text among the works of the Patriarch Nicephorus, the author of a *Contra Eusebium* in defense of images; ed. J. B. Pitra, *Spicilegium Solesmense*, I (Paris, 1852; anastatic reprinting, Graz, 1962), 383-386.

[11]See the analysis of the letter in G. Florovsky, *op. cit.*, 85-86.

[12]*Ed. cit.*, 384.

[13]Mansi, XI, col. 977-980.

[14]*De haeresibus et synodis*, PG, 98, col. 80 a.

[15]*Letter to John of Synada*, PG, 98, col. 157 bc.

[16]*Letter to Thomas of Claudiopolis*, PG, 98, col. 173 b; on these christological arguments, which appeared from the beginning of the controversy, see G. Ostrogorsky, "Soedinenie voprosa o sv. ikonakh s khristologicheskoi dogmatikoi," *Seminarium Kondakovianum*, 1 (Prague, 1927), 35-48.

[17]*Or.* I, PG, 94, col. 1236 c.

[18]*Or.* III, col. 1320 b.

[19]*Or.* I, col. 1245 a.

[20]P. J. Alexander, *Nicephorus*, 48.

[21]Mansi, XIII, col. 333 e-336 d; for a recent analysis of the decisions of 754, see M. Anastos, "The arguments for iconoclasm," 177-188.

[22]Mansi, XIII, col. 252 ab; 256 ab.

[23]*Ibid.*, col. 257 ab; the position of the soul of Christ in the Christology of the council of 754 is strictly Origenistic; cf. M. Harl, *Origène et la fonction révélatrice du Verbe Incarné* (Paris, 1958), 116-118.

[24]*Ibid.*, col. 336 c.

[25]*Chronique de Michel le Syrien*, ed. and tr. J. B. Chabot, vol. 2 (Paris, 1901), 521.

[26]('Η εἰκὼν) ταὐτὸν τῷ πρωτοτύπῳ ἐστί, Basil, *Ep.* 38, 8, *PG*, 42, col. 340 b.

[27]See the two long digressions on the different sorts of "images" in St. John Damascene, *Oratio* I, col. 1240-44; *Oratio* III, col. 1337 a-1348 b.

[28]*Cel. Hier.*, PG, 3, col. 124 a; the Eucharist as an "image" for the iconoclasts, in Mansi, XIII, col. 261 d-264 c; orthodox opposition to that notion, in Theodore the Studite, *Antirrh.*, PG, 99, col. 340 ac; Nicephorus, *Antirrh.* II, PG, 100, col. 336 b-337 a; *Contra Eusebium*, ed. Pitra, *Spic. olesm.*, I, 440-442.

[29]Apart from the article by G. Florovsky quoted above, there is no ʰudy on Origenist thought during the iconoclastic period; the relationships

are, however, quite evident; cf., for instance, H. Crouzel, *Théologie de l'image de Dieu chez Origène* (Paris, 1956), and M. Harl, *op. cit.*, 104-120, 139-160, etc.

[30]Theodore the Studite, *Letter to Athanasius*, II, 85, *PG*, 99, col. 1329 a.

[31]Council of Nicaea, *Definition*, Mansi, XIII, col. 377 d.

[32]Council of Nicaea, *ibid.*; John of Damascus, *Or.*, III, col. 1348 d-1359 b; Theodore the Studite, *Letters*, II, 167, col. 1532 a; 292, col. 1640 ab; 217, col. 1656 cd; Nicephorus, *Antirrh.*, III, *PG*, 100, col. 392 c.

[33]"En atteignant l'image, la proskynèse ne l'atteint pas pour elle-même, pour sa substance, mais pour la seule similitude qu'elle a avec le prototype, et par suite elle est et elle est dite σχετική. En atteignant le Christ lui-même, elle l'atteint pour lui-même pour sa substance divine et alors elle est et elle est dite λατρευτική," V. Grumel, "L'iconologie de Théodore Studite," dans *Échos d'Orient*, 20 (1921), 265.

[34]Mansi, XXXII, col. 103; cf. V. Grumel, *op. cit.*, pp. 265-268.

[35]*Or.* III, col. 1332 b.

[36]Theodore, *Antirrh.* III, *PG*, 99, col. 417 bc. The outcome is that it is impossible to represent God the Father himself; symbolic representations of God the Father appeared only late in Byzantine art.

[37]*Refut. poem. iconom.*, *PG*, 99, col. 457 d.

[38]*To John of Synada, PG*, 98, col. 157 bc; cf. John of Damascus, *Or.* III, col. 1320 b; 1332 c, etc.

[39]Ὁ ἀόρατος ὁρᾶται, Theodore, *Antirrh.* I, *PG*, 99, col. 332 a.

[40]*Antirrh.* I, *PG*, 99, col. 332 d-333 a.

[41]*Antirrh.* III, *ibid.*, col. 396 c-397 a.

[42]*Ibid.*, col. 409 c.

[43]*Antirrh.* I, *PG*, 100, col. 272 b.

[44]*Supra*, p. 87.

[45]*Antirrh.* I, col. 328 bd.

[46]Theodore Studite, *Antirrh.* III, *PG*, 99, col. 396 b.

[47]*Ibid.*, col. 409 b.

[48]*Ibid.*, col. 408 a.

[49]Cf. Theodore, *Problemata*, col. 477 b; *Antirrh.* III, col. 417 ac; *Letter to dispersed brothers*, II, 8, col. 1132 d.

[50]*Antirrh.* I, *PG*, 100, col. 628 a.

[51]*Ibid.*, col. 268 b.

[52]*Antirrh.* I, *PG*, 99, col. 344 ab.

[53]*Letters*, II, 169, col. 1532 d-1533 a.

[54]*Antirrh.* I, col. 252 b; cf. same evasion of theopaschism in col. 313 d.

[55]*Ibid.*, col. 285 a, 301 d, 305 a.

[56]*Ibid.*, col. 317 b.

[57]*Antirrh.* III, col. 400 d-401 a.

[58]*Ibid.*, col. 405 a.

[59]*Adv. Iconomachos Capita* VII, *PG*, 99, col. 489 a.

[60]*Letter to Naucratius*, II, 67, col. 1296 ab; cf. *Antirrh.* III, col. 420 d.

[61]Nicephorus, *Contra Eusebium*, ed. Pitra, *Spicilegium Solesmense*, I, 401.

[62]*Ibid.*, 424, 430, 433, 446-447.

[63]*Ibid.*, 415.

[64]*Or.* III, *PG*, 94, col. 1325 a.

[65]*Ibid.*, col. 1348 ab.

[66]*Antirrh.* II, *PG*, 99, col. 385 b.

[67]Cf. also "Becoming the Body of God, the Body of Christ does not cease to be a body," Nicephorus, *Antirrh.*, I, *PG*, 100, col. 272 d.

[68]*Antirrh.* III, *PG*, 99, col. 416 c.

[69]*Contra Eusebium, ed. cit.*, 440, 447 d.

[70]See about this matter the interesting observations of L. Ouspensky, "The problem of the iconostasis," in *St. Vladimir's Seminary Quarterly*, 8 (1964), 186-218.

[71]Θεῖόν τι χρῆμα ὑπάρχειν τὸ τῆς εἰκονοουργίας εἶδος, *Antirrh.* III, col. 420 a.

[72]*Or.* II, *PG*, 94, col. 1274 c; cf. *supra*, p. 179.

[73]*Ibid.*, col. 1296 a.

[74]*Or.* I, col. 1245 b.

[75]*Antirrh.* II, col. 34 d.

[76]*Antirrh.* III, col. 421 a; cf. col. 428 b; *Letter to Plato Studite*, col. 504 b, c (the authenticity of this letter is, however, doubted by N. Grossu in his important monograph on Theodore, *Prepodobnyi Theodor Studit*, [Kiev, 1907], 192); *Letter to Nicetas Spatharius*, col. 1504 b.

[77]E. Troubetzskoi, *Umozrenie v kraskakh* (Moscow, 1915-1916); Eng. tr. *Icons: Theology in Colors* (Crestwood, N. Y., 1974).

NOTES TO CHAPTER 10

[1]Cf. Basil Krivochein, *Syméon le Nouveau Théologien, Catéchèses*, 1, in the collection Sources Chrétiennes, 96, Introduction (Paris, 1964), 39-40. The critical work and the recent publication of the texts of Symeon by Archbishop Basil Krivochein makes possible today a general appreciation of Symeon's work.

[2]*Ibid.*, III, Sources Chrétiennes, 113 (Paris, 1965), 176-179. The editor notes that Symeon, in this passage, paraphrases Macarius, who also speaks of "those who consider as impossible the coming of the Spirit into man," *Epist. Magna*, ed. Jaeger, *Two rediscovered works*, 298.

[3] Acts of the trial of Italos in T. Uspensky, ed., in *Zapiski Russkago Arkheologicheskago Instituta v Konstantinople*, 2 (1897); about John Italos, see mainly T. Uspensky *Ocherki po istorii vizantiiskoi obrazovannosti* (St. Petersburg, 1891), 146-190; P. E. Stephanou, *Jean Italos, philosophe et humaniste*, in *OCA*, 134 (Rome, 1949); Joannou, *Christliche Metaphysik in Byzanz. Die Illuminationslehre des Michael Psellos und Joannes Italos*, in Studia Patristica et Byzantina, 3 (Ettal, 1956).

[4]Thanksgiving service introduced into the liturgy of the first Sunday in Lent ("Orthodoxy Sunday") on the occasion of the final liquidation of iconoclasm in 843. The service includes the solemn commemoration of the champions of orthodoxy, as well as anathemas against the heretics. The service has been regularly brought up to date after its composition in the ninth century. New critical edition and French translation, by J. Gouillard in *Travaux et mémoires*, 2 (Paris, 1967).

[5]The first of the anathemas of the *Synodikon* relating to Italos mentions those who introduce "novelties" in Christology and who "try to use dialectically the terms *nature* (φύσις) and *state* (θέσις)," ed. J. Gouillard,

56-57. This vague reference indicates that the christological problems were being discussed in Italos' circle.

[6]About Nilus, see Anna Comnena, *Alexiad*, X, 1, ed. B. Leib, Coll. Budé, II (Paris, 1943), 187-188; Uspensky, *Ocherki*, 189-192; J. Gouillard, *op. cit.*, 60-61, 202-206, 300-303 (new sources and new evidence).

[7]About Eustratius, see mainly the studies of P. Joannou, "Eustrate de Nicée, trois pièces de son procès," in *REB*, 10 (1952), 24-34; "Der Nominalismus und die menschliche Psychologie Christi: Das Semeoma gegen Eustratios von Nikaia (1117)," in *Byzantinische Zeitschrift*, 47 (1954), 369-378; cf. J. Gouillard, *op. cit.*, 68-71, 206-210.

[8]Critical edition by P. Joannou in *Byzantinische Zeitschrift*, 47 (1954), 374-378; Eustratius' treatise against the Monophysites, published in A. Demetrakopoulos, Ἐκκλησιαστικὴ Βιβλιοθήκη, (Leipzig, 1866, Repr. Hildersheim, 1965), 160-198, contains none of the condemned propositions.

[9]Ed. Joannou, 376. The fifth council spoke of the distinction of the natures τῇ θεωρίᾳ μόνῃ (c. 7); the distinction κατ᾽ ἐπίνοιαν was, however, in Justinian's confession.

[10]Soterichos, *Dialogue, PG*, 140, col. 141 a; Soterichos' *Dialogue*, as well as the Acts of both councils, are part of Book 24 of the *Thesaurus orthodoxae fidei* by Nicetas Choniates, part of which is published in Migne. A critical edition of the Acts of the second council can also be found in I. Sakkelion, Πατμιακὴ Βιβλιοθήκη (Athens, 1890), 316-328. The Acts contain a patristic anthology used during the councils against Soterichos, as well as the final condemnation. The theological argument which inspired the Synod is expressed by Nicholas of Methone, in a detailed treatise against Soterichos, ed. Demetrakopoulos, *op. cit.*, 321-359. The best theological analysis of the sources is that of the hieromonk Paul (Cheremukhin), "Konstantinopol'sky Sobor 1157 g.: Nikolai episkop Mefonsky," in *Bogoslovskie Trudy*, 1 (Moscow, 1960), 87-109; cf. also T. Uspensky, *Ocherki*, 214-224; J. Gouillard, *op. cit.*, 72-74, 210-215.

[11]Nicholas of Methone, *ed. cit.*, 326.

[12]Σὺ γὰρ ὁ προσφέρων καὶ προσφερόμενος καὶ προσδεχόμενος καὶ διαδιδόμενος.

[13]*Op. cit.*, 332-333.

[14]*Dialogue, PG*, 140, col. 141 d.

[15]Nicholas of Methone, *op. cit.*, 337-338. Nicholas' purely philosophical argument (difference between ἀνταλλαγὴ and καταλλαγή) has only a limited bearing, but the general sense of his thought certainly reflects the patristic tradition.

[16]Fifth anathematism, J. Gouillard, *op. cit.*, 74.

[17]Fourth anathematism, *ibid.*, 74.

[18]Nicholas of Methone, *op. cit.*, 335.

[19]Cf. P. Classen, "Das Konzil von Konstantinopel 1166 und die Lateiner," in *Byzantinische Zeitschrift*, 48 (1955), 339-368; A. Dondaine, "Hughes Éthérien et le concile de Constantinople 1166," in *Historiches Jahrbuch*, 77 (1958), 480-482.

[20]The conciliar texts were recently published by S. N. Sakkos, " Ἡ ἐν Κωνσταντινουπόλει σύνοδος τοῦ 1170" in Θεολογικὸν Συμπόσιον in honor of P. Khrestou (Thessaloniki, 1967), 313-352. On the paragraphs inserted, at the same time, in the *Synodikon* and the history of the debates, see J. Gouillard, *op. cit.*, 78-80, 216-226. The decision of the Council of 1166 was even inscribed on marble plates and placed in the vestibule of

St. Sophia. The original plates were only recently discovered (C. Mango, "The conciliar Edict of 1166," in *DOP*, 17 [1963], 317-330). The above-mentioned authors refer to other contemporary sources and mention previous bibliography on the debates.

[21]The *Triads in defense of the holy hesychasts*, by Palamas, constitute the essential text, including numerous quotations from Barlaam's works (ed. J. Meyendorff, in the collection Spicilegium Sacrum Lovaniense, 30-31, [Louvain, 1959], Greek text and Fr. tr.); cf. also J. Meyendorff, *Introduction à l'étude de Grégoire Palamas* (Paris, 1959), 173-279 (Eng. tr. [London, 1964], 115-201).

[22]About Barlaam see also my article "Un mauvais théologien de l'unité," *L'Église et les églises* (Mélanges L. Beauduin, Chévetogne, 1955), II, 47-64; for a more positive view on Barlaam, see G. Schirò, *Barlaam Calabro, Epistole greche* (Palermo, 1954) and "Gregorio Palamas e la scienza profana," in *Le Millénaire du Mont Athos*, II (Chévetogne, 1965), 81-96.

[23]*Triads*, II, 3, 29, ed. John Meyendorff, 444-446; cf. J. Meyendorff, "Notes sur l'influence dionysienne en Orient," in *Studia Patristica*, 2, *TU*, 64 (Berlin, 1957), 547-552.

[24]*Synodal Tome, PG*, 151, 722 b.

[25]Μυριϋπόστατον, Palamas, *Against Gregoras IV, Coisl.* 100, fol. 285; *Theophanes, PG*, 150, col. 941 a.

[26]Cf. J. Meyendorff, *Grégoire Palamas*, 252-256 (*A Study of Gregory Palamas*, 182-184).

[27]*Dialogue, Marc. gr.* 155, fol. 94.

[28]*Against Palamas, Monac. gr.* 223, fol. 69 v.

[29]*Refutation of the Confession of Palamas, Monac. gr.* 223, fol. 47.

[30]*Against Palamas, Monac. gr.* 223, fol. 74 v.

[31]*Ibid.*, fol. 173 v.

[32]See in particular the clear and irenic exposition by C. Journet, "Palamisme et Thomisme," in *Revue Thomiste*, 60 (1960), 448-449.

[33]J. Meyendorff, *Palamas*, pp. 252-253 (*A Study*, p. 182).

[34]*Refutation of the Letter of Palamas, Monac. gr.* 223, fol. 17, fol. 72.

[35]*Against Palamas, Monac. gr.* 223, fol. 17, fol. 76.

[36]Traditional christological formula directed against Apollinarianism.

[37]Baruch 3:38, text often used in the Byzantine liturgy; cf. *Theotokion* of the Saturday vespers (fourth tone plag.) and *heirmos* of the ninth ode of the canon for August 6th.

[38]The word σύσσωμος, which comes from Eph 3:6, is current in Athanasius (*Contra Ar.*, I, 42, *PG*, 26, 100 b; II, 74, *ibid.*, col. 305 a), in Gregory of Nyssa (*Hom. XIV in Cantic.*, *PG*, 44, 1112 c), and above all in St. Cyril of Alexandria, where it appears in the same Eucharistic context as in Palamas: "By giving his body for food in the mystic eulogy to those who believe in him, he makes them co-corporal (συσσώμους) with him and among themselves" (*Comm. on John* 11, 11, *PG*, 74, col. 560 b, ed. Pusey, II, p. 735, 12; cf. also *Adv. Nest.* IV, *PG*, 76, col. 193 b; *Glaphyra in Gen.* I, *PG*, 69, col. 29 b). We have seen above (p. 190) the importance of this concept in St. Theodore Studite's iconology.

[39]*Tr.* I, 3, 38, ed. J. Meyendorff, 192.

[40]Akindynos, *Against Palamas, Monac. gr.* 223, fol. 163 v.

[41]According to Akindynos, this term is used by the hymnographers as a poetic image, *ibid.*, fol. 109 v, 185, etc.

[42]*Hom. XL*, 6, *PG*, 36, col. 365 a.

[43]*Exaposteilarion* for Aug. 6th; *Apostikha* for Aug. 7th; cf. Palamas, *Tr.* III, 1, 12, ed. Meyendorff, 580-582.

[44]*Life in Christ*, PG, 150, col. 592 d-593 d (cf. tr. by C. J. de Catanzaro [Crestwood, N. Y., 1974], pp. 122-123).

NOTES TO THE CONCLUSION

[1]John S. Romanides, "Highlights in the Debate over Theodore of Mopsuestia's Christology and Some Suggestions for a Fresh Approach," in the *Greek Orthodox Theological Review,* 5, 2 (Winter 1959-60), 140-185; cf. especially 179-181.

[2]"Current Problems in Christology," in *Theological Investigations,* I (Baltimore, 1965), 183; cf. also "Considérations générales sur la christologie," in *Problèmes actuels de Christologie,* Travaux du Symposium de l'Arbesle 1961, recueillis par H. Bouesse et J. J. Latour (Paris, 1965), 21-22.

[3]*Ibid.,* p. 187; cf. also John Macquarrie, *Principles of Christian Theology* (New York, 1966), 274-275.

[4]"Faith Functioning in Human Self-understanding," in T. Patrick Burke, *The Word in History* (New York, 1966), 42.

[5]"La proximité et l'éloignement de la créature, sa dépendance et son autonomie, ne croissent pas en proportion inverse, mais égale. C'est pourquoi le Christ est le plus radicalement homme, et son humanité la plus autonome, la plus libre," K. Rahner, "Considérations," 30.

[6]"Current Problems," 181-182.

[7]Cf. K. Rahner, "Considérations," 25-26; cf. also J. Meyendorff, "Philosophy, Theology, Palamism, and Secular Christianity," in *St. Vladimir's Seminary Quarterly,* 10 (1966), 203-108, and V. Lossky, *In the Image and Likeness of God* (Crestwood, N. Y., 1974), pp. 111-123.

[8]"Considérations," 17; "Current Problems," 188.

[9]"Considérations," 19.

Index

243